INTO THE ARCHIVE

INTO THE ARCHIVE

Writing and Power

in Colonial Peru

Kathryn Burns

DUKE UNIVERSITY PRESS

DURHAM AND LONDON

2010

© 2010 Duke University Press
All rights reserved
Printed in the United States
of America on acid-free paper ∞
Designed by Amy Ruth Buchanan
Typeset in Dante by
Keystone Typesetting, Inc.
Library of Congress Cataloging-in-
Publication Data appear on the last
printed page of this book.

Frontispiece: Cuzco volume of sixteenth-century
notarial records (*protocolo*), ARC. Bound inside are some
two dozen *registros*, or notebooks, containing records
of clients' business. Photograph by the author.

To my family, with love

CONTENTS

Illustrations ix

Preface xi

Acknowledgments xiii

Introduction 1

1. Of Notaries, Templates, and Truth 20

2. Interests 42

3. Custom 68

4. Power in the Archives 95

5. Archives as Chessboards 124

Epilogue 148

Notes 153

Glossary 205

Works Consulted 209

Index 239

ILLUSTRATIONS

Figures

MAP 1. Map of southern colonial Peru   7

MAP 2. Cuzco   48

FIGURE 1. Guaman Poma depicts an indigenous notary   9

FIGURE 2. A choirmaster / schoolmaster, as depicted by Guaman Poma   10

FIGURE 3. An anonymous doodler decorates the cover sheet of a *registro de indios*   16

FIGURE 4. Quentin Massys's *Portrait of a Man*   23

FIGURE 5. Title page of Hernando Díaz de Valdepeñas's *Suma de notas copiosas*   28

FIGURE 6. Title page of Gabriel de Monterroso y Alvarado's *Pratica civil, y criminal, e instruction de scrivanos*   30

FIGURE 7. Judicial torture in Jean Milles de Souvigny, *Praxis criminis persequendi*   35

FIGURE 8. Guaman Poma depicts the imagined dialogue of Inca and Spaniard   43

FIGURE 9. The signature of indigenous notary Pedro Quispe   51

FIGURE 10. Guaman Poma's representation of "the poor Indians of this kingdom"   67

FIGURE 11. Anonymous notarial doodles   69

FIGURE 12. Satirical doodles   70

FIGURE 13. Satirical doodle of a notary's head assistant   71

FIGURE 14. Doodle of a heraldic lion peeing a scribal flourish   74

FIGURE 15. Doodle of a notary's head assistant with sarcastic verses and caption   75

FIGURE 16. The signature and *signo* of a Cuzco notary   76

FIGURE 17. The signature and authenticating marks of a Cuzco notary   77

FIGURE 18. A blank contractual page with signatures at the bottom   78

FIGURE 19. The squeezed handwriting of a penman who had to fit form language into a preallotted documentary space   79

FIGURE 20. A papelito sticking up inside a protocolo   81

FIGURE 21. A stylized hand drawn in the margin of a manual page   84

FIGURE 22. Marginal disclosure of the "truth" about a sales contract   103

FIGURE 23. Marginal annotation in manual highlighting a passage   115

FIGURE 24. Petition with plea for justice   135

FIGURE 25. A doodle with implied challenge to read between the lines   144

FIGURE 26. Outside a Cuzco notary's office   150

Tables

TABLE 1. Prices of notarial offices in Cuzco (in *pesos ensayados*), 1595–1692   60

TABLE 2. Prices of public offices sold at auction in Lima (in *pesos corrientes*), 1701–15   64

TABLE 3. Most frequently produced types of notarial documents (sampling ARC protocolos for the years 1600, 1650, 1700)   85

PREFACE

Scholars of Latin America have worked hard in recent years to challenge old assumptions about alphabetic writing as a cornerstone of civilization. As they tease the virtuosic inscriptions of Mesoamerican scribes from ancient stelae and study the knotted cords of Andean *quipus*, they reveal the power of what Elizabeth Boone and Walter Mignolo call "writing without words."[1]

But of course the colonial Latin American archive is also full of alphabetic writing, the bulk of it (though not all) in Spanish. We have recourse to it constantly, but have thus far asked relatively few questions about it and its makers. Who imposed this form of literacy and record keeping, when, and how? How did it work? Whose needs and ends did it serve? Roberto González Echevarría usefully reminds us, in *Myth and Archive*, that writing circa 1500 "took place within a grid of strict rules and formulae." And this grid was markedly legal. "Legal writing was the predominant form of discourse in the Spanish Golden Age," González Echevarría observes, and "it permeated the writing of history, sustained the idea of Empire, and was instrumental in the creation of the Picaresque."[2]

Legal writing also sustained the idea of the Archive—and the genealogy of the Latin American archive is not merely legal, but distinctly *notarial*. Not by accident is a stock figure in the picaresque narratives that flourished in Golden Age Spain and America that legal writer par excellence, the *escribano*, or notary. (He scampers on and offstage quickly in *Lazarillo de Tormes*, but steals major scenes in *Guzmán de Alfarache* and *La vida del Buscón*.) These men gave the colonial Latin American archive its shape, its characteristic forms. They were involved in records of all kinds, not just the contracts, wills, and other extrajudicial documents we recognize as "notarial records," but trial records, treasury accounts, and much more besides. Writing and power were inextricably joined in their hands: they (and their assistants) had the power to put other people's words into official form. These men thus hold power over us as well: the power to shape our histories of the Latin American past.

Why, then, are notaries not prominently featured in my title? Because, for one thing, notaries are very minor figures in the legality of the modern United States, so minor that those of us in academia in this country may overlook their considerable influence in other societies, past and present. Years of describing my work have convinced me that a project about writing and power sounds far more engaging to most friends and colleagues than anything I might have to say about notaries. And as my project grew and changed over time, the notaries who were its original subjects were joined by a host of other historical subjects—people who went to notaries and actively engaged with "things notarial," *lo notarial*— and my sense of notaries' primacy inside their own workshops changed. The further I went into the archive, in short, the less I was writing about notaries, and the more I was writing about writing and power.

I hope these words serve as an enticing invitation to follow me into the archive. Different readings are certainly possible here: those interested primarily in archives may want to skim or skip the details about Cuzco's history in chapter 2, for example, and head straight for the bustling notarial workshops of chapter 3 or the historiographical points of chapter 5. While I'm not out to dispel the obloquy that has historically attached to notaries, I do hope the pages that follow will put it in perspective. Notaries themselves may not have been major figures on the stage of history, but their words and characteristic forms of authority have had tremendous staying power—and not just in colonial places.

ACKNOWLEDGMENTS

It's an enormous pleasure to thank the many people who helped me turn inchoate musings about *escribanos* into a book. First I would like to express my gratitude to the institutions that gave me access to their holdings: in Cuzco, the Archivo Arzobispal, the Archivo Regional de Cusco, the Monasterio de Santa Catalina de Sena, and the Monasterio de Santa Clara; in Lima, the Archivo Arzobispal de Lima, the Archivo General de la Nación, the Sala de Investigaciones of the Biblioteca Nacional, and the Archivo de Límites of the Ministerio de Relaciones Exteriores; in Spain, the Archivo General de Indias in Seville, the Archivo Histórico de Sevilla, and the Biblioteca Nacional in Madrid; in Portugal, the Arquivo Nacional da Torre do Tombo in Lisbon and the Biblioteca Geral da Universidade de Coimbra; and in the United States, the Benson Latin American Library at the University of Texas at Austin, the John Carter Brown Library at Brown University, the Latin American Library at Tulane University, the Harvard Law School Library, the Houghton Library at Harvard University, the Wilson and Davis Libraries of the University of North Carolina at Chapel Hill, and Special Collections at the Duke University Library. I am deeply grateful to those who made me welcome in these places, often going beyond the call of duty.

I am also grateful to the institutions that funded my research and writing at various stages. The University of North Carolina provided support for summer research travel to Spain and Peru. I thank Peter Coclanis and Lloyd Kramer, chairs of the History Department, for helping me get the funds I needed, and I thank my colleagues in the department for making our work environment so congenial. A National Humanities Center fellowship in 2002–3 and a fall 2003 fellowship from UNC's Institute for the Arts and Humanities enabled me to begin drafting chapters; with a National Endowment for the Humanities fellowship in 2006–7, I was able to complete a first draft.

There are many others without whom I'd never have pulled this sprawling project together. For initial encouragement and help, I thank Donato

Amado Gonzáles, Jeremy Baskes, Jodi Bilinkoff, Sandra Bronfman, Vicenta Cortés Alonso, Alec Dawson, Carolyn Dean, Karen Graubart, Meg Greer, Marikay McCabe, Hortensia Muñoz, Margareth Najarro, Gabriela Ramos, David Sartorius, Karen Spalding, and Charles Walker; research trips to Peru and Spain would not have been half as much fun without them. Margareth Najarro did the research behind table 3, for which it's a pleasure to thank her. I also want to acknowledge those who stimulated my thinking by inviting me to visit their campuses and present portions of my work. Thanks to Frances Ramos, Ann Twinam, and colleagues at the University of Texas; to Rebecca Scott and Sueann Caulfield at the University of Michigan; to María Elena Martínez at the University of Southern California; to Hortensia Calvo, David Dressing, and colleagues at Tulane's Latin American Library; to James Green at Brown University; and to Sabine MacCormack at Notre Dame University, all of whom extended a warm welcome and asked great questions. I'm particularly grateful to Rebecca Scott for including me in the rich transnational dialogue that she, Jean Hebrard, and Michael Zeuske have had with colleagues in Cuba about "making the documents speak." Special thanks as well to Julie Hardwick, Tamar Herzog, and Laurie Nussdorfer, whose work on early modern notaries has so benefited my own. Laurie generously shared with me the complete manuscript of her book, *Brokers of Public Trust: Notaries in Early Modern Rome*, before it was published by Johns Hopkins University Press.

I gave shape to the chapters that follow through dialogue with my writing group, all current or former faculty at UNC: Jane Danielewicz, Judy Farquhar, Joy Kasson, Laurie Langbauer, Megan Matchinske, Rashmi Varma, Heather Williams, and Mary Floyd-Wilson. Their careful reading and steadfast support have mattered enormously to me. I'm also grateful to the National Humanities Center and UNC Institute for the Arts and Humanities reading/writing groups in which I took part in 2002–3 (and after), especially for the feedback and friendship of Erin Carlston, Grace Hale, Maura Lafferty, Shantanu Phukan, Joanne Rappaport, Moshe Sluhovsky, Helen Solterer, and Francesca Talenti. Thereafter, Louise Newman and Tamar Herzog took the time to read chapters and give me valuable comments. So, too, did my graduate students in a fall 2008 seminar on writing and power in colonial Latin America. My warmest thanks to all of them, and to Lisa Lindsay, Jolie Olcott, Cara Robertson, Mary Dodge Smith, and John Sweet, for helping me keep perspective on work and life.

It's been a pleasure, as ever, to work with Valerie Millholland of Duke

University Press. I deeply appreciate her patience and her confidence in this project. My thanks, too, to Miriam Angress and Mark Mastromarino, who have been excellent guides through the intricacies of the publication process; to William L. Nelson, who made the maps; to Sonya Manes for expert copyediting, and to the two anonymous readers for the press who gave me such helpful comments on the manuscript. I'd also like to thank the *American Historical Review* for permission to publish here, in revised form, portions of my article "Notaries, Truth, and Consequences," AHR 110:2 (April 2005), and Ashgate Press for permission to incorporate in chapter 4 portions of "Forms of Authority: Women's Legal Representations in Mid-colonial Cuzco," which first appeared in Marta V. Vicente and Luis R. Corteguera, editors, *Women and Textual Authority in the Early Modern Spanish World*, 149–63 (Burlington, Vt.: Ashgate, 2004).

Special thanks to the many other friends and family who have been part of my life in the course of this project. Hortensia Muñoz, Maura Lafferty, Roland Greene, Stephanie Stewart, and Kate Raisz kept me going with generous encouragement from the start, and Kate somehow found time to read and comment on the entire manuscript twice. No one read proto-chapters as generously and often as Sheryl Kroen, my dear neighbor from Gainesville. Her keen insight gave me what I needed to undertake the big manuscript overhaul of spring 2007. Whatever flaws remain in the chapters that follow are in no way her fault; whatever clarity and coherence they have owe quite a lot to her. The title was provided by Rebecca Karl, who saw exactly what I was up to. I've been fortunate to have around me other friends who feel like family, including Sarah Shields and William Merryman, Margaret and Sophie Wiener and Patricia Sawin, Marisol de la Cadena, María Emma Mannarelli, and Marianela Gibaja. Ned, Martha, Michael, and Alvin Burns have been loving supporters, going well out of their way to be my cheering section whenever possible. And thanks to the recent move to Durham by my sister, Stephanie Wechsler, and her husband Dan, I get to be a *tía* at close range to two of my three wonderful nieces—Caroline, Julie, and Violet—who mean the world to me. This book is for my extended family with heartfelt thanks and love.

INTRODUCTION

The image is an arresting one: Christopher Columbus on the beach at Guanahani in October 1492, claiming a new world for his sovereigns. No sooner did he go ashore with two of his captains than he "brought out the royal banner and the captains two flags," insignia they planted as part of a ritualized *toma de posesión*, taking possession.[1] Next, according to the journal of the voyage, came a series of actions crucial to the performance of the Genoese admiral's claims. He had a notary put the relevant specifics in writing. Thus the first thing Europeans made on American shores in 1492 was a notarial record:

> The Admiral called to the two captains and to the others who had jumped ashore and to Rodrigo Descobedo, the *escrivano* [notary] of the whole fleet . . . and he said that they should be witnesses that, in the presence of all, he would take, as in fact he did take, possession of the said island for the king and for the queen his lords, making the declarations that were required, and which at more length are contained in the testimonials made there in writing.[2]

Eager "discoverers" in the wake of Columbus went about extending this paper trail of possession. Vicente Yáñez Pinzón in Paria "jumped from the boat . . . [with] certain notaries," taking possession of the land for his sovereign by heaping up boundary markers and giving the site a Castilian name. He also "cut off many branches from the trees, and in certain principal places they drew crosses to signify possession and made other crosses out of wood."[3] Bartolomé de Celada, in what is now Honduras, had a notary record that his possession-taking acts involved moving about, "cutting branches from the trees and pulling up grass and digging into the land with his hands."[4] Perhaps most memorably, in 1513, Vasco Núñez de Balboa claimed for Castile not land but sea. On reaching the Pacific's shore Balboa and his party found that the tide was out and the timing wasn't right for a possession ceremony. So they sat on the beach and waited. When the tide was high, Balboa waded in knee-deep, drew his sword, unfurled the royal standard, and in the name of his sovereigns claimed the entire Pacific Ocean.[5]

In the beginning, for these men, was the word—the Castilian, notarial word. They brought other templates with them as well: those of Christian scripture, for example, and Petrarchan lyric. All of these would inform the voluminous stream of writing they sent back across the Atlantic.[6] But first, and out front, came the formulae of the notary, or *escribano*. His were the words that would constitute imperial claims as legally true.[7] Other sovereigns might contest these claims (and did). The exact form of the claims would change over time.[8] But from Guanahani to the Strait of Magellan and the California coast, it was the notary's written words—backed by all the power of Castilian enforcement—that first constituted Spanish American empire.[9]

Notaries were indispensable to possession, and possession in a Roman law sense permeated Europeans' worlds. Whether they were Jewish, Christian, or Muslim, Europeans lived in intimate contact with the law of things, its distinctions, and its enforcers.[10] They were answerable to its claims. (A thing, *res*, might be possessed without being owned; it had to be publicly conveyed, and so forth.) And writing offered security for these claims. The Jewish *sōfer*, the Muslim *sāhib al-wathā'iq*—these men as well as Christian notaries cast possession in written forms, Hebrew and Arabic as well as Latin.[11] By the time Columbus claimed Guanahani, people had been using such forms for centuries, both in the Mediterranean world and beyond. And in the words of M. T. Clanchy, they had come to trust writing—to believe that "property rights depended generally on writings and not on the oral recollections of old wise men."[12] Only after a protracted historical process were Europeans (the vast majority of whom did not read or write) prepared to honor written records over oral tradition. Traces of prior practices remained, however, in the forms they used. Columbus (or the buyer of a house) still had to signify possession by saying things aloud and performing "corporal acts": marking the sand with a sword, or slicing off tree branches; opening and shutting windows and doors, and so forth.[13] These actions had to be certified as uncontested, "without any contradiction or protest." But the actor could not simply write these things down in whatever words came to his or her mind. The memory that mattered most by 1492 was the version shaped by the notary.

Who was this essential person? The notary (*escribano*) was a kind of ventriloquist—someone who could give other people an official "voice."[14] He knew the state-sanctioned forms through which agency could be constituted in writing, whether the agents were claiming an ocean or doing something much more mundane: transacting a sale, loan, or dowry; making a will; giving testimony in a lawsuit. People might know how to read and write, but they couldn't produce binding documents on their own. It took the notary's mediation to turn their desires and actions into legally valid records (*instrumentos*). His signature and his *signo*—his unique sign—attested that records were true ("I, María Ramos, do agree to lend this sum . . ."). And true records gave the parties named in them the standing to take future action: María Ramos might collect on her loan, for example, and the Castilian crown might defend its claim to Guanahani.[15]

It was largely through these men's agency that the colonial Latin American archive was formed.[16] Even the documents that seem to range furthest from the notary's formulae—such as witnesses' testimony in lawsuits—bear his shaping influence, as we'll see in the chapters ahead. And the reach of his legalistic templates can be seen across other privileged cultural forms. "In the sixteenth century writing was subservient to the law," as Roberto González Echevarría reminds us in *Myth and Archive*. Thus the lively, expansive realm of sixteenth-century Spanish narrative, "both fictional and historical," depended on legal writing, which "permeated the writing of history, sustained the idea of Empire, and was instrumental in the creation of the Picaresque."[17] Notaries in this sense attended the birth of the novel—the narrative form par excellence.[18]

Yet notaries were not, in period terms, *letrados*: a *letrado* was someone who knew Latin and had studied for a law degree. Advocates (*abogados*) were letrados; notaries and the legal paper-pushers known as *procuradores* were not.[19] Still, these men had to work together closely and knew much about each other's (and their clients') business. They all participated in the workings of what Angel Rama has called "the lettered city," *la ciudad letrada*—an urban concentration of men, comparable to "a priestly caste," wielding dominion over the official channels and instruments of communication.[20] Here I will argue that the lettered city had a much bigger city plan and was much less exclusive than we might suppose. For as Armando Petrucci has pointed out, the world of literacy extended well beyond those who were in detailed technical command of its forms. Through what Petrucci calls "delegated writing," notaries' workshops were the gateway through which others made their entry into the record, the courts, the archives.[21]

So when he called Rodrigo de Escovedo ashore, Columbus could hardly have done otherwise. He needed the notary's words to stake his claim. "To history's gain," writes James Lockhart, "there was hardly anything that the Spaniards did not notarize."[22] When someone died, a notary might be called in to record the details for a death certificate: how the deceased was clothed, how many candles burned at the bier. When people wounded each other, he might register the wounds' severity and specific location. And when they hit each other with lawsuits (as they often did), a notary would take charge of the judicial records that resulted. Yet we tend to look right past him—over his shoulder, so to speak, at the documents he made. What if instead we looked at the notary as an intriguing stranger? If he recorded truth, just whose truth was it?

Here I take Escovedo and his fellows to be the "secret agents" of the archives, productive figures central to my inquiry into writing and power. Most of this study will be concerned with these men and the practices that grew up around them. The overall argument is quite simple: if we want to understand the agency of colonial Americans, and it is largely represented to us in documents made by notaries, then we first need to understand this realm of representation. We need to go into the archive, deeply into the conditions of its making. Who had the power to make other people's deeds and desires legally true? What was silenced and what made salient? Just how did people get their versions into (or out of) the record?

Europeans did not consider these things transparent or neutral. To the contrary: they recognized a built-in tension between the notary's role as *fides publica*, "a writer endowed with credibility (*fides*) by public authority," and his need to make a living from his pen.[23] Many notaries by Columbus's day had purchased their offices and lived off the fees they charged for their services. As Laurie Nussdorfer observes, this regime of venality (i.e., office purchasing) put the notary "at the curious junction between what we would call the private and the public spheres. . . . He was a broker of public trust."[24] He was also, as we'll see, often suspected of violating his neutrality for personal gain and reviled as a crass manipulator of the documented word—all the more reason to study Escovedo and his fellows as they participated in the claiming of a "new world." But we must first consider the knowledge and truths they papered over.

What of indigenous archives? In his search for gold, Columbus could see only lack. As far as he could tell, the islanders of Guanahani had no religion and lived "without weapons and without law."²⁵ But as Europeans poured across the Atlantic in search of the gold Columbus had glimpsed, they soon saw otherwise. Mainland peoples had vast trading networks, prosperous cities and states, commoners and lords—the latter dubbed indiscriminately "caciques" by the Spaniards, using an Arawak word. They spoke hundreds of different languages. Their capacious memories held lengthy, elaborate speeches and songs.²⁶ And they had "paintings," complex, colorful records brushed on carefully prepared deerskin, bark, and other surfaces. This was writing as Spaniards weren't used to seeing it: writing without words.²⁷

The sophistication of native writing systems was dazzling. Aztec *tlacuilos*—"painters" or scribes—could record everything from royal genealogies to solstices to dreams. To Spaniards, however, the tlacuilos were instruments of the devil; their archives held only barbarous "superstition," worthy of being destroyed. The Franciscan friar Motolinia described five types of books he had seen: "The first speaks of the years and times; the second of the days and feasts they had all year; the third of dreams, illusions, superstitions, and omens in which they believed. The fourth was about baptism and the names they gave children; the fifth, of the rites, ceremonies, and omens related to marriage." In Motolinia's estimation, these heathen accounts still merited some credit: "Only one of all these books, namely the first, can be trusted because it recounts the truth, although barbarous and not written in letters. . . . Thus they recorded the feats and histories of conquests and wars, and the succession of lords; bad weather, noteworthy signs in the sky, and epidemics; when, and under which lord these things occurred. . . . All this they have in symbols and pictures that render the account intelligible."²⁸

After the Aztec Triple Alliance succumbed to Hernán Cortés and his indigenous allies in 1521, amid a devastating epidemic of smallpox, Spaniards began to press their customs (as well as their germs) on the Mexicans. By the mid-1520s a Spanish-style city council and a corps of Spanish notaries had been installed atop Tenochtitlan—as they had been previously on the islands of Hispaniola, Puerto Rico, and Cuba.²⁹ And Franciscans and other mendicants who reached the heartland of central Mexico in the 1520s launched a determined campaign of destruction. "The years 1525 to 1540," writes Serge Gruzinski, "were the age of violent and spectacular persecutions" in which "whole aspects of indigenous culture sank into clandestinity, to acquire in the light of the Christianity of the conquerors the cursed and demonic status of 'idolatry.' "[30] Among them were the arts and knowledge of the tlacuilos. The persecution would continue farther south, among the Maya. Diego de Landa writes laconically of his years at the helm of the Franciscan mission in the Yucatan, "We found a great many books in their writing, and because they were about nothing more than superstition and diabolical falsehood, we burned them all, which upset them greatly and caused them much sorrow."[31] By such means the friars and priests assailed knowledge systems that had taken centuries to refine, reducing Mesoamerican archives to ashes. This destruction was a vital part of what Walter Mignolo has called the "colonization of memory"—a project that would extend throughout the Americas and beyond.[32]

At the same time, new ways of writing were being devised. Friars and priests worked busily with their first native converts in the 1530s and 1540s to cast Christian messages in alphabetic Nahuatl, Maya, Mixtec, and other American languages. Soon significant numbers of Nahua, Maya, and Mixtec writers—perhaps some of the same men who had once made intricate codices—began adapting these alphabetic literacies for other purposes. The importance of the Spanish notary and his archives had not been lost on them. As their communities confronted Spaniards' devastating diseases and demands, and set up the kinds of local leaders that Spaniards recognized and encouraged, they began to produce home-grown notarial records: land titles, loans, wills.[33]

By the mid-1500s, then, Mexicans were generating a hybrid notarial culture all their own. Its products show marked Spanish influence. But the new forms did not simply sweep away the old. Gradually, by uneven stages, central Mexican notaries worked the new and the old together, taking on more loanwords and developing transculturated forms.[34] Nahua culture has received the bulk of the attention thus far, and Lockhart has identified a "golden age" of Nahuatl literacy in the years 1580–1610.[35] Well into the 1700s, however, some Mesoamerican notaries still wrote in Nahuatl, Maya, and Mixtec. A flourishing movement among Mesoamericanist scholars now seeks to understand Mexican ethnohistory through the painstaking work of locating and translating such sources.[36]

Yet indigenous-language sources are not plentiful, compared with the voluminous Spanish documentation from colonial Mexico and Central America. One reason for this is surely official neglect. For while Spanish notaries' records were carefully preserved, periodically inspected, and in-

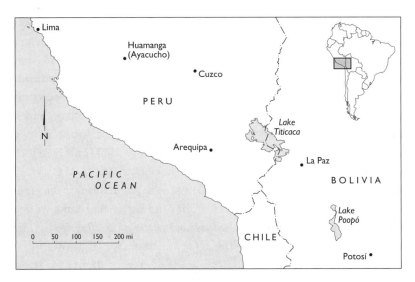

MAP 1. Map of southern colonial Peru, formerly the
heartland of the Inca empire of Tawantinsuyu.

ventoried (at least in theory), indigenous notaries' records were left out of
these inspections (even if they wrote in Spanish). Theirs was a subjugated literacy—a colonial byproduct that from the point of view of Spanish officialdom held little or no interest. Its scarcity today speaks eloquently to the
relative standing of Indian and Spanish notaries under Spanish colonialism.

What of the Andes, where the gold of the Inca empire lay? There, too,
the Spaniards continued their hunt for treasure in 1532, aided by the biolog-
ical weapons they unwittingly carried. Epidemic disease had preceded
them, killing the Inca ruler, Huayna Capac, and precipitating a vicious
struggle between rival heirs. Francisco Pizarro and his men took full advantage of the turmoil. In less than a decade, they ransomed and killed the new
Inca ruler, Atahualpa; claimed the rich highland city of Cuzco; then moved
to the coast to found a new base of operations: Lima, the "City of Kings."
There, as in Mexico, a demographic disaster continued in their wake.[37]

But much was different about the multiethnic empire that lay along the
spine of the Andes. Andeans had no markets, yet their towns and cities
were well provisioned. An astonishing road system linked the empire's
distant quarters. Massive Inca palaces, temples, and administrative centers
had been built without the use of wheeled vehicles of any kind, their finely
worked stones so tightly joined that a knife's blade could not be slipped

between them. All this clearly required enormous amounts of labor power and coordination—yet Andean peoples appeared to have no books, nor anything else the Europeans could recognize as writing. Instead, they wove messages into textiles in abstract, colorful bands (*tocapu*), inscribed them on ceremonial cups (*queros*), and knotted them into massed cords (*quipus*).[38] Quipu literacy was much older than the Inca empire, and it fascinated and baffled the Spaniards. The Jesuit José de Acosta in 1590 described quipus as "memory aids or registers made up of cords on which different knots and different colors signify different things," and marveled at their capacity: "What they [i.e., Andeans] achieved in this way is incredible, for whatever books can tell of histories and laws and ceremonies and accounts of business all is supplied by the *quipus* so accurately that the result is astonishing."[39] According to the Mercedarian friar Martín de Murúa, Andeans had once "had great heaps of these cords, like the registers our notaries have, and those were their archives."[40]

Meanwhile, Dominican friars and their converts worked from the 1550s to put Andean languages—Quechua, Aymara, and others—into alphabetic writing.[41] This joint effort proved highly productive, as in Mexico: the latter half of the sixteenth century saw the printing of grammars and dictionaries, sermon collections, and confessional manuals. (Many more circulated in manuscript.) Integrally involved were *indios ladinos*, bilingual Andeans who had studied the ways of the Spaniards at close range.[42] But they do not seem to have produced a home-grown notarial culture centered on Quechua or Aymara. As Tom Cummins has argued, the cultural distance between Andean and Spanish literacies was too great for the quipu keepers, the *quipucamayoc*, to bridge.[43]

There were native Andean notaries, however, and they wrote in Spanish. Dozens of these indigenous notaries were practicing by the late 1500s in the Inca heartland of Cuzco, both in the city's indigenous parishes and in the towns of its hinterland.[44] Their prototype figures in the copiously illustrated chronicle that Felipe Guaman Poma de Ayala sent to his Spanish sovereign around 1615.[45] Guaman Poma depicts a culturally ambidextrous notary or "quilcaycamayoc," a paper keeper (figure 1). How such men might have learned Spanish forms appears in another of Guaman Poma's drawings: indigenous pupils are taught by a local *maestro* (figure 2). Yet colonial Andean archives hold almost no writing by indigenous notaries, even though sixteenth-century Spaniards complained constantly about

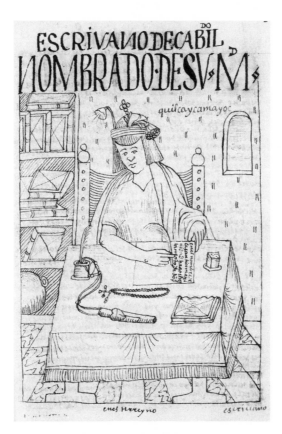

FIGURE 1. Felipe Guaman Poma de Ayala depicts an indigenous notary with his archive of papers (*quilca* in Quechua). The ceramic jar on the lowest shelf may contain bunched quipus; I thank Gary Urton for this insight into Andean archives. Artwork in the public domain. Photograph supplied by The Royal Library, Copenhagen, Denmark, from manuscript GKS 2232 4°, *El primer nueva corónica y buen gobierno* (1615 / 1616), "29. The chapter of local native administrators of this kingdom," drawing 307, p. 828. See http://www.kb.dk/permalink/ 2006/poma/info/es/frontpage.htm.

"litigious Indians." What happened to this paper trail? As in Mexico, part of the answer lies in the official neglect Spaniards accorded indigenous communities' records. Another part seems to involve the little-studied Indian courts (*juzgados de indios*) created in the 1570s by the Peruvian viceroy Francisco de Toledo to channel Indian justice through a local, summary process. Argumentation before the Spanish "judges of Indians"

FIGURE 2. A choirmaster and schoolmaster, as depicted by Guaman
Poma. The indigenous pupil in the front row appears to be drawing up
a notarial record; he begins, "Sepan quantos" (Be it known to all). Artwork
in the public domain. Photograph supplied by The Royal Library, Copenhagen,
Denmark, from manuscript GKS 2232 4°, *El primer nueva corónica y buen gobierno*
(1615 / 1616), "23. The chapter of the parish priests," drawing 266, p. 684. See
http://www.kb.dk/permalink/2006/poma/info/es/frontpage.htm.

(*jueces de naturales*) was conducted orally; only a brief written summary of
the proceedings was kept by the notary. This (so they said) was for the
Indians' own good.[46]

Thus in the Andes, too, a distinctly colonial archive was produced by
deliberate exclusions. For the vast majority of Andeans, Spanish justice
was rendered "summarily" (i.e., orally), largely bypassing the written
word. The colonial state did not see to the gathering of the results as it did
with other kinds of records; thus the papers of indigenous courts and

"council notaries" turn up only episodically in Peru, wherever they happened to intersect the dominant courts' and notaries' workings and enter their paper trail. The distinctively Andean quipus did not disappear.[47] But their use became a subjugated literacy, firmly relegated to the margins.

Archives have become strikingly visible in recent scholarship.[48] This is very much a consequence of the "linguistic turn," brought about since the 1970s through the rich interdisciplinary dialogues among historians, anthropologists, and literary scholars.[49] Before, as Natalie Zemon Davis writes, "we were ordinarily taught as scientific historians to peel away the fictive elements in our documents so we could get at the real facts." Now, however, Davis and many others focus on "fiction in the archives" for what it can reveal about the narrator's world. By fictional elements Davis means not what is feigned or false, "but rather, using the other and broader sense of the root word *fingere*, their forming, shaping, and molding elements: the crafting of a narrative. . . . I think we can agree with Roland Barthes, Paul Ricoeur, and Lionel Gossman that shaping choices of language, detail, and order are needed to present an account that seems to both writer and reader true, real, meaningful, and / or explanatory."[50]

From here it is an obvious step into the archives' own past, toward the relations and shaping choices that formed them. Increasingly, scholars are taking up anthropologists' calls for "an ethnographic approach to the archive."[51] The focus so far has been mostly on modern archives. And scholars tend to think up and out, toward these holdings' connections to the state.[52] If, for many, "modern history—or rather the modern idea of history—was born with the French Revolution," writes Nicholas Dirks, "it is perhaps even more true to say that the modern archive was born with the French Revolution . . . and, as befits that tumultuous event, the modern archive was as much about the destruction as it was about the preservation of the past."[53] In particular, as Carolyn Steedman notes, "the colonial archive has been much scrutinised as a source of imperial power."[54] Imperial bureaucrats' desire for control at a distance produced protocols of control over information: of recording, archiving, and retrieval. The result is the Foucauldian panopticon writ large, with archives all about knowledge and power, surveillance, and control. The emphasis is on centripetal movement: bureaucrats' data-gathering impetus, and their tendency to draw things in toward imperial institutions (e.g., the British Museum or Public Record Office).[55]

But premodern archives worked rather differently. Although our por-trait of Philip II burning the midnight oil in the Escorial to pore over manuscripts from all over his late sixteenth-century empire is deeply in-scribed in the historiography, the "lettered city" of the Indies was not built solely to enable Philip and his counselors to "see like a state."[56] It was meant, above all, to impose the forms of a monarchy that aspired to go Rome one better and create an orderly, Christian *imperio universal*.[57] Where there were no Christians and no property or justice in forms that Spaniards could recognize, these had to be diligently cultivated.[58] The focus of Vice-roy Toledo and many others was thus on fixing the forms of orderly, Chris-tian "good customs," *buenas costumbres*. These contained the lineaments of everything proper and right. If they were firmly in place, the rest would follow.[59]

Just who might "speak" through these forms is the subject of my inquiry. My approach to colonial archives thus moves, not up and out (toward the State, writ large), but in a different direction: down to the material itself, to the paper, ink, and inkblots that seem to disclose things and to the habitual movements of thoughts and bodies produced in practice.[60] This is not to say that the state is not interesting, however, as it certainly is—and thinking about the early modern European state and its workings has changed dra-matically in recent years. Monoliths of absolutism now look considerably less monolithic. My approach is in broad consonance with the work of those who, like Tamar Herzog, show that beneath the trappings of absolutism, early modern monarchies were far less centralized than they might appear, relying heavily on lower-level functionaries for whom there was no clear distinction "between private and public behavior or between private and public ends."[61] This revisionism about sixteenth- and seventeenth-century states and social networks puts many things in fresh perspective: the sale of offices, for example, becomes less a matter of corruption than one of blurred boundaries, overlapping interests, and a mutable moral economy of fair practice.[62] The state not only couldn't oversee all instances; it never tried to. In modern parlance, Spanish sovereigns and their successors dele-gated; they subcontracted things out.[63]

This subcontracting and delegating can be seen quite clearly from the angle of colonial archives. Indeed, this is what the existing historiography highlights about Spanish American notaries: that as the overstretched Spanish treasury slid into bankruptcy in the late 1500s (not once but several times), the sale of public offices took off, with overseas notaries' posts the initial bestsellers.[64] The numbers and variety of notaries grew rapidly at this time. Those of the ecclesiastical estate, the *notarios eclesiásticos*, were not the crown's to distribute, but significant funds could be raised by selling titles to public notarial offices—and under Philip II, this became big business. Posts for qualified applicants came in two main varieties. *Escribanos públicos y del número*, numerary notaries public, were appointed to serve in a specific town or city (and the *escribano público y del concejo*, or town council notary, was responsible for keeping the records of the town council, or *cabildo*). By contrast, *escribanos de Su Majestad* (or *escribanos reales*), royal notaries, might act as notaries anywhere in their sovereign's domain as long as they did not encroach on the business of the numerary notaries.[65] Those who received title to join the ranks of Spain's *fedatarios públicos*—those who held the power to cast other people's words and deeds into official documents—had to pass an examination before their possession of notarial office was confirmed to them.

The crown, then, oversaw the admission of those interested in going into archives for a living. After that, notaries for the most part were on their own to sustain themselves and their families by charging customers a fee for their services.[66] The history of Spanish American archives is thus business history: that of men whose record-making activities were neither supervised nor funded by government in the modern sense, but undertaken (with royal rather than guild license) more in the spirit of a trade. Like artisans' livelihoods, those of notaries required a lengthy apprenticeship, as we'll see. And the social status of notaries in Spanish America also resembled that of artisans, as well as that of notaries across contemporary western Europe. As Julie Hardwick puts it in her study of the notaries of early modern Nantes, these were "middling men."[67]

Middling men, men in the middle: that was precisely what was called for in the great legal code of medieval Castile, the *Siete Partidas*. Notaries in the king's service "should not be very poor or very lowly; neither should they be very noble, or very powerful . . . because poverty induces men to be very greedy, which is the root of all evil, and low birth causes them not to know what is good." Noble and powerful men, for their part, "would disdain quotidian service" in the office of notary, and might dare to do things that would redound to its harm. Notaries should instead be *omes medianos*, men located between the extremes.[68] As Bartolomé de Carvajal puts it in his sixteenth-century manual, they should be the *fiel del peso*: the guarantor of correct weights and measures, above particular interests and partisanship.[69]

But all these recipes for probity did not resolve the basic contradiction of the notary's place. He wasn't supposed to be powerful in a contemporary sense—that is, well born, aristocratic. Yet he was entrusted with the making and keeping of archives that held the official records of the affairs of his sovereign's subjects. This, too, was power, especially at a time when Spain's bureaucracy was rapidly growing (as it was from the reign of Isabella and Ferdinand) and its judicial system was experiencing a dramatic increase in litigation.[70] That notaries' de facto powers struck contemporaries as contradictory and excessive is evident in the rising chorus of complaints about notaries in the 1500s, from popular sayings (*refranes*) to the pages of the prescriptive legal literature that began to pour from Spanish presses.

The great Golden Age writers had a veritable field day with the stock character of the venal, partisan notary. Take Miguel de Cervantes's curious tale of "The Glass Graduate," in which a law school graduate named Tomás, after a traumatic accident, is convinced he is made of glass and always in danger of shattering. He becomes a kind of loony oracle, trailed by crowds of people curious to hear his next utterance. Asked why he has never criticized notaries, "when there is so much to be said," Tomás mounts a rare defense:

> The notary is a public figure and the work of the judge cannot be carried out effectively without his aid. . . . They pledge secrecy and loyalty and swear that they will not draw up documents in exchange for money. They also swear that neither friendship nor enmity, profit [n]or loss will prevent them from performing their duty with a good, Christian conscience. If the profession requires all these good qualities, why should we expect that from more than twenty thousand notaries working in Spain the devil should reap the richest harvest, as if they were shoots on his vine? I am unwilling to believe it. . . . The fact is that they are the most indispensable people in a well-ordered state.[71]

Yet this ringing endorsement comes from Tomás, a madman. Cervantes (as usual) is working fine irony here. The Glass Graduate's defense of notaries is made for knowing laughs.[72]

A flourishing literary stereotype shouldn't simply be taken for a historical subject, but the great Golden Age ironists are excellent guides to their society's tensions and flashpoints. It was not necessarily easy to be a notarial man in the middle in Golden Age Spain. Advocates, doctors—these men, too, came in for their share of opprobrium in popular sayings as well as fiction. But the notaries, less exalted and more middling, got especially skewered in Spain for supposedly skewering other people "with the shafts of their quills." If occupying this middling spot was dicey in Spain, what was it like in the place Spaniards called the Indies?

This book is about writing and power, and about the peculiar efficacy of archives to make us forget that they, too, are historical artifacts—not simply clear panes through which can see the past, but the products of particular people's labor. Who made the archives we have now—the documents we now think of collectively as "the colonial archive?" What did people expect such records to do for them? How did things that to us now look comic, or tragic, or simply strange, once form part of people's basic common sense?

The focus here will be largely on escribanos públicos in the 1500s and 1600s and on Cuzco, the city with whose colonial archives I'm most familiar. Public notaries are relatively visible in Cuzco's archives. Moreover, because they were required to obtain royal confirmation of their titles, their dossiers and credentials can be found in abundance (though only for the 1500s and 1600s) in Seville's Archivo General de Indias. I should note that Cuzco had other notaries as well; those attached to the church, known as notarios eclesiásticos, handled ecclesiastical lawsuits and generally operated under the purview of the archbishop. Unfortunately, the careers of these men proved very difficult for me to trace, though archival bits suggest their training closely resembled that of their public counterparts.[73]

Cuzco is an especially good place to pose the question Gayatri Spivak asked, "Can the subaltern speak?"[74] The richness and grandeur of the city's Inca past is still obvious today. For three colonial centuries, Cuzco was home to Inca nobles as well as commoners, and it is still the center of a thriving "Incaism" constantly reinvented over time.[75] The bulk of the colonial papers in Cuzco's Archivo Regional (the former Archivo Departamental) was made by escribanos públicos and their assistants. These archives deliberately marginalized indigenous cuzqueños. Indeed, notaries from the mid-seventeenth century segregated "Indian registers" at the back of their books (figure 3). But Cuzco's notaries were immersed in a multiethnic city

FIGURE 3. An anonymous notarial doodler decorates the cover sheet of a *registro de indios*, or register of Indians' affairs, with stylized birds and a portrait of an Inca. The distinctive headdress, or *mascapaycha*, signifies the bearer's royal blood. ARC-PN, Gregorio Básquez Serrano, protocolo 52 (1705), register 11. Photograph by the author.

that was always demographically more Indian, and linguistically more Quechua, than anything else.

Many years ago I began to think these men were protesting too much. Everything they signed was insistently proclaimed to be true, *la verdad*. But there were documents in Cuzco's archives that made me wonder. What about those empty pages in several notaries' registers with their strange orphaned signatures at the bottom? Contracts signaled agreement, sealed by signatures and reached in the notary's witnessing presence—so why would anyone sign a phantom contract? Did that not leave them open to possible fraud? Then there was Don Francisco Mayontopa, the cacique of Ollantaytambo, who in the 1550s agreed on behalf of his community to donate land to the nuns of Santa Clara. According to the notarized record, the land was donated "voluntarily." That seemed straightforward enough until other documents turned up indicating that his hand had been forced.[76]

So whose truth was this? Gradually the archive itself began to be a research question. We historians are fond of regarding archives as windows on the past, or repositories of long-ago "voices." But now I was looking *at* an archive, not through it—and it was starting to look anything but transparent. I began taking notes on the things about documents that struck me as strange and in need of explanation: blank pages with nothing but signatures; documents crossed out with the words *no corrió* (did not go forward); volumes of records missing large chunks of their former contents.[77] I also became a makeshift ethnographer, taking notes on the things I saw and heard. Sometimes people came in to hold intense conversations with the archivists; these might be in Quechua. Rumor had it that some colonial land titles recently entrusted to the archive's care had disappeared. Over the years I had heard that documents were sometimes offered to researchers for sale, and the day it happened to me, I was shaken but not surprised. After all, the person who made the offer had been pressing me for "loans" we both knew would never be repaid. People whispered that he had a powerful political protector and could basically do whatever he wanted. In short, power plays in the contemporary archives of Cuzco were anything but subtle. It became harder and harder to think of their colonial antecedents as windows on the past.

But if the archive was not simply a clear pane to look through, or data waiting to be harvested, then what was it, and how to read its contents? One day I came across a manual that seemed to contain a very complete instruction kit for notaries: Gabriel de Monterroso y Alvarado's *Pratica civil, y criminal, e instruction de scrivanos* (1563). Here were the rules, or what Monterroso called the *teoría*, of official record making: what notaries were supposed to do in theory.[78] Once I started looking, many more such manuals turned up (including a neatly hand-copied one in the Cuzco archives). All of them began by lamenting the yawning gap between theory and practice. So I began to pay attention to this gap myself: whose interests did it serve? In a colonial place where few people knew the dominant language of officialdom, who might take advantage of it? And what exactly did people *do* in practice?

Getting to know the law and its forms was obviously one key to finding out. In chapter 1, I draw on legal literature of various kinds, especially the remedial self-help manuals for notaries that began to thrive in the mid-sixteenth century, to examine the way notaries were supposed to do their job.[79] The lives of actual notaries were clearly another key, and in chapter 2, I move from Castilian prescription to American practice, tracing the careers of Cuzco's sixteenth- and seventeenth-century notaries (mainly through wills and lawsuits) and their place in the complex webs of colonial relationships that Steve Stern has aptly called "power groups."[80] Many notaries were surprisingly active outside their workplaces, investing in everything from sugar and coca to mules and playing cards. Who, then, was minding the shop? In chapter 3, I take the reader inside the notarial workplace, into the apprenticeship hierarchies and "custom" that constituted everyday practice for young men learning the *ars notariae*. Here I trace the shortcuts and back alleys of the lettered city, some of them well outside the bounds of what was legally prescribed. And in chapter 4, I consider what clients might do to control the way their versions of things were registered. A close reading of Cuzco's colonial archives shows that cuzqueños had plenty of clever archival strategies of their own—such as bogus, "confidential" contracts (*confianzas*) and notarized documents that protested against other documents (*exclamaciones*).

Lastly, in chapter 5, I address the obvious historiographical question posed by the preceding chapters: if we can't simply take our archives at face value, how then to take them? The notion of archives as bearers of objective truths has been under scrutiny for some time now. In particular, scholars of colonialism have been devising ways to read "against the archival grain"—to recover subaltern voices and perspectives from sources that omit or paper over them. This approach is necessarily deconstructive in greater or lesser degree, and has provoked more than a little scholarly anxiety; it highlights the indeterminacy of meaning in our sources and challenges us to raise our tolerance for ambiguity.[81] But to regard archives and sources as in some sense "constructed" is not to throw up one's hands and accept any interpretation. Rather, it is to look for the patterns behind the construction—as Ann Stoler puts it, "the conditions of possibility that shaped what could be written . . . what competencies were rewarded in archival writing, what stories could be told, and what could not be said"— and then take these into account in the work of interpretation.[82]

That's precisely what I try to do in chapter 5. In a series of close readings of documents, putting to use the patterns traced in chapters 1 through 4, I show how more interpretive possibilities open up if we analyze our sources with an eye both to how they were made and to what their makers wanted. (What *we* want when we go into archives is quite different.) To understand an early modern world of "delegated writing," to borrow Petrucci's phrase, we need to know who might delegate official writing to whom, how, and why. The more we go into the archive—and grasp the expectations, templates, "custom," and inside knowledge of notaries, their assistants, and their clients—the richer our sources become.

Many of the specifics here are thoroughly redolent of Cuzco and of colonialism under Spain's Habsburgs. But my brief excursions into the archives of Coimbra and Lisbon indicate that notaries had a similar hand in constituting Portugal's colonial empire. And my sense is that despite the many late colonial reforms and upheavals, much about notarial practice remained the same in the 1700s and early 1800s (and even long after).[83] In any case, my overarching concerns—with "fiction in the archives," and the collaboration and conflict that went into archives' making—are, I think, of much wider interest. I hope this book provokes fresh thoughts about agency, writing, and power. If it pushes people to go further into these things than I have, I'll be immensely pleased.

CHAPTER I

OF NOTARIES, TEMPLATES, AND TRUTH

Los libros y letras andan por todo el mundo.
—B. de Albornoz

La Edad de Oro, the Golden Age: this resonant phrase names a time when Spanish imperial might reached its apogee. Galleons full of American silver sailed the seas, from Mexico and Peru to Manila and Seville, giving ballast to the Spanish monarchs' heady sense of themselves as "lords of all the world."[1] Spanish arts and letters flourished, and fashionable people throughout Europe wore severe black garments so as to look more Spanish. When in 1584 workers put the finishing touches on the monumental monastic palace of El Escorial, the power of the Spanish Habsburgs had never seemed greater. But this was also an age of notorious extremes and tensions. Visitors to the peninsula saw deepening poverty, haughty aristocrats, and a virulent "religious racism" that made life especially dangerous for the descendants of Jews and Moors. Rapid price inflation quadrupled the cost of basic commodities. Disease and famine carried off thousands, especially in Castile. Litigiousness increased dramatically; so, too, did the presence of beggars.[2]

Into this world of sharpening contradictions a new literary antihero was born: the rogue, or *pícaro*. Like the biblical Lazarus, the picaresque narrator of *Lazarillo de Tormes* (1554) revives after being laid low, not once but several times. His first-person immediacy instantly draws the reader in. Fatherless young Lázaro goes out into the world to live by his wits, and proceeds to serve a series of masters. These include a beggar, a priest, a petty nobleman, and a seller of papal indulgences, each of whom turns out to be an artful con man, worse than the last.[3] *Lazarillo* succeeds brilliantly as a send-up of the supposed pillars of Spanish society while posing deeply troubling questions: Can anyone be taken at his word? Behind the façade of appearances, who or what is true?

This was the perfect literary expression for an age of anxiety.[4] And *Laza-*

rillo had many literary progeny, including the enormously popular two-part *Guzmán de Alfarache* (1599, 1604).[5] Its eponymous narrator must also make his way in an uncertain, unstable world, without benefit of family ties or wealth. Guzmán is the son of a shady merchant, and pursues one dubious get-rich-quick scheme after another (all the while denouncing the pervasive influence of money, and the arrogance and power of the rich). He attaches himself to a series of masters and learns to beg, borrow, and steal. Along the way, he sees much greater rogues than himself—merchants, clergymen, captains at arms—engaged in the large-scale equivalent of begging, borrowing, and stealing. Guzmán constantly gets into trouble, but they do just fine, even though from Guzmán's perspective they are the true leeches of society's lifeblood.[6]

Everything is potentially for sale in the pícaro's world—even the sworn, documented truth produced by notaries. The figure of the notary makes only a brief walk-on appearance in *Lazarillo*, but appears early and often in *Guzmán*. He is a particular kind of merchant, a word merchant. And he is most emphatically not to be trusted. "Before it slips my mind," Guzmán narrates in the novel's opening pages, "listen to the Good Friday sermon preached by a learned priest in the church of San Gil in Madrid." The priest (in Guzmán's reported speech) inventories the many different kinds of sinners he has steered toward reform in the course of his long career. All showed signs of true redemption, except for notaries.

> I really don't know how they confess or who absolves them—those who abuse their powers, that is—because they report and write down whatever they please, and for two coins or to please a friend or lover . . . they take away people's lives, honor, and property, opening the way for countless sins. They are insatiably greedy, with a canine hunger and an infernal fire that burns in their souls, which makes them gobble up other people's assets and swallow them whole. . . . So it seems to me that whenever one of them is saved—since they can't all be as bad as those I've described— the angels must say joyfully to one another as he enters paradise, "*Laetamini in Domino*. A notary in heaven? That's new, that's new."[7]

With *Guzmán*, the picaresque took off in popularity, along with the stock figure of the greedy, conniving notary.[8] In Francisco de Quevedo's *Vida del buscón llamado don Pablos* (1626), another highly successful contribution to the genre, the protagonist Pablos falls into jail and bribes a notary to help him. First Pablos gets an earful of the man's boastful omnipotence:

" 'Believe me, sir, it all depends on us. . . . I've sent more innocent men to the galleys for pleasure than there are letters in a lawsuit. Now trust me and I'll get you out safe and sound.' "[9] Next the notary makes sure entire clauses are expunged from the trial record, and gets his man released on probation. But Pablos immediately falls into the clutches of another notary, whose roof tiles he has accidentally broken. He is thrashed and bound by the man and his servants. Then the notary starts drawing up a written indictment of Pablos: "There were some keys rattling in my pocket, so he said, and he wrote down that they were skeleton keys, even though he saw them and it was obvious they weren't. . . . All this was happening on the roof. It didn't matter that they were a little nearer heaven; they still told lies."[10] Pablos spends a sleepless night considering his cruel fate. Recalling the notary's "pages and pages of indictment" of him, Pablos concludes that "nothing grows as fast as your guilt when you're in the hands of a notary."[11]

Nor was the stereotype of the bad notary limited to high cultural products. Notaries were the butt of dozens of common sayings, as picked up in early modern compendia of popular adages. They gave people a close shave: "Escribano, puta y barbero, pacen en un prado y van por un sendero" (Notaries, whores, and barbers: all pasture together and follow the same path). They had no souls or human warmth: "Escribano y difunto, todo es uno" (Between a notary and a dead man, there's no difference). By their pens they could make black appear white, then turn it back again: "Pluma de escribano, de negro hace blanco; y a la vuelta de un pelo, de blanco hace negro." You couldn't hope to win a lawsuit (*pleito*) unless you had the notary on your side: "Pleito bueno, pleito malo, el escribano de tu mano."[12]

Notaries were not the only men on the receiving end of popular barbs, to be sure. But there is an especially strong argument coming out of early modern Spain that notaries are powerful and not to be trusted.[13] Cautionary tales about them obtrude with sudden violence like geological upheavals, as though authors can't contain themselves. Mateo Alemán abruptly inserts into the first chapter of *Guzmán* the priest's rant against "incorrigible" notaries who will confound the angels if one ever makes it to heaven. Similar passages abound in texts of all kinds. In his biography of a saintly Spanish nun, for example, the Franciscan friar Pedro Navarro swerves into a narrative annex about an incident in an Italian town in the year 1601 in which a dead notary emerges from his coffin in the midst of his

FIGURE 4. Images of Iberian notaries are scarce, but these men might have resembled the subject of Quentin Massys's *Portrait of a Man* (ca. 1510–20). Reproduced by permission of the National Gallery of Scotland.

own funeral to tell horrified onlookers where he hid the money he had stolen from someone's pious bequest.[14]

Why the notary? Did he become a scapegoat for the anxieties of an early modern empire in the midst of severe growing pains? Something of the sort does seem likely. The notary (figure 4) was a more familiar, accessible target in the legal profession than the more exalted figures of advocates and judges.[15] And he stood at the confluence of several trends that were making people feel extremely vulnerable. Costs were increasing, bureaucracy was growing, and lawsuits were thriving as never before in Golden Age Spain.[16] Most Spaniards could not read or write, and did not know the inner workings of the legal system. Yet even small fry might be caught up in the bureaucratic traps of legalese.[17] Like the fictional Pablos, they might suddenly have to place their fate in the hands of a notarial intercessor for their case to reach an advocate or a judge. No wonder the notary seemed to wield control over others with the shaft of his pen. But there was more to the charged stereotype of the bad notary than convenient emotional displacement.

Greed and power: these are the two main characteristics entwined in the stereotypical notary. If we tease them apart and set aside the villainous greed (which is all but impossible to gauge in archival sources), we are left with the notary's power—and that was much more than a literary mirage. The notary *was* a powerful figure in Golden Age Spain.[18] The very structure of Spanish justice made him so. Documents of all kinds—contracts, wills, legal petitions, and depositions—were crucial to obtaining justice, and the making of valid documents was the exclusive province of the notary. He acted, to quote Herzog, "as a bridge between the formal, public, technical world, on the one hand, and on the other, the circumstances, desires, and interests of individuals."[19] For urban dwellers especially, he must have seemed ubiquitous. He actually might troll the city jail for customers. (In Seville, he could have come across Alemán or Cervantes, both of whom did time for debts and got to know the notorious city jail from within.)[20] He might also have some pull with the local judge. Just how effective one's papers were, in or out of court, depended significantly, if not exclusively, on him. The reader who got a good laugh out of Pablos's notary in *El Buscón* ("Believe me, sir, it all depends on us") might be laughing in rueful recognition.

As for those of us used to filtering archival evidence to reconstruct the past, there's much to ponder here. The filtering process began long ago, *in the very making of the archival record itself.* Filtering and shaping the contents of documents was basically what notaries did for a living. This was what clients expected them to do: cast the essential details of their business in the standard, well-worn forms.[21] If we know what notaries were empowered to do, we can see that even the most seemingly spontaneous archival "voices" often obey submerged but quite specific scripts. The archive becomes an echo chamber of blended, collaborative agencies.

In this chapter, we will go into these men's jobs—both as prescribed by Spanish justice and as exercised by Spanish notaries in practice. Notaries' work featured prominently in the extensive "how-to" literature for legal professions that began to thrive alongside *Lazarillo*, *Guzmán*, *Don Quijote*, and other bestsellers of the early modern book trade. To understand the notary's powers fully, however, we begin with a look at the deep historical roots of his craft.

Spanish notaries' powers, like those of other Mediterranean notaries, were deeply rooted in the history of writing, as their name implies: *escribanos* were meant to write, *escribir*.[22] But this was not just any kind of writing; it was legal writing, conspicuously rooted in Roman private law. The Roman notary (*tabellio*) made written records of people's testaments and transactions—contracts of sale, leases, loans, dowries, and more.[23] He might also prepare petitions (*libelli, preces*) for presentation to Roman officials.[24] He was not a legal scholar (*iurisconsultus*) or advocate; those men could be called on to solve a legal problem or present well-crafted arguments to a magistrate.[25] The Roman notary dealt instead in well-worn forms. By the late Roman empire he might be found working in public markets and fora across a wide swath of Europe, from Byzantium in the east to the Iberian peninsula and the British isles in the west.[26]

Roman law is the most esteemed source of Spanish legality, but not its only source. When Germanic peoples invaded the Roman province of Hispania in the early fifth century AD, they introduced elements of a legal culture that privileged spoken words, tokens, and gestures over written records. Old forms remained, but gained new terms. Whoever purchased property, for example, was expected to perform symbolic acts to signify possession. (Traces of Germanic law could still be seen centuries later in gestures like Columbus's.)[27] When North African armies invaded in 711 AD and brought most of the peninsula under Islamic rule, Arabic notaries began to influence local practice.[28] They used detailed formularies to make written records of all kinds of things: maritime and other transactions; marriage, dowries, legacies, and so on.[29] Among the most advanced medieval formularies in Europe were those produced in Islamic Spain.[30]

As Mediterranean cities and economies grew, so did their need for reliable records. The northern Italian "legal renaissance" of the twelfth century reinvigorated the Roman law tradition—including, eventually, its notarial forms and practices. Bolognese notaries Salatiel (d. 1280) and Rolandino dei Passaggieri (d. 1300) wrote influential manuals of notarial practice that circulated widely in Europe.[31] These directly shaped the *Siete Partidas*, the great Castilian legal code attributed to Alfonso X "el Sabio" (d. 1284). Large portions of Partida 3.18 are basically a notarial formulary.[32] As Alfonso and his successors gradually brought most of the peninsula under Christian rule, the *Partidas* increasingly became the law of the land.

So it was that Iberian legal culture in the late middle ages came to bear a striking resemblance to that of northern Italy (and that of ancient Rome). Legal scholars played an esteemed role. These were the advocates, known in Spain as *abogados* or simply *letrados*, "lettered ones." They were expected to have studied law at a university, perhaps at Bologna, Paris, Salamanca, or Alcalá de Henares.[33] There were also attorneys, known as *procuradores*, to shepherd clients' cases through the workings of the judicial system.[34] They did not hold prestigious degrees but were adept at routine judicial business. Then there were the ubiquitous notaries public, the *escribanos públicos*. By the late middle ages these men had state sanction to act as *fides publicae*, authenticating a wide variety of judicial and extrajudicial records. They held title to their offices by virtue of royal appointment. Each city had a fixed number of municipal notaries, known as *escribanos públicos y del número*, and each of these "numerary" notaries inherited and enlarged the archives of his predecessors in office. (Large cities, like Toledo and Valladolid, might have 30 or more; Burgos had 38.)[35] In addition, monarchs created *escribanos reales* (or *de Su Majestad*), "royal notaries" who might perform notarial duties in any part of the realm as long as they did not infringe on the numerary notaries' terrain.[36]

When exactly did one meet up with a notary? That depended on one's *condición*, one's place in the order of things. Urban dwellers were by far the most likely to see notaries in action. Notarial workshops, or *escribanías*, might be found in conspicuous spots such as neighborhood plazas, and were especially thick wherever merchants gathered to trade—places like the steps of the enormous Gothic cathedral of Seville.[37] (A typical Iberian workshop probably looked much as it does in Dutch engravings: a room with a large table, writing implements, shelves and chests for storing documents.)[38] An artisan might see a notary often, whenever he took on a new apprentice or contracted for delivery of his goods. A mother superior or anyone who lingered near the entryway to a convent would have seen a notary constantly. Dowries had to be contracted for the novices and nuns; properties had to be bought, sold, renovated, and rented; services had to be engaged for delivery of foodstuffs, care for the sick, and any number of other things. And merchants might see notaries on a daily basis—especially if a trade fair had just happened or a ship laden with merchandise had just docked at the quay.

For most people, however, a close encounter with a notary was unusual and bound up with a major turning point of some kind. Parents might call on a notary public to formalize the dowry agreement for a daughter's marriage. The spouse or kin of the dying might call for a notary—perhaps with last-minute urgency—to record a will, a power of attorney, or a deathbed confession. A major purchase or transfer of property was considered more secure if the parties involved got a notary to document it. Putting people's important, even intimate, business in legal language was the notary's everyday job, his bread and butter.

Not surprisingly, the laws of Castile and elsewhere insisted that notaries be men of unquestionable rectitude. The *Siete Partidas* stressed the notary's *lealtança*: he must be faithful and true to those he served (*leal*).[39] His own interests must not come into play, nor should he favor one party over another; he must be evenhanded. He had to keep the business confided to him a professional secret.[40] And he should be of a middling sort, as we have seen. Poverty and low status (*vileza*) were thought to make men greedy and ignorant, while nobility made them too impatient for ordinary, day-to-day business.[41] The notary should be at neither extreme. He had to immerse himself in the particular interests of others, yet remain neutral, disinterested.

By the late 1400s, however, Iberian notaries had reached a kind of professional nadir. Titles to notarial offices had proliferated beyond royal control and were routinely rented, bought, and sold in a lively traffic in notarial posts.[42] Things grew particularly lax in Castile under King Juan II (1406–54), who allowed titles to be sold in blank for the names of the recipients to be filled in later. These *cartas blancas* were then used to create notaries with few or no qualifications. The result was a marked decline in the quality of documents. At the 1469 Cortes at Ocaña, for example, Juan's successor, Enrique IV, was warned, "many false documents are drawn up by the many notaries that in recent years your lordship has created and authorized; here many children and men who do not know how to write hold titles to the office of notary which they purchased in blank."[43]

Like so much else, this situation attracted the reforming energies of the monarchs Ferdinand and Isabella, who set out to discipline a refractory notariate. In 1480 efforts were made to reduce notaries' numbers and to improve their quality by requiring them to pass an examination.[44] The Pragmatic Sanction of 1503 went much further, reforming the way notaries made and kept their records.[45] Notaries were required to certify that they knew the people whose business they recorded. They had to apprise their clients fully of all the specifics their documents would contain, to prevent misun-

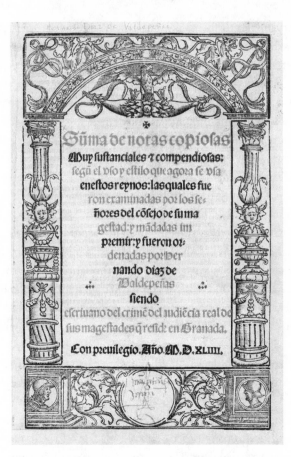

FIGURE 5. Title page of Hernando Díaz de Valdepeñas's *Suma de notas copiosas* (Granada, 1544), an early printed formulary for notaries public. Reproduced courtesy of Special Collections Department, Harvard Law School Library.

derstandings or fraud. And notaries had to keep documents in bound, orderly volumes (*protocolos*), "declaring the persons who enter into them, the day, month, year, and the place where they are made, and what is agreed to, specifying all conditions, understandings, and clauses."[46] The crown would set the fees that notaries might charge for their services, the better to shield royal subjects from harm.[47] This was thorough reform that reached deeply into everyday practice.

The Pragmatic Sanction of 1503 marked a major watershed in Castilian notarial history—what one legal historian has called the "birth of the protocolo."[48] It regulated the production of notarial records right down to the type of paper and the number of lines to be written on each sheet. The protocolo had to contain complete records, not just hasty notes (*notas*). In many Castilian cities, to judge from historians' findings, the reforms appear to have been well enforced.[49] Notaries' records became more uniform and rigorous, and notaries themselves seem to have been held to higher standards. A notary public in Córdoba, for example, had to be at least twenty-four years of age and possess at least 20,000 maravedis; candidates for the post were also required to demonstrate their abilities in an examination given by officials of the city council.[50] Notaries in the newly conquered city of Granada had to work in the presence of an Arabic translator when necessary, and identify recent converts in their documents by both their Islamic and Christian names.[51]

By the early 1500s, then, reliable archives were one of the Spanish crown's priorities, and this meant greater notarial discipline. This new rigor coincided with the emergence of a Spanish publishing industry. Before long, peninsular publishers could supply a variety of early modern self-help titles (see, e.g., figure 5), many of them directed to a particular kind of imagined reader: the aspiring notary.[52] Some notarial manuals were pocket-sized editions designed for easy reference. Others were weighty tomes full of legal citations and advice. Thanks to this tutelary literature, we can imagine notaries' work in everyday detail, and also why it might excite strong feelings.

Disciplining the Notary

El pleytear se [ha] conertido en arte para lucro
aviendo sido inventado para solo remedio.
—Monterroso, *Pratica civil, y criminal,*
e instruction de scrivanos

In 1563, in the old Castilian city of Valladolid, a notary named Gabriel de Monterroso y Alvarado brought out a comprehensive manual of civil and criminal procedure, *Pratica civil, y criminal, e instruction de scrivanos* (figure 6). Monterroso claimed to have been raised "from my earliest years in the Supreme Courts of these Kingdoms, dealing and conversing with the most capable, expert officials and the famous Doctors who reside there."[53] His *Pratica* soon became a bestseller and a model for works of its kind. It was at

FIGURE 6. Title page of Gabriel Monterroso y Alvarado's *Pratica civil,
y criminal, e instruction de scrivanos* (Valladolid, 1563), which quickly
became a transatlantic bestseller. Reproduced courtesy of Special
Collections Department, Harvard Law School Library.

heart a *formulario*, a compendium of useful forms notaries needed to know
to do their job well. Such formularies had been around for centuries;
indeed, the *Siete Partidas* contained one. But Monterroso did more, il-
lustrating step by step the notary's crucial role in civil and criminal cases.
What moved him was a sense of urgency. "Every day there are more lawsuits and conflicts," he writes, and "the world is so engulfed and plagued
with them that almost nothing is decided without going to court."[54] And
while he finds high court officials reasonably competent to handle the
flood of litigation, Monterroso laments that "in many lower jurisdictions

(especially where the judges hold no degree, are not instructed in the style and practice of Civil and Criminal suits, and are ignorant of the law), the entire administration of justice depends on the notary (whose ignorance often impedes Justice, harms the polity, and makes lawsuits infinite and immortal)."[55]

Thus Monterroso, like the authors of the picaresque then coming into vogue, casts the notary as a powerful, strategic figure in the administration of Castilian justice. He's a potentially dangerous actor, too, but due less to greed than to ignorance and sloth. "In many parts of these Kingdoms," according to Monterroso, "it is commonplace for notaries, without working or studying, to use their offices however they please. This sows all manner of errors and barbarity (by contrast with foreign Kingdoms, where the notaries know Latin and are well-read)."[56] As a result he finds a veritable garden of contractual and judicial tares: botched dowries, contracts, and wills, dubious depositions and confessions, and more. No one should expect to do the job well, warns Monterroso, unless he invests plenty of hard work and study. He offers his *Pratica* as a means by which the aspiring notary can hone his skills and pass the required exams.[57]

Monterroso gives pride of place to lawsuits. This makes sense, as litigation was rapidly increasing in Monterroso's day. Obviously not all suits were alike: some were criminal, while most were civil (thus Monterroso begins with civil suits, *causas civiles en la vía ordinaria*); some were initiated by plaintiffs, whereas others were brought by the authorities themselves (*de oficio*); some were conducted in abbreviated format (*sumariamente*), while others extended into a proof phase involving interrogatories and witness depositions. But all suits involved writing. For a case even to begin, the initial allegations and petition for justice had to be put into written form—perhaps by an advocate (*abogado*) or by one of the less expensive attorneys, a *procurador*.[58] Then a notary had to present this document to a judge, who would decide whether to pursue it.[59] All testimony and legal motions thereafter had to be written down for the judge's consideration. In Spanish justice, unlike that of the English, no juries were involved.[60] Oral argumentation did have its place, but a great deal happened away from the courtroom and had to be conveyed to the judge on paper.[61] The very structure of justice thus made the notarial go-between a crucial participant.

Moreover, the parties to a dispute had to work through the same notary. It took two sides to tangle in a lawsuit, but only one notary. He compiled the written records on the basis of which the judge would decide who won. Typically he acted like a shuttlecock, moving among legal actors and weaving together the multiple writings (not all of them his)—the accusations, notifications, testimony, pleadings, recusations, and other forms—upon which a judge would base his decision. The notary was supposed to be studiously neutral, and to keep case records secret and safe.

The notary's mediating job became especially crucial when the judge ordered witness depositions. In theory, a judge was supposed to attend and conduct these.[62] "It is very important for the Judge to see the Witness's face," Villadiego Vascuñana explains in Instruccion politica, y práctica judicial (1612), the better to determine "how much faith to put in them." The judge should observe "the form and manner in which [witnesses] speak: whether they become alarmed or confused, or speak with passion, or very deliberately."[63] In practice, however, judges leaned heavily on notaries instead, given the clogged condition of the Spanish judicial system.[64] Judges only judged for a limited term of office, after all, whereas notaries were professionals permanently engaged in record making. Monterroso is thus quite clear:

> The best and principal part of the office is to know how to examine a witness, and the greater part of justice for the parties depends on it, because lawsuits are decided by the depositions (at least all those that consist of depositions). And since it is mainly notaries who examine the witnesses and not judges, who do so only rarely, it is very important that they be specialists in this, and find out as much about it as they possibly can.[65]

So the notary had to be prepared to be an everyday inquisitor, a specialist at producing trial-ready truth for a judge's consideration. He might have to confront a recalcitrant debtor.[66] Or he might be among the first to arrive at a crime scene; he had to know just what to do to capture witnesses' testimony while their memories were still fresh.[67] Mistakes put everyone's conscience at risk. Indeed, their very salvation was at stake. So serious was the job of judicial record making that Bartolomé de Carvajal, in his 1585 manual Instruction y memorial para escrivanos y juezes executores, compares notaries to priests. Making sworn depositions, he writes, "is like going to confess."[68]

For Carvajal, doing a good job began with proper swearing-in technique. The notary should take witnesses' oaths "copiously, because the words of the oath instill fear in them and move them to tell the truth."[69] Once a witness was sworn in, the notary's next task was to administer a series of questions known as the "general" ones mandated by law (las *preguntas generales de la ley*).[70] First the witness was asked whether he or she knew about the substance of the case. The next questions served to identify the witness: age, whether the witness was related to one of the parties (and if so, in what way), whether the witness was a friend or enemy of one of the parties. Last but not least, had anyone bribed, begged, or otherwise induced the witness not to tell the truth? The details of these preliminaries were not recorded, just brief mention of administering the oath (*juraron en forma*) and the "general questions required by law." From this point on, the notary was supposed to "take great care to find out the truth just as it happened."[71]

But just the intention to learn the truth was not enough. Specific techniques of interrogation and legal ventriloquy had to be studied and learned. To keep witnesses from perjuring themselves and do one's Christian duty by them, writes Monterroso, a notary must break down each question. Does the witness *know* something, or *believe* it? (Why, for what reasons exactly?) Did he actually *see* it (and if so, when, where, and who was present)? Or did he only *hear* about it (from whom, how, etc.)? If you break the question down with this four-part technique, instructs Monterroso, even someone who wants to answer badly will answer reasonably. This technique, he indicates, is especially useful for witnesses who are simpletons and "need to be dragged by the beard."[72] It will also catch out those who have been bribed and simply "want to repeat everything that the question says," and will trap clever fabricators in contradictions.[73]

What of recording—what exactly should be written down? Notaries "are interpreters," according to Francisco González de Torneo's 1587 manual *Pratica de escrivanos*, whose account of witnesses' words is the governing one in a case.[74] When it comes to taking initial testimony in a criminal case (*sumaria información*), the notary must write down what witnesses say in the same order that they say it, even if they blurt out a disorderly mess, "without subtracting or changing anything of substance." For example, if a witness says that someone bashed someone else with a club (*garrote*), the notary should not write down that the weapon was a stick (*palo*). That is, unless the witness testifies in "very rustic" words, "like *ru, ru,* or *gangarrillo,* or other similar terms people use when word gets around about something shameful." Here González de Torneo seems to leave some room for interpretation. What he insists should not be altered are the gestures or words the witness says he saw or heard.[75]

Since most early modern Spaniards could neither read nor write, the issue of the "rustic person" was more than hypothetical—and as we'll see in later chapters, it bulked large in Spanish America. Later writers frankly acknowledged a gap between prescription and practice. Yes, the notary was supposed to record exactly what the witness said, however crude it might be. Yet according to José Juan y Colom's highly successful *Instruccion de escribanos en orden a lo judicial* (1736), "the usual practice is to put the substance of what the witness says in better-sounding, clear terms, because if the witness is a rustic person, his testimony will otherwise be utterly confusing, and a complete fabrication, as often occurs; thus it is permissible . . . to purify what the witness says, and write it down properly."[76] For Juan y Colom, the notary not only converts a witness's words from speech into writing, but acts as the arbiter of decency: he converts improper, "rustic" speech into propriety. With his pen, ink, and specialized knowledge, he himself is a kind of pre-judge, filtering testimony for the judge to weigh.

The authors of manuals were also concerned by what notaries did *not* write. Monterroso complains that ignorant notaries, when eliciting witnesses' testimony, "leave the best parts unwritten, multiplying words where they're useless and leaving the necessary ones in the inkwell." Some, he claims, are even so lazy that they merely take down a list of witnesses' names and write up their responses to the questions later, "when the witnesses are not present."[77] González de Torneo particularly cautions notaries about recording the initial round of testimony in criminal trials. He warns them not to edit out crucial portions of witnesses' words, a practice he describes as commonplace: "There is a common practice in the *sumarias informaciones* the reason for which I fail to understand, and I think it must have been introduced by notaries, and it is that even though the witness says something that exculpates the accused, they only put [in writing] what makes him look guilty, when they should put down everything he says."[78] Even in the sensitive opening stage of a criminal case, then, notaries produced a shaped, collaborative truth—one that might shave, bevel, and polish witnesses' words a bit here, a bit there, as they were "translated" into writing.[79]

But what if a witness refused to talk? In certain situations accused persons might avoid testifying and incriminating themselves: under ecclesiastical immunity, for instance. No one (at least in theory) could go after a man or woman who had claimed refuge in a church.[80] However, if defendants or witnesses refused to testify, or gave dubious or contradictory testimony,

FIGURE 7. Jean Milles de Souvigny, *Praxis criminis persequendi*
(Paris, 1541), depicts the *estrapade*, a form of judicial torture especially
common in early modern Europe. Also known as "the strappado, *corda*,
or *cola*," it was "called by jurists the 'queen of torments.' " Peters,
Torture, 68. The notary, seated before the judge, writes down the
tortured subject's confession. Reproduced courtesy of New
York Public Library, Sterling Collection.

the judge could order the truth forced out of them. Judicial torture was not
an oxymoron; *tormento* was part of the administration of early modern justice. The use of ropes and stretching of limbs, water torture, and other
techniques was not confined to the Spanish Inquisition.[81]

Leading manuals of practice such as Monterroso's are gruesomely specific and serious about ensuring that torture, when prescribed, was orderly,
legitimate. And when it came to torture, the notary was an indispensable
technology of power. Monterroso could not be more chillingly clear on

this: "You must know that the notary is the execution of torture."[82] He should register the precise location of the tourniquets on the defendants' thighs, calves, biceps, and forearms, and the exact number of turns given to them; the precise amount of water poured through a thin cloth and down the defendant's throat; and so on (figure 7). If he failed to do this grisly duty, the parties to a lawsuit might be "gravely harmed." For example, Monterroso explains, if "the judge ordered someone to be given eight turns of the tourniquet, or twelve *quartillos* of water, on account of the crime and the quality of his person, and then at the time of execution of the sentence of torture they gave him half or a third more turns and too many quartillos of water, such that by so exceeding his sentence of torture the defendant died, or they made him say something that was not true," no one would know unless the notary had written it all down precisely.[83] The notary was an indispensable part of torture.

Everyone but the plaintiff might in theory be subjected to violence of some kind to get at the truth. That was the way this system of justice worked: the truth of the crime scene, the courtroom, the jail, and the dungeon could *legally* be extracted through leading questions and careful, calibrated applications of fear and intimidation. Castilian laws and manuals go to great lengths to restrain officials and keep their behavior within the bounds of the licit—but they are clear that fear and force should be used and documented. Hence what reads like an oxymoron: legitimate torture. Records of the resulting violence and its "truths" are especially stark and chilling in Inquisition cases.[84] But the Inquisition's repertoire of techniques was in much wider use. No wonder early modern Spanish sayings insistently juxtaposed legal professionals and doctors. Both engaged in extraction; both had economic interests at stake; both might well gouge. "If you dislike someone," as the saying went, "sue them; if you hate someone, sue them and send a doctor."[85]

The manuals of later centuries would show a shift away from the institutionalized infliction of fear and pain. Torture "only serves to reveal the greater or lesser robustness, the sturdier or weaker spirit of the defendants, and not to uncover the truth that is looked for," as José Marcos Gutiérrez's 1826 manual on criminal practice puts it—thus exposing physically frail innocents to a high risk of falsely incriminating themselves while giving hardened criminals a good chance of getting off for crimes they actually committed.[86] It might also be inefficient. Those who had made statements under torture were required to ratify them later, and might seesaw back and forth between versions. Late eighteenth-century critiques led eventually to change, but copies of manuals by Monterroso and others still circulated from Madrid to Manila, their torture sections intact.

Truth by Template

Notarial records of an extrajudicial kind consist overwhelmingly of stylized accord: "Be it known to all who read this that we . . . do agree. . . ."[87] They also insistently proclaim their truthfulness, textually guaranteed by the notary's presence. Though we never remark on it, there is something extraordinary about this. How did centuries of very unequal, often exploitative relations—including feudal relations of tribute and labor, slavery, and the abusive exercise of authority—leave behind so many millions of pages attesting to true agreement? And by what superintending notarial magic did a land sale, legal proxy, or credit deal come out looking virtually the same across centuries, from frontier outposts to Madrid or Granada? If Spanish notarial records were a musical score and we could play them, we would get something very long and dull but strangely harmonious.

Clearly this is truth by template—a truth recognizable not by its singularity, but by its very regularity.[88] The overwhelming textual impression conveyed by notarial records is one of the unity of event and recordation: the tag phrases "before me (*ante mí*)" and "which I certify" (*de que doy fé*) recur throughout, as though the notary were drawing up documents himself at the very moment of agreement.[89] But as we'll see, document production happened in stages, and might involve various writers and multiple scenes of writing. The unities are textual artifacts of this historical process.

The basic steps of the process, regulated by the 1503 Pragmatic Sanction and subsequent Castilian laws, were supposed to proceed as follows: If someone wanted a notarized public record of a sale or some other business, she or he made arrangements for a notary to draw one up.[90] This might happen at the notary's workplace, or it might involve a house call for a little extra charge.[91] A draft, called the *nota* or *minuta*, would be written for the client(s), with all its clauses fully filled out (*en extenso*) so that clients would be apprised of the details of the agreements to which they were committing themselves. The draft would then be read to the parties. If they agreed with its contents, they were supposed to sign it (or have a witness sign for them).[92] Then the notary had a fixed allowance of days within which to deliver an exact final copy to the parties involved. What he himself kept, bound into his registers should it later be needed, was the duly authorized draft. Thus what we are reading in the notarial archives is the chronologically ordered drafts (*minutas*) of the transactions drawn up before notaries. (Copies went to the parties who had commissioned and paid for them.)[93]

These were the rules. Knowing how to get the details right in each kind of record was the notary's weighty responsibility. And as Monterroso lamented from his lofty perch in the Castilian legal system, "in contracts, entails, wills . . . there are many errors, nullities, lacks, contradictions, and obfuscations; and what is worse, falsehood results from the lack of good order and the ignorance of the notary who tries to do what he does not understand. . . . Most are happy to know from memory just the badly ordered beginning of a simple proxy, obligation, sale, or custody record . . . and to earn money, they fake what they are not."[94] These themes were picked up with variations by other authors. They proclaimed themselves seasoned experts while clearing a place for their manuals by decrying the evils of their day—the ignorance, the greed, and (more to the point for boosting sales) the shortcomings of earlier works like Monterroso's. Some authors tailored their contributions to concentrate on particular audiences or types of documents. Tomás de Mercado's influential *Tratos y contratos de mercaderes y tratantes* (1569), for example, addressed the special requirements and dilemmas presented by mercantile contracts.[95] And Juan de la Ripia's *Practica de testamentos, y modos de subceder* (1676) took on wills and other aspects of inheritance, beginning with a detailed list of "objections" to previous authors' advice on the subject.[96] No two notarial manuals are alike—but the authors all proclaim the importance of getting the details right, so that notaries might avoid endangering their salvation and that of their clients through grievous malpractice.

This led to the introduction, in some Castilian cities, of prefabricated forms for certain contracts. They contained blank spaces in the appropriate places for the client's name, place of residence, and so forth; the rest was already written out. With the increased availability of printing, such forms might be made up in bulk at a local print shop and used as needed.[97] Notarial assistants must have appreciated this labor-saving improvement. The use of printed forms sped up the rate at which notaries could deliver relatively simple, formulaic contracts to clients, such as powers of attorney (*poderes*), which were among the documents most in demand.

The crown also tried to standardize the amount notaries might charge clients for their work. This had long been a concern of the monarchs. By the late fifteenth century, matters had gotten quite out of hand, and thus sixteenth-century reform efforts sought to make the price of documents reasonable and predictable.[98] The Pragmática of 1503 ordered notaries to charge ten maravedis for each page.[99] Before long, however, rapid inflation and rising costs of living made it necessary to issue adjustments.[100] Official price lists (*aranceles*) were decreed for various kinds of documents, and notaries were required to display these prominently so that their clients might know the fixed rates. But the issue remained a vexed one, and a standard feature of popular sayings lambasting notaries.[101]

The sixteenth-century push for standardization of notarial practice had some unintended effects. The historian José Bono notes what others noted at the time: that the use of manuals and printed forms, while it unified notaries' style, also "favored the multiplication of irrelevant clauses, and the maintenance of antiquated ones out of servile addiction."[102] Knowing the forms was not enough; the notary had to know when and how to apply them, and that depended largely on his informal apprenticeship. The crown could not suddenly boost the level at which young men learned through everyday practice. Changing legal prescription was one thing; changing deeply ingrained customs was another.

Conclusions

How, then, to interpret the boast that Quevedo inserts into the mouth of a notary, "Believe me, sir, it all depends on us"? This is celebrated early modern fiction. Yet Gabriel de Monterroso in his bestselling manual basically asserts the same thing: the centrality and importance of the notaries who made people's judicial and extrajudicial records. For those of us who rely on the archival results to gain access to long-ago "voices," this is a bracing reminder that spoken words did not pass unfiltered into the record. Notarial agency (perhaps undeclared and invisible) gave records their words and final form. We thus have to modify the imagined subjects of our archives to make room for a blended, composite agency that includes the notary, even in the records that seem most spontaneous. For notaries, to paraphrase Monterroso, were the instruments of the early modern archive.

Thus we need to grasp the rules, interests, and customs of the notary's craft—and, happily, early modern Spanish publishers provide important pieces of the puzzle. Monterroso's *Pratica* and other notarial manuals give us a thorough rendering of the notary's business as it was supposed to be practiced *en teoría*, in theory, according to contemporary Castilian legality. What about notaries overseas, in America and beyond, where Spaniards invaded and imposed their empire? There, too, Castilian standards applied. As authoritative works like Monterroso's *Pratica* became available in the late sixteenth century, they quickly spread throughout Spain's empire. Monterroso became a bestseller of the transatlantic book trade.[103] Nor were Spanish notaries the only customers: by 1588, a Spanish priest working in the Andes complained to the crown that some Indians—generally caciques and their sons, trained in Spanish by priests—used their linguistic skills "to penetrate our usages, the better to resist us."[104] He cited examples with which he was familiar, including "a Spanish-speaking Indian from a town called Andamarca, in the province of Los Carangas [now Bolivia]" who "bought a Monterroso."[105]

As for interests and customs—that is, notarial *práctica* as opposed to *teoría*—we are about to see how large they bulked. But before we turn to the American side of the Atlantic, we should recall further Spanish exigencies. Philip II had to deal with a bankrupt imperial treasury almost as soon as he was crowned king. Keeping Spanish armies in Flanders would prove thereafter to be a vastly expensive royal project.[106] Thus Philip and his advisors constantly had to find new sources of revenue, the most long-lasting and notorious of which was the crown's sale of public offices in its Spanish American realms.[107] This commerce grew gradually, starting with the sale of notarial offices. In 1559, a qualified applicant might purchase a lifetime post as a notary public in the viceroyalties of New Spain and Peru.[108] By 1581, if the owner of such a post paid a third of its value to the crown, he might transfer it (along with his archives) to a buyer-successor through a formal "renunciation."[109] By 1606, to make the investment even more attractive to potential buyers, the crown allowed officeholders to transfer offices in perpetuity, as long as they made payments to the royal treasury: half an office's value for the initial renunciation, and on subsequent renunciations, a third of the purchase price.[110]

Thus by the beginning of the seventeenth century, according to J. H. Parry, salable public offices "became pieces of private property, reverting to the Crown only when the conditions of sale or renunciation were violated."[111] Whenever a post reverted to the crown, royal officials auctioned it off as soon as possible to the highest bidder. The higher the price, the better for the royal treasury—but the more officeholders needed to earn while in office to recoup their initial investments. A cycle was launched that would continue for centuries, leading to the sale of ever higher and more responsible posts. In the process, Spanish American notarial archives were thoroughly "patrimonialized": they became part of notary publics' property, bought and sold for profit.[112]

This created a dilemma of the crown's own making: how to ensure bureaucratic discipline in Spanish America if public offices were commodities, bought and sold in perpetuity? A notary public was supposed to be beholden to no one. His prices were not to exceed official limits, and the neutrality of his conduct while drawing up judicial and extrajudicial records should be beyond question. But if office buyers bought posts on credit —sometimes at high prices—were they not bound to recoup their investments, perhaps by gouging or favoring their customers? The sharp-eyed Mateo Alemán did not miss this potential source of discord. Guzmán, his picaresque protagonist, mocks the greedy notary that was a fixture of popular lore:

> He'll know how to defend himself and make excuses; after all, an iron shaft can always be gilded. And they'll say that the price lists are outdated, that basic necessities cost more each day, that taxes are also going up, that they didn't get their offices for nothing, that their income has to cover the rent and the time they've invested. . . . It must always have been so, since Aristotle says that the worst thing that can happen to a republic is the sale of offices.[113]

The dilemma would only grow in Spanish America. Spaniards did not go there with low expectations, and the cherished hope of many was to make a quick fortune and live in style as a successful *indiano*. Hernán Cortés, after all, was a notary—and look what he had achieved.[114] Disciplining notaries, never an easy task in Castile, would grow even more difficult in the Americas once a massive gold rush was on.

CHAPTER 2

INTERESTS

Interese: El provecho, la utilidad, la ganancia
que se saca o espera de una cosa.
Indiano: El que ha ido a las Indias,
que de ordinario éstos buelven ricos.
—Sebastián de Covarrubias

From Americans' point of view, the Spanish invaders initially had one big interest: gold. They simply couldn't get enough of it. Columbus had gone from one island to another asking about it; the earliest settlers had forced people to find it for them. After the fall of the Aztec empire, Francisco Pizarro had raised a following to pursue rumors that even more of the precious metal could be found. When he and his men reached the Inca empire, they were dazzled beyond their wildest dreams. Guaman Poma later depicted an imagined dialogue between the Inca ruler and a Spanish conquistador (figure 8). The Inca inquires, "Is this the gold you eat?" and the Spaniard confirms, "We eat this gold."[1]

More abundant, however, was silver. By the 1540s, Spaniards were finding rich veins of it across the area they called New Spain, from Taxco to Zacatecas. And by 1545, Spaniards in Peru had learned of a big silver mountain high in the Andes, the "cerro rico" of Potosí. So great was their appetite for its riches that they made a city at its base—even though it was far from the coast, at an altitude of over 13,000 feet, where cold winds blasted and crops could not grow. By 1600, Peru's registered silver production had grown to around 70 million pesos a year, and Potosí, with a population of around 100,000, had suddenly become one of the world's largest cities.[2]

Notaries were in the thick of this restless quest. Cortés himself was a notary who had not been content to remain in the Caribbean. And of the 169 men who in 1532 accompanied Pizarro to Peru, writes James Lockhart, "there were ten notaries . . . and there is little reason to think the propor-

FIGURE 8. Felipe Guaman Poma de Ayala represents the invading
Spaniards' boundless appetite for precious metals in this imagined
colloquy. Artwork in the public domain. Photograph supplied by The
Royal Library, Copenhagen, Denmark, from manuscript GKS 2232 4°,
El primer nueva corónica y buen gobierno (1615 / 1616), "19. The chapter
of the Spanish conquest and the civil wars," drawing 147, p. 371. See
http://www.kb.dk/permalink/2006/poma/info/es/frontpage.htm.

tion diminished later."[3] To Spaniards, the handsomest prize of all was a
grant of indigenous peoples' labor power, an *encomienda*. Such grants were
the key to extracting local resources. Notaries involved in the early mili-
tary stages received encomiendas "as a matter of course," and those who
played their cards right in the complicated Peruvian civil wars of the 1540s
and '50s might also attain encomiendas for loyal service.[4] Some of these
men were of relatively high standing in the Iberian communities they had
left, but some were humble men who had achieved spectacular feats of
social climbing.[5]

Meanwhile, American populations were plummeting, due to epidemic disease as well as the violence of war and settlers' brutality.[6] As the toll of Spaniards' invasion became clearer, the crown made efforts to protect its indigenous subjects from Spaniards' "bad example." In 1529, Charles V took the remarkable step, given the great (and growing) litigiousness of Spanish society, of banning lawyers from his American realms.[7] The prohibition would not last long, but is as good an indication as any of the monarch's alarm at the rapid spread of litigiousness overseas.[8] Notaries were never banned; they were needed to produce the most basic truth of possession. But by mid-century the crown was increasingly concerned about them: that notaries were unqualified; that they battened on Indian communities, stirring up trouble among them the better to charge exorbitant fees.[9]

Gradually, the crown began to rein in the *encomenderos* (the holders of encomienda grants) and put in place two juridical estates or "republics"— the *república de españoles* and the *república de indios*—each governed by its own institutions.[10] Spaniards were supposed to stay in cities with orderly urban grids, create stable marriages and households, and lead orderly, Christian lives. They had their own magistrates (*corregidores*), as well as municipal councils (*cabildos*) and notaries.[11] As for "Indians"—still the vast majority in New Spain and Peru—they were to live under the jurisdiction of a rural magistrate (known in New Spain as *alcalde mayor*, and in Peru as *corregidor de indios*) and the spiritual supervision of a local priest. They were also supposed to govern themselves in their own towns and villages through a separate system of indigenous mayors, municipal councils, and notaries (*escribanos de cabildo*). Thus in theory, at least, the indigenous population would resolve many of its own disputes.[12]

In practice, the crown's orderly design never worked out so neatly.[13] Yet the two estates, or *repúblicas*, long served as a juridical framework for governance, leading, among other things, to the creation of special Indian defenders and some Indian courts (*juzgados de indios*).[14] Encomenderos did not disappear during the late 1500s, but their powers were significantly curtailed. Meanwhile, Philip II increasingly shifted responsibility for effective local governance to the corregidores, salaried bureaucrats with fixed terms of office. He also issued various orders aimed at controlling the quality of the overseas posts—primarily notarial offices—that he was starting to sell. Those holding Spanish American notarial office could not simultaneously be encomenderos; no mestizo or mulatto might be a notary, and so forth.[15]

Still, the stereotype spread of the bad American notary—the greedy, grasping officeholder ready to sell the best truth money could buy. Guaman Poma offers a scathing portrait that situates him among other stereotypically villainous figures preying upon "the poor Indian." He denounces corregidores' notaries in particular: they "receive large bribes" from caciques and commoners, and so on. These deceitful men even turn on their own superiors, the corregidores, for gain, "and then they walk away laughing."[16] Friar Antonio de Calancha, in his 1638 chronicle of Augustinian friars' labors in Peru, provides an even more vivid cameo. He depicts people in the northern Peruvian city of Trujillo gathered around a table in a notary's workshop, drawing up a contract, all of them aware that one of the parties is in the process of defrauding the other. "The notary favored the cause of the evildoer," writes Calancha, "and all the other witnesses and people present were partisans, cooperating in the fraud." But just as they were winding up, an earthquake hit.

> The defrauded one said, "Let's get out, it's an earthquake," to which his defrauder replied, "It'll pass, let's finish this." As the furor grew and chunks of the roof began to fall, the innocent man tried to flee but was stopped by the malicious man, who said, "Don't be a coward, it'll be over soon." As the notary could tell the earthquake was getting worse, he tried to leave the table that was blocking their passage, but the defrauder moved to stop him, which allowed the innocent man and a friend of his to escape into the plaza. As the entire building collapsed, a beam caught the notary's head between the corner of the table on which he was writing and his hands, and sliced off his hands like a knife.[17]

The elements of the stereotype are remarkably consistent: the notary is greedy, partial, *interesado*; he is thus open to illicit, "unholy alliances" of convenience. And the stereotype would be very long-lived. Antonio de Paz y Salgado, for example, author of the Guatemalan manual *Instruccion de litigantes* (1742), cautions his readers to avoid spending money on lawsuits if at all possible. But should they engage in litigation, "of all the officials involved, the one whom the litigant should take the greatest care to please is the Notary of the case, not only because he tends to be the greatest *Satrap*, but because, as the Spanish maxim says, *good lawsuit or bad, get the*

Notary well in hand."[18] The Mexican author José Joaquín Fernández de Lizardi makes ample use of the stereotype as well in *El Periquillo Sarniento* (1816), regarded as the first Latin American novel. He devotes a chapter to the malpractice of a notary nicknamed Chanfaina (Chili Stew) who "would commit the dirtiest tricks for just an ounce or two of gold, and sometimes for less."[19] The message conveyed by these and many other Spanish American writers is the same as Quevedo's and Monterroso's: the notary is a powerful, consequential actor you cannot afford to ignore. Be sure to get him on your side if you can.

The rapid diffusion in Spanish America of the stereotype of the greedy, gouging notary, I'll argue, points to further anxiety. As in Europe, notaries in the Americas represented the potent, troubling link between writing and power—specifically, the power of archived documents cast in durable "officialese." But this was colonial terrain. Those for whom Spanish was not a native tongue—that is, the vast indigenous majority of the American population—had especially good reasons to be concerned about this nexus. Guaman Poma illustrates well the challenge and the threat of getting words into official legal forms. It was not straightforward or simple. And whether you were situated in the Quechua hinterland of the "lettered city" or in its urban centers, your petitions for justice had to be mediated by writing.[20] Extrajudicial business was best committed to notaries, too, if you wanted to be able to avail yourself of the colonial justice system for enforcement of your claims. Notaries were the gateway to the colonial archives.

Moreover, notaries did not act alone. In Spanish America, as in Europe, the exercise of their powers depended for its efficacy on a set of local and extralocal officeholders, including corregidores (who acted as judges) and other judicial personnel. For these men the boundaries of public and private affairs were not sharply drawn.[21] And the longer Spanish families remained in one Spanish American place and cultivated a sense of belonging to it—that is, became more *criollo*—the more interconnected they became, as well as jealous of their hold on local power. From an indigenous point of view, these "power groups," as Steve Stern has called them, constituted networks of "mutually cooperative exploiters."[22] He traces their rise around 1600 in the Andean region of Huamanga (modern-day Ayacucho) as they grew to include corregidores, caciques, priests, merchants, municipal officials, and others interested in profiting from the business opportunities and the indigenous labor-power in their region.

Notaries, as we've seen, were required to be upstanding and free from selfish motives. Integral members of the lettered city, they were expected to serve their sovereign's justice daily in a thousand routine ways. Yet in this chapter I'll argue that Spanish American notaries could not do their jobs, or do them successfully, at any rate, independently of their region's "power groups." This does not mean that they (or anyone else) were walking villainous stereotypes. But it does mean they were thoroughly immersed in the local scene, and thoroughly invested in it. Using wills and other sources, I will examine the interests that moved notaries, and the stakes for them in belonging to a particular place. The focus will be on Cuzco—the largest and most important Inca city, refounded as a Spanish city in 1534—and the Spanish notaries who forged notarial practice there.

Early Notarial Interests

Cuzco was especially alluring to Spaniards, as its region held some of the richest encomiendas in all of Peru. Many among the Inca elite had decided in the 1530s that it was best to get along with the invaders, and thus an abundant labor force could be mustered—despite the resisting Incas, who had established an enclave in nearby Vilcabamba, and the ravages of disease. Cuzco was also strategically located along the royal road to Potosí, which was fast becoming the world's largest silver producer. Local entrepreneurs could do booming business in the upper mining districts, especially with the sugar loaves produced in the nearby temperate valleys of Abancay and the coca leaf grown around Paucartambo.[23]

The city itself, a monument of Inca stonework and engineering, was stunning to behold. Cuzco was full of imposing palaces and the *panacas*, or kin groups, of the former Inca rulers. "It also had a magnificent and solemn temple to the sun," wrote Pedro de Cieza de León, one of the first Spaniards to reach Cuzco, "which they called Curicanche, one of the richest in gold and silver to be found in the whole world."[24] By mid-century, Spaniards were actively refashioning the city to make a place for their own temples. They put Andean stonemasons to work erecting massive stone churches, monasteries, and convents (many atop Inca structures), as well as one of Spanish America's most imposing cathedrals. The large central plaza of the Incas was subdivided and a portion of it turned into residences and storefronts. Cabildo chambers were set along the new Plaza del Regocijo, which had once been the northwestern portion of the much larger Inca plaza. Cuzco's "numerary" public notaries (*escribanos públicos y del*

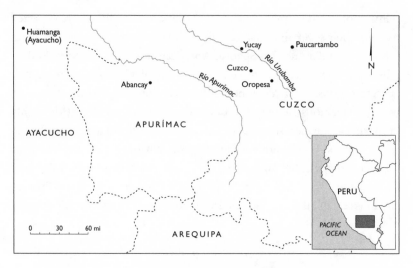

MAP 2. Cuzco, its hinterland, and neighboring cities
and towns mentioned in the text.

número) had their offices right next door, in the bustling *portal de los escribanos*, close to power.[25] Cuzco seems to have had six of these posts throughout the colonial period, as well as an indeterminate number of royal notaries, men who might eventually obtain a numerary post. (In the meantime they could do notarial work wherever they did not jostle the monopolies of the numerary notaries.) Thus in the heart of Cuzco, as in other Spanish American cities, Spaniards built the ramparts of their lettered city.

Who were the first notaries to inhabit this newly lettered city, and what interests moved them? These things are hard to trace, as notarial records from Spanish Cuzco's earliest decades have been lost.[26] But portions of the sixteenth-century paper trail remain. An entry in the crusty 1545–51 book of minutes of the Cuzco cabildo notes that on June 9, 1548, a man named Sancho de Orue came before the assembled councilmen to present his appointment as notary of Cuzco's cabildo.[27] Orue was qualified as a royal notary.[28] Moreover, he had "served his majesty as a good and loyal vassal" in the bloody civil wars that had broken out among rival Spaniards, fighting on the crown's side in the crucial 1548 battle of Jaquijaguana.[29] This post was clearly his reward, and he clung to it for decades, often naming a substitute to perform his notarial duties while he was away on other business.[30] Typically a Spanish city's cabildo notary (*escribano público y de cabildo*) occupied the highest rung in the local hierarchy of notarial offices, followed by the "numerary" notaries and the royal notaries.[31] So there was a spatial order to the most archivally visible, prestigious notarial posts, and at the peak (figuratively) and in the middle (literally) sat Sancho.

Not everyone gained notarial office in sixteenth-century Cuzco through daring feats of arms: Pedro Díaz Valdeón, for example, received a post because he was on good terms with the king's apothecary.[32] But at least one other man, Luis de Quesada, fought and then narrated his way into royal favor, becoming a numerary notary of Cuzco. By the time Quesada began petitioning in the 1560s, the crown was less interested in granting new privileges than in reining in those it had already rewarded. To get anywhere, one's story had to be good, and Quesada's certainly was. He seemed to have been everywhere, showing up just as trouble broke out to help put down rebellions against the crown.[33] But the pièce de résistance of his petition concerned the famous mines of Potosí. He, Luis de Quesada, had introduced to the Andes the technique for extracting silver from its ores with mercury, thus reviving production and boosting the crown's revenue by hundreds of thousands of pesos. This breakthrough had been credited to another man, but it was really Quesada who had taught him what to do and dispatched him to Potosí. For his pains, he was awarded official title to notarial office in the city of Cuzco.[34]

These men were was still around when a landmark visit took place. In 1571, Peru's fifth viceroy, Francisco de Toledo, came to town to settle old business and impose royal authority as firmly as possible. This was the first time a viceroy had come to Cuzco. He made sure that Túpac Amaru, leader of the Inca resistance at Vilcabamba, was captured and executed in a grisly public ceremony, killing Incas' hopes of a return to power. The viceroy also broke local encomenderos' lock on the Cuzco cabildo, forcing them to accept an alderman from outside their ranks. Toledo, in short, changed many things, upending many people's positions—but not that of Sancho de Orue. He was allowed to stay on as cabildo notary even though "he was very old and crippled in hands and feet by the disease of gout, and failing eyesight which kept him from exercising personally the [duties of] office."[35] Toledo gave him open-ended permission to act through a series of substitutes since Orue "wished to set aside his papers and attend to calmer things."[36] Not until 1581 did the old notary meet his match. That year his designated substitute, the royal notary Pedro de Cervantes, alerted the cabildo that Orue was trying to remove him to "avenge his passions."[37] The cabildo strongly endorsed Cervantes and ordered Sancho de Orue either to use his office personally or lose it. The old man tried for a few weeks—and the handwriting in the cabildo minute book goes wobbly—before giving up. Shortly thereafter, Luis de Quesada also stepped down, renouncing his post in favor of his son. No one thereafter would get to be a high-level notary quite the way these men had, by daring feats of arms.[38]

Orue and Quesada were among the earliest occupants of high-ranking notarial offices in Spanish Cuzco—the kinds of position desirable enough to be granted as favors or rewards, or (after 1571) sold to raise revenue. But Cuzco was also the workplace of men like Pedro Quispe (see figure 9). In a couple of loose notebooks from the 1580s that once belonged to a much larger *protocolo*, Quispe kept records of indigenous parishioners' business, signing himself "I, Pedro Quispe, public and council notary for His Majesty in the parish of Our Lady of Purificación of the Hospital de Naturales."[39] Such offices were not bought and sold, nor did the crown attempt to control their records, so their occupants are an all-but-forgotten part of the lettered city—though by Quispe's day Cuzco had several indigenous parishes, and probably at least as many parish notaries. What remains of Quispe's archive consists mostly of wills, codicils, death certificates, and *inventarios* (property lists). Clearly he spent a lot of time in the hospital around priests and sick and dying patients. But Quispe also made other kinds of records, such as the sale he notarized in 1586 for a woman named Isabel Tocto Coca, which notes her need to settle a debt of thirty-eight pesos left by her deceased first husband, Antón Aymara. This contract is by Spanish standards unusually explicit about the motive: "Because she could hardly afford to pay because she had no money and even less [did she have] movable assets of any kind of which she was not in great need, she considered it the best remedy to sell a small house which the said Anton Aymara her husband left in the said parish."[40]

A few years later, the notary Pedro Quispe was wearing another hat. He worked alongside Cuzco's *juez de naturales*, a Spanish judge elected annually by the cabildo to hear Indians' legal cases.[41] The Cuzco archive contains bits of the written records Quispe kept of the summary justice dispensed in these cases. His material, all of it in excellent Spanish, points to the day-to-day frictions in urban indigenous life. For example, on June 10, 1595, Juan Tupia, an alderman in the Cuzco parish of Belén, lodged a complaint against Don Gerónimo Chanca Topa for drunkenly resisting his orders to contribute labor to the church. Quispe recorded the plaintiff's

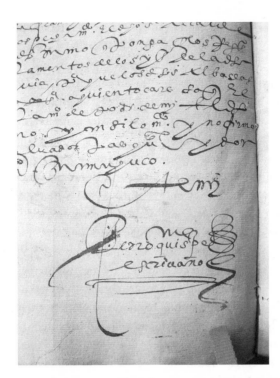

FIGURE 9. The signature of the indigenous notary Pedro Quispe.
ARC-PN, Pedro de la Carrera Ron, protocolo 4 (1586–96).
Photograph by the author.

account of Don Gerónimo's conduct as follows: "He resisted and mis-treated [Tupia], joined by some *montañeses* who were his kinsmen, and they tore his shirt, and thus he displayed it before the judge and asked him to order [Don Gerónimo] punished." The term *montañés* was used in sixteenth-century Cuzco to signify "mestizo," but apparently the term did not stick or enter into wider usage.[42] We cannot be sure whether this was Tupia's usage or Quispe's. But this is definitely not legalese. In a few fragments, Quispe provides some remarkable glimpses not only of local dilemmas and frictions, but of local terms for those involved in them.

What interests did these men pursue on the side, when they absented themselves from their duties and from Cuzco? The records, unfortunately, are missing. But around 1600 the notarial records thicken substantially, making it possible to trace some *cuzqueños'* interests and investments in detail. By this time Potosí was booming, absorbing foodstuffs from around the region and countless bushels of the coca leaf that Andean miners chewed to overcome exhaustion and hunger. Coca had once been mainly a ceremonial substance, consumed on ritual occasions. By the seventeenth century, however, coca chewing was spreading fast, and Spaniards were investing heavily in its cultivation in the Paucartambo region just north-east of Cuzco in the intermediate zone between high and lowlands.[43] They also began investing large sums to create sugar plantations in the relatively mild Andean valleys near Abancay. Much of the sugar produced on these *ingenios* would likewise be transported by mule trains and sold in Potosí.[44]

Cuzco's numerary notaries did a great deal of business for cuzqueños involved in trade: they drew up the contracts for overland shipping (*fleta-mentos*), the powers of attorney needed to transact deals at a distance (*poderes*), the credit agreements that facilitated deals (*obligaciones, censos*), sales contracts (*ventas*), and more. One gauge of the boom times is the bulkiness of the notarial registers in Cuzco's regional archives: those from the early to mid-seventeenth century are notably thicker than those dating from later in the century and thereafter. And notaries themselves might get profitably involved. Take the last will and testament of Pedro de la Carrera Ron, from 1617. A native of the town of Porcuna, near Jaen in southern Castile, Carrera Ron had become a numerary notary in Cuzco by the end of the sixteenth century; a few years later, he was also cabildo notary.[45] His will discloses his investments in the coca trade, both as a purchaser of the right to collect the tithes assessed on coca production (along with two fellow investors, "compañeros de la coca") and as a buyer and seller of coca leaf to be transported and sold.[46] He seems to have married a local merchant's daughter and managed their assets well, acquir-ing a livestock ranch at Jaquijaguana in addition to a residence in Cuzco.[47] By the end of his days Pedro de la Carrera Ron was a wealthy man. He was able to endow over 600 masses for the good of his soul and purchase 40 *bulas de composición*, indulgences that enabled a sinner to make blanket restitution for his sins through direct payment to the church. Such bulls were popular at the time because, as historian Victoria Hennessy Cum-mins notes, "the sinner would not have to proclaim his wrong-doing pub-licly in order to make amends." Better still, "the bulls were also a bargain, since restitution was made at a fraction of the actual profit accrued."[48]

Carrera Ron's contemporary, the Cuzco notary Joan de Olave, moved to profit from the expansion of sugar production. In 1609 he petitioned the viceroy for a year's leave of absence from his office of numerary notary, arguing that he owned "important estates in the valley of Abancay" that were deteriorating. If he could not attend to them personally, "they would be completely lost." The viceroy ordered Cuzco's corregidor to inquire. He reported that Olave did indeed have estates in Abancay, where wheat, maize, and other crops were grown. The notary also owned a cattle ranch, and was "in the process of putting in sugarcane for [the production of] sugar and rebuilding an inn . . . all of which constitutes important property, and to repair and build houses and [outbuildings] and mills he needs to be there in person, because to do otherwise would incur high costs, losses, and damage to the said estates."[49] Permission was granted for a four-month absence. In April 1610, Olave named the royal notary Miguel Mendo in his stead, and presumably left town to oversee his expanding rural estates.

Cuzco notaries invested in a variety of other things as well, from pack mules to playing cards. The notary Alonso Calvo's investment of choice was the mules that moved trade goods throughout the Andes. In his 1637 will he declared that he owned "a mule train of seventy-eight mules," which his overseer had just taken to Lima to collect "the clothing and other merchandise" that a Lima merchant had contracted with Calvo to transport.[50] Calvo also bought and sold mules, as well as horseshoes, tack, and other things necessary for his freight business. His fellow numerary notary José Navarro diversified in a different direction, investing in the entertainment business of his day: playing cards. Navarro, on his sickbed in 1643 due to unspecified wounds, declared in his will that he had purchased the right to hold the local playing card monopoly (el estanco de los naipes) for a ten-year period. This was no small investment; it cost a yearly bar of silver worth 1,700 pesos.[51] An inventory of Navarro's property listed several relevant items: printing plates, a wooden press, large scissors used to make playing cards, and crates containing over 4,300 decks of cards.

Were notaries breaking the law if they devoted their energies to such non-notarial business? Not as long as they did the notarial work that was expected of them. They were not supposed to engage in the kind of petty trading known as regatonería: buying goods in bulk and then, acting as middleman, selling them off in smaller quantities.[52] But other forms of business—like running ranches or sugar mills, freighting mule trains, or making playing cards—were not prohibited to them. As they pursued enticing opportunities, the notaries of mid-colonial Cuzco put down deeper roots in the city's and region's businesses, and in the institutions and relationships that made them run.

Until the early 1600s, most of Cuzco's titled notaries—the city's numerary notaries and the royal notaries working there—were peninsular Spaniards. They might use their American profits to help out relatives back in Spain. Sebastián de Vera, a native of Llerena, ordered in his 1592 will that his largest bequest, 600 *pesos ensayados*, be sent "as soon as possible" to his mother, and should she be dead the money should go to his sisters, "those who have not yet married or professed."[53] Pedro de la Carrera Ron had his brother in Baeza, Alonso de la Carrera Ron, purchase high municipal offices in 1611 for him and his heirs. In Carrera Ron's 1617 will he ordered Alonso to sell the offices and give part of the proceeds to Alonso's children, his niece and nephew.[54] Remitting money to be invested in one's relatives or business in Spain was not a guaranteed success, however: José Navarro tried in 1642 to send to Spain a silver ingot worth 1,300 pesos, but the merchant taking it died in Panama before making the transatlantic voyage.[55]

Many notaries did what they could to leave their positions to a relative or close associate. Prior to the sale of transferable notarial offices, authorized in 1581, their efforts might be frustrated: Sancho de Orue's 1571 petition to have his son, Martín de Orue, take his place received only the inconclusive royal response, "Have a report prepared and we will see."[56] (Nothing seems to have happened.) The new terms of sale after 1581 made it easier to leave one's notarial post to a designated successor. Thus a notary might raise a son, nephew, or cousin in his profession and see him obtain title to a numerary post—if not his father's, then that of another local notary. This was the case with the Cuzco notary Alonso Beltrán Lucero, whose son Cristóbal de Lucero took over the position vacated by Antonio Sánchez on the latter's death in 1595. Years later Alonso's grandson and namesake, Alonso Beltrán Lucero, would also become a numerary notary.[57] The line seems to have ended with Alonso the younger, who died unmarried and childless.[58]

By the mid-seventeenth century, most Cuzco notaries were criollos— locally born men considered to be of Spanish descent. Peninsular immigrants might still become notaries in the city, like Antonio Pérez de Vargas, a native of Sevilla who settled in Cuzco and married a *criolla*. When title to a numerary office was sold at auction in 1687, his was the successful bid.[59] (Thereafter he tried to launch his son Ventura in trade. This bid failed spectacularly because, according to Pérez de Vargas's will, "he is a bad man

[who] has completely destroyed me, because everything he touches he ruins with his terrible ways.")[60] By then, however, Cuzco was producing its own bountiful crop of legal writers—men such as Lorenzo de Mesa Andueza, active as a numerary notary from the 1640s to the early 1680s.[61] Mesa Andueza proudly claimed descent from one of Cuzco's *conquistadores*, Alonso de Mesa, and from the highest ranks of Inca society. So proud was he of his bloodlines that, according to his 1686 will, he made sure to remind his children of them from his deathbed.[62]

The value of land is especially clear in Mesa Andueza's will. He had a considerable amount of it, including the hacienda Guandoja, adjacent to the nearby town of Anta, and urban lots in Cuzco inherited from his Inca ancestors.[63] Such assets not only bolstered one's status but made it possible to obtain that all-important resource, credit. For real estate was an especially acceptable form of collateral for taking out a *censo*, the period equivalent of a mortgage or a loan. Cuzco's largest institutional lenders, its convents and monasteries, required real estate (urban or rural) as collateral.[64] Notaries were not supposed to use their offices as collateral or in any way encumber them. (Some, like Cristóbal de Bustamante, ignored the prohibition: he declared in his 1704 will that he had imposed a censo of 3,000 pesos on his.)[65] Real property might thus give them access to credit. Lorenzo de Mesa Andueza, for example, listed in his will the censos he owed to the nuns of Santa Clara and the friars of Santo Domingo and San Agustín.[66]

Mesa Andueza's contemporary, Martín López de Paredes, allegedly came by his rural assets otherwise, by egregious land-grabbing. In 1647, his brother Juan had purchased the post of chief constable (*alguacil mayor*) for the province of Quispicanche, which contained rich croplands in the valley just south of Cuzco.[67] Juan López de Paredes had then managed to obtain land near Andahuaylillas that belonged to the indigenous kin group (*ayllu*) of Coscoja and given it to the mother-in-law of an associate of his.[68] The bishop of Cuzco had intervened and ordered restitution, but the conflict continued. Don Juan Marca, cacique of the Coscoja ayllu, went to the Cuzco cabildo in 1655 to denounce Martín López de Paredes for usurping the same piece of land as before. According to witness testimony, the notary had called together local indigenous leaders and told them in Quechua that "he had orders from the viceroy to return the lands of Coscoja to his brother Juan López de Paredes."[69] The priest of Andahuaylillas, Diego Hernández Machón, added that the notary had formed an alliance with

Don Marcos, head of another local ayllu, to sell land fraudulently with trumped-up testimony; Don Marcos thus "despoiled the people of his own ayllu . . . with Martín López securing the sale."[70] When pressed on how he knew such things, the priest cited "the reputation Martín Lopéz de Paredes has for diligently, painstakingly keeping the Indians of this town so subjected that they will do whatever he wants"—monopolizing the local wood supply, for example, so that they did not have a stick left.[71]

The outlines of a local power group seem to emerge here in the alleged collusion of constable, notary, and cacique (though in this case the priest firmly opted out). And from the available testimony, López de Paredes looks like the bad notary personified: greedy, duplicitous, using his office and knowledge to make fraudulent deals and shady alliances. But the record is very incomplete; his side of the story is missing, as well as the eventual outcome. A few years later, though, another case involving López de Paredes came before Cuzco's corregidor. This time the notary was the plaintiff, appealing a judgment requiring him to give up a small tract of land near the town of Oropesa (basically the same place as before; if not the same land, very near it). And this time his adversary was quite different. He was up against the Duke of Alba, absentee encomendero of Oropesa and one of the highest-ranking men in all of Spain.[72] The issue was whether land belonging to Alba's indigenous tributaries had been illegally sold to the notary. Alba's proxy argued that Spaniards such as López de Paredes preyed on the region's ayllus, buying up their land while promising to make tribute payments on their behalf, then forcing them to work the land. López de Paredes told a different version: he'd bought just a tiny tract from Don Diego Gualpa Nina and Don Bernabé Gualpa, "barren, mountainous, rocky, and uncultivable," and of course he had done so to help them out with their tribute payments.[73] Moreover, he asserted, land was abundant in the area, and the people who had lived there and paid tribute to the duke no longer existed.[74]

The verdict in this case is unclear, but Martín López de Paredes certainly comes across as a wily and tenacious legal adversary. The title he adduced to the land in question (which had cost him only thirty pesos) contains an unusually explicit description of the land as barren, rocky, and uncultivable. López de Paredes no doubt knew the crown had prohibited the sale of indigenous communities' lands. Nevertheless, he had obtained title to a piece by having its caciques explicitly sell it to him as useless. His notarial skills clearly served him well as he boldly poached resources from the Duke of

Alba's tributaries.[75] The Cuzco notary held other lands in the area as well. By the time he died in 1676, López de Paredes had amassed significant wealth.[76] He and his wife, Doña Catalina Ruiz de Garfias, had a daughter who professed as a nun in Santa Catalina, and their five other legitimate children (four sons and a daughter) each received an inheritance of 13,228 pesos. Their daughter Doña Josefa López de Paredes would eventually marry three times without leaving an heir. During the early 1700s she become involved in a lengthy legal battle with Cuzco's Jesuits over an estate called Vicho. The rector of the Jesuit academy claimed Doña Josefa had formally made over Vicho to his institution in a letter of donation. For her part, Doña Josefa claimed—ironically, for the daughter of a notary—to have been swindled, harassed by the rector, and duped into signing a blank page.[77]

The Ties that Bind: Notarial Relationships

As we have seen, notaries were in theory neutral, unswayed by particular interests or partisan loyalties. Yet those holding numerary posts might perform the duties of office in the same place for years, even decades, and they were expected to know the locals whose records they made—well enough, at least, to certify the truth of their identities and transactions. They and their clients lived in a world of complex webs of relations that bound people together: ties of kinship, spiritual solace, business partnership, and good credit. Their social networks also segmented and segregated cuzqueños: religious confraternities (*cofradías*), for example, were organized by ethnicity, although the boundaries do not seem to have been vigorously policed.[78] Notaries took part in these relationships; in Cuzco or elsewhere, it would have been impossible to do otherwise.

These ties and relationships took various forms. Collectively, Cuzco's notaries sponsored an altar in the annual Corpus Christi procession, a major ritual occasion that brought the city's authorities out in full splendor (and in hierarchical order).[79] They otherwise seem to have had few collective investments or traditions. As individuals, however, they made spiritual investments much like those of other cuzqueños. Notaries belonged to confraternities (Pedro de la Carrera Ron belonged to nine), and might help each other out with loans to cover funeral expenses.[80] Many placed children in religious orders, like Lorenzo de Mesa Andueza, who had three sons in the clergy, and Martín López de Paredes, who had a daughter living as a nun in Santa Catalina and a son in the priesthood.[81] And some notaries seem to have formed especially close ties to a particular religious order. Alonso Beltrán Lucero, for instance, lived in a house that belonged to the nearby Order of La Merced and asked to be buried inside the order's church in the chapel of Our Lady of Solitude, to whose confraternity he belonged.[82]

Notaries' wills also disclose other close business ties and special friendships. These included formal partnerships, or *compañías*, for trading purposes, like those of Pedro de la Carrera Ron and his "compañeros de la coca." But many cultivated less formal relations with specific local people who might be their business partners, relatives, or both. Lorenzo de Mesa Andueza, for example, placed a lien on his residence to support his son-in-law, presumably a merchant or shopkeeper, "when he was working with his merchandise."[83] Antonio Pérez de Vargas had close ties to Captain Juan Francisco Centeno, a wealthy man who did all his notarial business with Pérez de Vargas, paid funeral expenses for the notary's wife, and sold him a choice piece of local real estate in which the notary lived. The relationship soured, according to Pérez de Vargas, after Centeno took advantage of the notary's absence to arrange for the house to be resold.[84]

What about notaries' relations with local authorities? What kinds of ties or relations did they maintain with the corregidores, aldermen, alcaldes, and constables, the officials in whose proximity and under whose orders they did much of their work? As the stereotypes would have it, these men fit hand in glove. But are there traces of actual practice? A logical place to look is the records of *residencias*, the official inspections carried out when one magistrate's term ended and another took over. Extensive interviews were conducted to determine whether the outgoing officials had done their job properly.[85] If not, they might be subject to fines and lawsuits. Unfortunately, the records of three colonial centuries of Cuzco residencias are missing from the city's archives—all but one, a bulging volume misclassified as a sixteenth-century notarial register.[86]

As it happens, this 1596–97 Cuzco residencia is largely devoted to the alleged malfeasance of one man: the cabildo notary, a Spaniard named Francisco de la Fuente. De la Fuente had only been in Cuzco since 1592. Before that he had been in Lima in a variety of offices: first he was secretary for the criminal cases brought before the Audiencia, Peru's highest court, and then he became the court's reporter (*relator*); next he was notary in the provincial court.[87] He had married well while in the viceregal capital, wedding a criolla named Doña Isabel de Soto, who brought him a substantial dowry. That had enabled him to buy the office of cabildo notary of Cuzco when it was auctioned off in 1592. De la Fuente bid the grand sum of 16,000 pesos for the post—more than anyone had ever paid for it before or would ever pay again (table 1). He moved to the highlands and was received in his new position in 1592. But when the new magistrate, Gabriel Paniagua de Loaysa, arrived late in 1596, De la Fuente was already in jail. Tensions had been building for years between him and the clique of men who controlled the city's high offices. They were the Espinosas of Potosí: Don Cristóbal de Espinosa, who had purchased the position of alguacil mayor of Cuzco; his brother Juan, whom he had made his lieutenant; their brother-in-law, Don Luis Ponce de León; and various assorted kinsmen and retainers.

Matters had come to a head on July 19, 1596, when De la Fuente and his brother, the Cuzco procurador Juan López de Solórzano, had a run-in with Diego de Espinosa. De la Fuente fought with Espinosa, a permanent member (*regidor perpetuo*) of the cabildo, over an irrigation ditch the notary was having installed to bring water from the plaza to his house. He claimed Espinosa had overreached his authority by violently charging him on horseback and having him arrested. (Espinosa claimed he had acted within his authority and that De la Fuente had violently and insolently resisted arrest, screaming such epithets as "villainous Jewish dog.") Whatever happened on the plaza that day, the notary paid a high price for it. His workplace was closed down, and he could not manage to win quick release.

His back now probably against a cold, hard wall, De la Fuente decided to sue. He knew Paniagua de Loaysa was about to arrive and conduct a residencia. But he also knew the new magistrate had married into the Espinosa clan and would probably favor them. Suing from jail in mid-1596, he portrayed himself as the knight in shining armor who would save the city from their menacing presence. He charged that the Espinosas had "so tyrannized the city and region that its people find it preferable to let their property be taken away from them than to ask for relief from the extortions and injuries they receive."[88] Juan de Espinosa, for example, had gone around publicizing the fact that he had paid the crown 50,000 pesos for his post, and so planned to take full advantage of it.[89] Luis de Espinosa told people who brought lawsuits "that he was the mayor's advisor and that the mayor wouldn't do anything except what he [Luis] wanted, and that they should keep him happy." Thus "the word around town was that they sold Justice to whoever paid them the most."[90] But one of De la Fuente's

TABLE I. Prices of notarial offices in Cuzco (in *pesos ensayados*), 1595–1692

Office (year of royal confirmation) and occupant	Price (at auction [A] or via renunciation [R])
Cabildo notary (1595): Francisco de la Fuente	16,000 pesos ensayados[a] (A)
Notary public (1596): Gaspar de Prado	*4,000 pesos ensayados (R)*
Notary public (1601): Cristóbal Beltrán Lucero	4,000 pesos ensayados (R)
Notary public (1607): Pedro de la Carrera Ron	4,000 pesos ensayados (R)
Notary public (1610): Bartolomé de Montoya	**10,500 pesos corrientes★ (A)**
Notary public (1612): Alonso Herrero	*9,000 pesos corrientes (R)*
Notary public (1617): Francisco Hurtado	***9,000 pesos corrientes (R)***
Notary public (1617): Luis Díez de Morales	9,000 pesos corrientes (A)
Notary public (1619): Domingo de Oro	**9,000 pesos corrientes (R)**
Notary public (1625): Marcelo de Aicardo	*9,000 pesos corrientes (A)*
Notary public (1628): Gabriel de Villa	***9,000 pesos corrientes(R)***
Notary public (1629): Francisco de Espinosa	*9,000 pesos corrientes (R)*
Notary public (1637): José Navarro	**9,000 pesos corrientes (R)**
Notary public (1640): Alonso Calvo	*9,200 pesos corrientes (A)*
Notary public (1642): Juan Flores de Bastidas	**7,000 pesos corrientes (R)**
Notary public (1648): Lorenzo de Mesa Andueza	8,000 pesos corrientes (R)
Notary public (1650): Martín López de Paredes	6,000 pesos corrientes (R)
Notary of the Indian tribunal (*juzgado de naturales*) (1652): Juan Flores de Bastidas	7,000 pesos corrientes (A)
Notary public (1680): Alfonso de Bustamante	6,000 pesos corrientes (R)
Notary public (1686): Pedro López de la Cerda	4,000 pesos corrientes (A)
Cabildo notary (1692): Antonio Pérez de Vargas Machuca	10,000 pesos corrientes (A)

Sources: AGI, Lima, 179A, n. 53 (1595) and n. 69 (1596); Lima, 179B, n. 46 (1601); Lima, 180, n. 35 (1607); Lima, 181, n. 8 (1610) and n. 32 (1612); Lima, 182, n. 1 (1617), n. 18 (1617), and n. 35 (1619); Lima, 183, n. 66 (1625); Lima, 184, n. 2 (1628) and n.

TABLE I. *Continued*

29 (1629); Lima, 185, n. 62 (1637); Lima, 186, n. 35 (1640) and n. 54 (1642); Lima, 187, n. 44 (1648) and n. 107 (1652); Lima, 194, n. 19 (1680); Lima, 195, n. 17 (1686); Lima, 196, n. 29 (1692).

Each typeface represents a specific office that can be traced clearly through several occupants (for example: italics show that Prado, Herrero, Aicardo, and Espinosa held the same office, each adding his protocolos and judicial records to its archive before it passed to his successor), except for roman, which is used when the path of transmission of office is unclear.

[a]The conversion rate of peso ensayados to pesos corrientes is 1 to 1.6544, according to John Jay Tepaske and Herbert S. Klein, *The Royal Treasuries of the Spanish Empire in America.*

grievances was much more personal. He had once defied them by making a bid on behalf of a local widow at a public auction. According to him, Luis de Espinosa had roughed him up at his workplace, then had him jailed "as if I were a delinquent." Two other clan members had then barged into his house and threatened his wife, "angrily telling her that I was just a poor little man, poor and very alone, and they were many and very Rich, and that when I least expected it they would give me a blow that I wouldn't know where it had come from, and that after I was dead they would turn everything to silver"—a reported speech De la Fuente claimed was so effective that his wife had run screaming from the house.[91]

Once the residencia began, De la Fuente's situation went from bad to worse. In January 1597, after hearing copious testimony, Paniagua y Loaysa lodged formal charges against the notary. De la Fuente was given the opportunity to contest several pages' worth of infractions that he had allegedly committed—everything from overcharging clients and keeping sloppy records to registering the wills of people who were mentally or physically incapacitated. (One was indeed mute, De la Fuente testified; he had suddenly fallen ill and thereafter could only say "mamamamama," but was still very astute in the management of his affairs, and able to communicate through "signs" what he wanted in his will, although he wasn't literate.) Other Cuzco notaries faced charges too. The standard ones were keeping sloppy registers, overcharging clients, and delegating too much work to assistants. But while the others would face fines of 10 to 100 pesos, Francisco de la Fuente would be condemned to lose his office and spend six years in the galleys.[92]

Had De la Fuente gone that much further than his fellow notaries? Like the others, he systematically refuted the standard charges. He argued that his fees had always been reasonable: "Besides being no more than what people customarily paid my predecessor . . . the said fees were very moderate for this city."[93] But De la Fuente was also accused of using his position to make others trade with him at disadvantageous prices. And this he did not entirely deny. His pledge to pay 16,000 pesos for Cuzco's highest-ranking notarial office, he declared, "had made it necessary for me to sell off my assets at bargain prices to make the payments at the times that I promised." Yes, he had sold wine, sugar, and other goods through an agent, but "never by my own hand, nor was anything sold to any local storeowner on my orders."[94] For good measure, he added, "I am not among those persons the law prohibits from trading."[95] He claimed never to have had as much as a hundred pesos to invest because of the large installments he regularly had to pay for his office.

Here is the nub of the notary's dilemma, in a kind of limit case. Francisco de la Fuente had purchased notarial office for a high price. He was required to be scrupulously neutral—to favor neither side in lawsuits and contractual dealings. But like anyone else who paid a significant sum for an office, he needed to recoup his investment. That meant doing business locally, which required special relationships, understandings, and favors. The price of offices (notarial and otherwise) reflected the amounts people thought they could get. And here De la Fuente's defensive retort that he only did what was *customary* is key. He seems to gesture toward an archivally all-but-invisible world of local understandings, made through the kind of give-and-take he understandably did not claim as his because it truly wasn't just his. It was also that of all the other cabildo notaries and the people with whom they dealt in their inspection rounds of the city's marketplaces and stores.[96] Cabildo notaries were supposed to charge fees fixed by law in a fee table that if strictly followed would make no one rich.[97] And their salaries were modest. Why did De la Fuente invest as heavily in his office as he did? Maybe, coming from Lima, he had been misled or had let his imagination run wild. But most likely he was buying into a set of possibilities (perhaps known to him only in broad outline) of local knowledge, access, and leverage. He seems, in short, to have paid the opportunity cost of getting into a local power group. Since he soon met every merchant in town and could expect them all to welcome a chance to court his favor, why not ask them to sell wine for him? There would be the occasional inspection visit. But as long as he stayed within the limits of local "custom," he could expect only petty fines. A nuisance, but probably an acceptable opportunity cost for doing business in such a rich environment.[98]

By around 1600, all Cuzco's numerary notaries had purchased their offices—some, like De la Fuente, for prices they were not easily able to afford. With the ever-expanding sale of offices in the seventeenth century, more and more crown officials, from constables to aldermen and corregidores, needed to make payments on the sums they had pledged for their posts. The most appetizing offices might cost several thousand pesos (table 2). Thus, as Parry puts it, in a colonial society "where officials were normally paid by fees and perquisites rather than by regular stipends, the distinction between perquisites and bribes, between fees and tips, was difficult to draw exactly."[99]

Conclusions

Occasionally the archives disclose glimpses of very picaresque characters, such as Don Diego Laso, a royal notary caught naked in bed in the town of Huanta near Huamanga in 1658 with a woman who was not his wife. The corregidor Sebastián Florescano had gone to arrest Laso, not for philandering but for taking part in contraband: he had learned that Laso "had stolen a large quantity of silver and mercury in which the Royal Treasury has an interest, and he has committed a very serious crime." Unfortunately for the corregidor, Laso had managed while he was getting dressed (no doubt very slowly) to send a servant racing to tell his friends of the impending arrest. The case records are badly damaged and incomplete, but they hint at another local alliance stirred to defend its interests. By Florescano's testimony, "Captain Don Alonso de Araujo Sotomayor, provincial mayor, appeared . . . with his assistants and a total of some fourteen other people, who with shotguns, pistols, and drawn swords . . . took from me the said prisoner."[100]

Rarely are notaries' lives this juicy. For the most part, their own archives depict Cuzco notaries' lives as comfortable, middling, and not especially piquant or picaresque. The cameos I have presented of notarial (and other) interests, these *semblanzas*, do suggest a notariate that gradually changed

TABLE 2. Prices of public offices sold at auction in Lima, 1701–15
(in *pesos corrientes*)

Office (year)	Sale price at auction
Notary public (*escribano público y del número*), province of Canta (1701)	300 pesos
Criminal court notary, Real Audiencia (1702)	1,500 pesos
Notary public, city of Ica (1702)	800 pesos
Cabildo notary (*escribano público y de cabildo*), villa of Cañete (1702)	300 pesos
Accountant (*contador*), Real Caja [royal treasury office] de Guayaquil (1703)	12,000 pesos
Treasury official (*tesorero*), Real Caja, Potosí (1705)	28,000 pesos
Accountant, Real Caja, province of Tucumán (1705)	2,100 pesos
Notary public, province of Cajatambo (1705)	500 pesos
City councilman (*regidor*), Lima (1706)	11,320 pesos
Treasury official, Real Caja, city of Cuzco (1706)	24,000 pesos
Notary of inspections (*visitas y residencias*) in six *corregimientos* of Huancavelica (1706)	1,100 pesos
Notary public, province of Yauyos (1708)	140 pesos
Notary of Indian affairs (*escribano de naturales*), Cercado de Lima (1708)	3,500 pesos
Cabildo notary, city of Huamanga (1713)	3,400 pesos
Notary public, city of Lima (1714)	2,000 pesos
Notary public, city of Lima (1715)	3,025 pesos

Source: AGN, Superior Gobierno, legajo 6, 1701–59, cuaderno 104, "Libro donde se asientan los remates de minas, de oficios, nombramientos de receptores, escribanos, tesoreros, fundidores, etc."

over time. The peninsular immigrants who dominated local offices during the first century or so of Spanish Cuzco's existence—Sancho de Orue, Pedro de la Carrera Ron, and the like—seem on the whole to have gained considerable material resources.[101] The criollo notaries who began taking over in the early 1600s appear, not surprisingly, to have had more local knowledge than their predecessors, such as the Quechua fluency of Martín López de Paredes.[102] Beyond such generalizations, though, it is hard to describe a typical Cuzco notary. These men did not have predictable interests; they might make a wide range of urban and rural investments. Some of them lived comfortably and left sizeable legacies. Others, such as Cristóbal de Bustamante, ended up relatively poor.[103]

All, however, were close to merchants and other cuzqueños involved in large-scale trade. These were the notaries' most constant day-to-day customers, as their business required frequent use of contracts: credit arrangements, shipping and sales agreements, powers of attorney, and more. In Spain, nobles or aspiring nobles (hidalgos) would not stoop to associate closely with commerce, at least not too closely. But Cuzco was different. There everyone seemed to be involved in commerce; everyone seemed to be, to some degree, a merchant. Indeed, notaries themselves are perhaps best thought of as word merchants, men who served their clients within the informal understandings Francisco de la Fuente glossed as "custom."[104]

If we piece together the archival traces of these men, it is not hard to see why they provoked the kind of anxiety that marks period literature and popular sayings. Notaries knew people's intimate business, as well as the formulae in which to set down their transactions; they kept the archival paper trail. They might be party to local power-sharing arrangements. And should a notary choose—the way De la Fuente and López de Paredes allegedly did—to exploit his position beyond what was accepted local "custom," his words were registered as the official truth. This was all threatening enough to those with something at stake (and these are the people whose records turn up in the archives). Such a figure could not be allowed to get too far out of the bounds of local custom, whatever these were in a given place.[105] If one of them did, from the point of view of his allies, he might seriously jeopardize the smooth workings of the whole.

Serious discord over alleged notarial malpractice is relatively rare in the archives, but when it turns up, it is very revealing. What got Francisco de la Fuente into trouble was showing a dangerously independent disrespect for his superiors. He defied an Espinosa: that was how he landed in jail in the

FIGURE 10. The kneeling figure of Felipe Guaman Poma de Ayala's allegorical drawing represents "the poor Indians of this kingdom," preyed upon by hungry animals, including the notary, or "gato escriuano." Artwork in the public domain. Photograph supplied by The Royal Library, Copenhagen, Denmark, from manuscript GKS 2232 4°, *El primer nueva corónica y buen gobierno* (1615 / 1616), "24. The chapter of the church inspectors," drawing 272, p. 708. See http://www.kb.dk/ permalink/2006/poma/info/es/frontpage.htm.

first place. (The rest, trumped up or not, came later.) Perhaps the Espinosa clan's members and allies jailed him once he seemed to become uppity, afraid that if they did not move first he would spill what he knew about them.[106] His contemporary Miguel Ruiz, cabildo notary in the coastal Peruvian town of Cañete, was denounced in 1585 by Cañete's cabildo for allegedly incorporating part of its premises into his own house by means of spurious contracts. The stakes were monetarily miniscule—Ruiz failed to pay five pesos annually into the cabildo's coffers—but bulked large locally: "since he [Ruiz] is the notary of the cabildo and there is no other notary in town, everyone has great respect for him and does whatever he wants, and no one dares collect what he owes."[107]

These men seem to have defied "power groups," those informal-yet-potent alliances that Steve Stern sees as bulwarks of local power-sharing and profit-taking. Such arrangements are not on the books; formalizing their terms was out of the question. But colonial history—in the Andes and elsewhere—was filled with these tacit understandings. They are usually studied from the perspective of those most ground down by them. In the colonial Andes, for example, indigenous communities understood by the seventeenth century that priests would not perform the sacraments for them without charging extra fees, and corregidores would not leave them in peace unless they purchased a certain amount of their merchandise every few years (through the infamous *reparto*, or forced distribution of goods). They also understood that their own caciques might help to enforce compliance.

Guaman Poma's representation of the "poor Indians" of Peru (figure 10) hints that similar understandings were reached from an early date regarding colonial notaries.[108] Exactly how these tacit bargains got established is likely to remain a mystery. Elsewhere in his chronicle, Guaman Poma imagines the questions that might have been posed by a notary eager to do business among Indians; what if someone complains, he asks, and I'm found guilty during a residencia? As imagined dialogue continues, the notary instructs caciques to cooperate with him: "I'll help you, but you must help me out with llamas," and so forth.[109] How many similar deals were struck by Cuzco's colonial notaries? There is no way to know. Clearly, however, by 1600 a Cuzco notary might know a great deal about the unwritten rules of doing business, as well as the best business opportunities. As de la Fuente, López de Paredes, and others moved to exploit these, they developed a hands-off style that relied on their notarial assistants. They called it simply "custom." This, too, did not happen by the book, but relied upon local knowledge of tacit understandings. As we'll see in the next chapter, custom was something that had to be carefully taught.

CHAPTER 3

CUSTOM

La costumbre hace ley.
—Spanish proverb

The notarial page is a remarkably disciplined space. Its size was standard-ized throughout Spain's empire, as was the way it was bound into books at the end of each year. Notaries' books were not supposed to contain abbre-viations, but they did, and the same ones tended to be in use from place to place.[1] Even the handwriting looks strikingly similar from Madrid and Seville to Lima and Cuzco.[2] One proxy or sale thus looks much like any other contemporary one registered elsewhere in the empire. This was, after all, what people paid notaries to do for them: discipline the messy particulars of their business into the approved legal forms.[3]

But the cover sheets of the registers inside these bound volumes are a different matter. No rules governed these spaces, and those from colonial Cuzco hold riotous life. A menagerie of fanciful creatures cavorts across the page: stylized birds and heraldic lions, a man in a fantastic headdress twice as big as he is (figure 11), a disembodied hand, a fish, a face. A quill-wielding faun turns his head and grins (figure 12), displaying his haunches. A cartoon couple floats in the air: "A kiss, *taitay*," says the woman to the man, and he replies, "I don't want to, sister" (figure 13). Then there are the insults, some of them bilingual and not easy to understand. Beneath the name of Bernardo de Benavente, for example, an assistant in the 1680s to the notary Lorenzo Jaimes, someone wrote *"otorongo* hombre enfermo borracho"—making Benavente both a sick drunk and a jaguar. Elsewhere are inscriptions calling Jaimes an Inca hunchback and a false Inca.[4] There is plenty of pee and shit (*mierda*). To judge by the cover sheets of their registers, Cuzco's colonial notaries must have been a bunch of giggling, prepubescent boys.

Cuzco's notaries were not boys; they were men in their mid-twenties or older who had been through extensive training. But boys were an essential part of their workforce. To become a notary, one began as a boy—whether

FIGURE 11. The work of anonymous notarial doodler(s). The dandy with cane and headdress is labeled Don Joaquín de Gamarra, probably a relative of the notary's; another caption locates him in the town of Anta, just outside Cuzco. Below is a chase scene, perhaps a self-portrait of the doodlers. ARC-PN, Bernardo José Gamarra, protocolo 74 (1809–10), cover sheet, registro de indios. Photograph by the author.

in Spain or in the American colonies.[5] Bartolomé González, petitioning in the 1570s to serve as a notary in Peru, had people in his Spanish hometown attest that "from the age of twelve he had resided in this city in notaries' offices."[6] (Most were less specific, indicating that the applicant had served notaries "from his tenderest years.") González had worked as a copyist and assistant (*escribiente y oficial*) until he had left for Peru, by which time he was "a young man with a beard who appeared to be at least twenty years old."[7] Eventually he had worked his way up to head assistant (*oficial mayor*) and sought to become a notary himself. Centuries later this would still be a common pattern. The Cuzco native Pedro José Gamarra, for instance, petitioned for his own credentials in 1782 after fifteen years of doing notarial

FIGURE 12. More satirical doodles have survived from the late 1700s and early 1800s than from earlier years. Here are "D[on] Juan Joseph Ledo," a faunlike *plumario* with prominent hindquarters, and the "lowly Porroa," head official of the Cuzco notary Ambrocio Arias de Lira. ARC-PN, Ambrocio Arias de Lira, protocolo 44 (1790–92), cover sheet. Photograph by the author.

work for others "very diligently and accurately."[8] Becoming a notary might easily take over a decade of training, starting in childhood.

Early apprenticeship meant living so close to the notary that one might be more or less his servant.[9] The boundaries between a notary's residence and his workplace were often not entirely clear, and it was not unusual for notaries to keep portions of their papers at home.[10] There, or in the notary's workshop, a young penman would start learning his craft by writing down dictated documents or making clean copies from drafts. By night he would curl up on the floor; by day he would do whatever tasks his master or the head assistant assigned him. No documents describe an apprentice's routine, but some of it can be imagined: sharpening quills, mixing ink, fetching papers the master left at home, and delivering finished documents, loitering a little along the way. Sometimes there would be a house call. The master would go in person to the home of someone important (or too weak and incapacitated to make it to his workshop), bringing an assistant or two in tow. These outings might be ticklish: business transpired in private places, unlike the busy *portal de los escribanos*, and witnesses might

FIGURE 13. The unfortunate Antonio Porroa y Sánchez, much lampooned by his subalterns, is refusing the request for a kiss by his sister Doña Asencia Porroa ("Un besito taitay"). ARC-PN, Ambrocio Arias de Lira, protocolo 41 (1784–85), cover sheet of 1785. Photograph by the author.

be few.[11] With enough at stake, someone might later start a judicial inquiry alleging that the resulting document had not been lawfully made.[12] One had to learn to be careful.

Gradually, one's responsibilities would increase. A rank beginner was more servant than penman. He might be confined to a specific corner of his master's workshop so he could be easily located when needed and out of everyone's way the rest of the time. If physical labor was required—for example, if someone was needed to carry the master's draft book and implements to a client's house—he would perform it.[13] If he showed aptitude for the work, proving himself a diligent and quick learner, he would be given more advanced tasks: from writing out ("extending") short, almost entirely formulaic documents such as powers of attorney, he might graduate to writing longer ones with more tailor-made elements, such as censos and wills. At the end of the year he might help the head assistant organize the previous twelve months' business into bound volumes (*protocolos*) with a detailed, alphabetic index.

Not everyone who started out as a notary's penman would become a notary himself. Some became attorneys (*procuradores*), an office that cost significantly less than that of numerary notary in the city of Cuzco. Others became personal secretaries, like Juan Francisco Luyardo, who spent years doing the bidding of the bedridden corregidor of Paucartambo, teaching his son to read and write.[14] (Such positions might be stepping-stones on the way to holding notarial office in the city, but they did not guarantee it.) Some penmen did not get very far at all. Sloppy work or a bad attitude could end one's career before it had even begun. In 1773, the royal notary José de Tapia y Sarmiento sued Francisca Cusipaucar for protecting her son, his young mestizo apprentice Manuel. The boy had allegedly stolen over a hundred pesos' worth of small sums from his master's strongbox, stealing the keys from his pants pocket while he slept, "until one night I caught him in the act of taking my pants from the place where I usually put them."[15]

Some serious pilfering on the part of penmen was aimed at the archive itself. Cases from both Lima and Cuzco suggest that a tempting source of income for young *plumarios* was a thriving secondary market for old paper —specifically, as a source of fiber for the making of fireworks.[16] Some of the colonial archive, in other words, literally went up in flames. A Lima case from 1739 began when a notary brought suit against his assistant "for having stolen from my office various papers that turned up in a fireworks shop."[17] Similarly, in 1746, the Cuzco notary Juan Bautista Gamarra sued his young assistant Juan José Palomino for stealing old papers that later appeared in the hands of "an Indian or mestiza fireworks maker."[18] The eighteen-year-old Palomino claimed to have had no idea the papers were valuable. Pressed on the point, he testified that "even though he was a penman, he did not know the papers were important because he could not read or understand them, they were so garbled and old, and . . . [he was] a poor fellow who was just beginning to write only what was dictated to him and nothing more."[19]

As these cases suggest, notaries might not know in detail what went on inside their own workshops. They were busy men who might have other business to tend. Having worked their way up through the ranks over the years and made it to the top, they were ready to hand off the close, day-to-day supervision of the shop to a trusted, experienced head assistant, an oficial mayor. These senior associates were their right-hand men. They oversaw such crucial tasks as the proper indexing and binding of the notary's annual volumes; they directed the flow of filing and knew where everything was supposed to be kept.[20] (If something went missing, they were the ones most on the spot.) They were on hand to administer discipline to the apprentices. And they were men, not boys. They went home at night to their own residences and families, and might have their own small-time business deals on the side.[21] Their positions, too, might be stepping-stones on the way to becoming a full-fledged notary. But achieving that feat required resources and a certain amount of luck. One might also spend one's career as a notary's oficial mayor.

Not surprisingly, these men—the authority figures most consistently present in notaries' workshops—were the targets of the doodlers' most pointed slings and arrows. Cuzco's doodling plumarios were up to many things, as Carolyn Dean has pointed out. Many of their doodles are decorative, eye-pleasing embellishments of the margins. Some evince an esprit de corps: practice signatures with elaborate flourishes, for example, and the proud heraldic lions found on many Gamarra registers' cover sheets (figure 14).[22] There is plenty of friendly ribbing and bad verse. But the doodlers could also be resentful, sarcastic, and mean. The head assistant Antonio Porroa, for instance, came under sustained fire as an old, irascible incompetent (figure 15).[23] Men like the belittled "Porroitas" represented discipline to the boys working under them. The doodles thus comment on power in the archives: whether playful and silly or stinging and sarcastic (or all of the above), they point to the hierarchies that formed both writers and writing. Technically the notary was in charge inside his own workshop, but in day-to-day practice, from an apprentice's perspective, the heavy hand of the boss often belonged to his chief assistant.

This was all part of the complicated world of practice. Manuals such as Monterroso's are written as though each notarial word had to be penned by the notary himself. But inside notarial workshops, things were quite otherwise: the higher one rose in the notarial order of things, the less one actually wrote.[24] Behind each of Cuzco's escribanos was a small schoolhouse powered by the document-making labor (and sometime doodling) of boys and young men. What exactly did they learn? Certainly dozens of variations on the theme "Be it known to all" (*Sepan cuantos*): the forms of proxies, sales, loans, and dozens of other standard notarial transactions. And they picked up the fine points of making depositions for a trial. But they also absorbed crucial lessons that went beyond the contents of the forms. They came to understand the ample social margins surrounding their use, the vast realm cuzqueños glossed simply as *costumbre*, "custom."[25] This was not in Monterroso or the other well-known manuals. It had to be learned over the years in practice.

FIGURE 14. Gamarra plumarios often drew proud heraldic lions on the cover sheets of their bosses' registers, as Carolyn Dean notes in "Beyond Prescription," 302–3. This lion lightens the effect by peeing a scribal flourish. ARC-PN, Bernardo José Gamarra, protocolo 119 (1794), cover sheet of registro #6. Photograph by the author.

"Ante mí": Truth and Witness

The heart of the notary's job was to bear faithful witness to other people's doings. As the *Siete Partidas* puts it, the most basic duty of notaries public was to "write the documents of the sales, and of the purchases, and the lawsuits, and the dealings which men bring amongst themselves in the cities and towns. And the good that comes from them is very great when they perform their office well, and faithfully . . . and a remembrance remains of past things, in the notes that they keep in their registers."[26] The notary's authenticating marks included his signature, his *rúbrica* (a practiced flourish), and a seal-like emblem called the *signo*. On obtaining title to notarial office, each notary gained his own signo—typically in the form of

FIGURE 15. This full-length portrait of Porroa is accompanied by
sarcastic verses and a caption belittling its subject as a big-eared little
old man: "Porroitas machucha, biejesito maldito orejudo." ARC-PN,
Ambrocio Arias de Lira, protocolo 41 (1784–85), cover sheet
of 1784 registro. Photograph by the author.

a square or star, embellished with a unique pattern of some kind (figures 16
and 17).[27] These inscriptions promised that he had been there, a superintending presence, as deals were struck and agreements were sealed. If he
certified that something had taken place, then it became a legal fact, "true
in law."[28] Proving otherwise was almost impossible to do. The notary's
marks were the linchpin of notarial culture, its sine qua non. The boys and
adolescents who worked for notaries practiced making their own flourishes over and over.[29] For them, this marked the summit of a career path,
the moment when they would not have to write much of anything else.

What to make, then, of Pedro de Cáceres? In his registers from the years
1696–97, this aging Cuzco notary bore witness with his signature to page
after page of absolutely nothing—just blank space. His clients' signatures

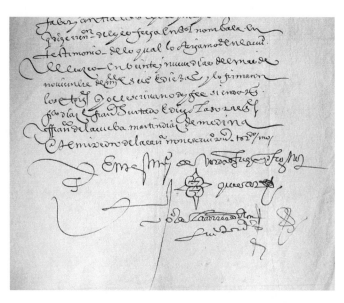

FIGURE 16. The signature and unique *signo* of the Cuzco notary Pedro de la Carrera Ron. ARC, Cabildo, Justicia Ordinaria, Causas Civiles, legajo 2 (1606–26), cuaderno 6, expediente 33 (1614), fol. 4. Photograph by the author.

appear alongside his, even though their documents' terms had not yet been filled in. The abbess and several nuns of Santa Clara, for instance, had signed off on several *censos*, mortgage-like transactions that extended credit to local borrowers (figure 18). This went against royal provisions: notaries were never supposed to have people sign documents in blank.[30] Such pages, if they somehow fell into the wrong hands, could be made to say (and legally bind the signatories to) anything.

This might seem an isolated instance of notarial negligence. Yet a closer look at Cuzco's records suggests Cáceres's clients were hardly alone in signing blank pages for someone to fill in later. Many documents conclude in tiny, crabbed handwriting that hints that the penman had to struggle to fit everything in (figure 19). Others contain huge, loopy handwriting that seems designed to fill an overly ample preallotted space. These, too, are traces of the habitual, accepted divergence of prescription and practice. Strange and counterintuitive as it may seem, people in the Andes often signed blank pages in their notaries' registers for copyists to fill in later. Clients perhaps found it convenient, since signing a blank page meant they did not have to wait around while copyists drafted each legalistic word of

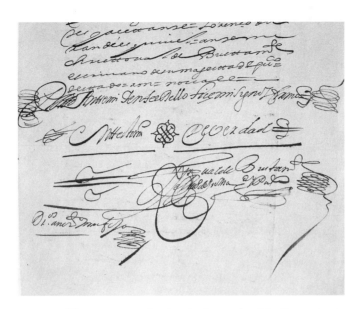

FIGURE 17. The signature and authenticating marks of the Cuzco notary Cristóbal de Bustamante. ARC, Corregimiento, Causas Ordinarias, legajo 26 (1691–92), cuaderno 4, expediente 523 (1691), fol. 12. Photograph by the author.

their business. More importantly for notaries, it was profitable: this practice enabled them to do more business in a given amount of time.[31]

So how did notaries and their assistants remember what to put in their clients' records? And what assured their clients that they would get it right? In practice, for efficiency's sake, notaries might have an assistant jot down the essentials of a document in a draft book, then ask the client to sign a blank page in a register on which the complete draft would be filled in later.[32] This method explains the squeezed lines with tiny, crabbed handwriting and enormous lines with huge, loopy handwriting to which copyists resorted when they had to make a draft fill the space allotted for it.[33] (The technique will sound familiar to anyone who has met a required number of pages for a writing assignment by fiddling with the size of fonts and margins.) Notaries were definitely not supposed to handle the writing process this way, and it was a punishable offense if they were caught.[34] But practice was deeply rooted and resilient.

This shortcut relied on the key expedient of the draft book, variously called the *manual*, *libro de minutas*, *minutario*—something that was not illegal, but which rarely shows up in an archive.[35] Before 1503, such draft

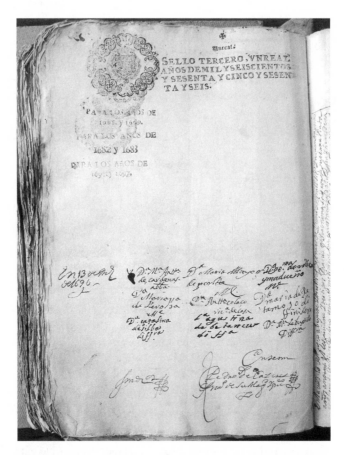

FIGURE 18. The egregious case of the Cuzco notary Pedro de Cáceres reveals a common practice among Andean notaries: having clients sign blank pages for the contents to be filled in later. This blank page awaits the form language of a credit transaction (*censo al quitar*); at the bottom are the signatures of the abbess and advisory council nuns of the Cuzco convent of Santa Clara. ARC-PN, Pedro de Cáceres, protocolo 39 (1696), fol. 398, December 13, 1696. Photograph by the author.

books were the norm in Castilian notarial practice. Clients signed only the abbreviated versions of their business which draft books contained. The 1503 reform aimed to prevent fraud by phasing out, or at least deemphasizing, such draft books and ensuring that clients instead signed a complete draft (*en extenso*) of their business in the notary's register.[36] Yet the draft books hung on in practice. The Cuzco notary Francisco De la Fuente explained in 1597 that they were absolutely common and essential to doing business:

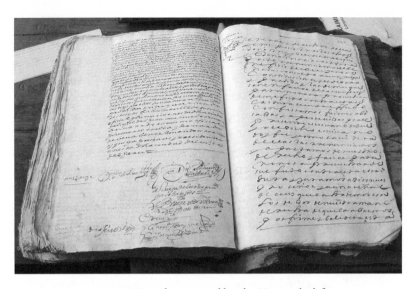

FIGURE 19. Note the squeezed handwriting on the left, where the plumario had to cram in the contents of the last page of a November 1689 sales contract. ARC-PN, Lorenzo Xaimes [Jaimes], protocolo 312 (1687–91), first volume (1687–89), fols. 443v–444. Photograph by the author.

All of us notaries customarily and in keeping with the law of the kingdom draw up documents in the presence of the parties, and if the document is prolix and long and requires time and space to fill out, when there is other business and it can't be taken care of, we ordinarily have— as I do—a manual in which the essentials for the document are taken down with the parties present, and that is where they give it, to be filled in later accordingly, and I keep this manual with as much care as I do my own registers, and it makes it possible to run this business because otherwise it would be impossible; and this is so general in all the kingdoms and jurisdictions of His Majesty that there is nothing contrary to it, and thus we are able to keep track of, and not lose the essentials of, said documents, and there is only some carelessness in the filling in of them, and that is the fault of the assistants who work on salary for me, and mine for trusting them.[37]

De la Fuente is right about colonial Andean practice.[38] But he elides the other standard practice coupled with the use of a draft book: asking clients to sign a blank page for later completion in a notary's register. This clearly contradicted the spirit of the 1503 reform, which aimed to prevent fraud by requiring notaries to apprise their clients fully about the wording of the documents they commissioned.

Obviously this roomy notarial drafting process might leave clients feeling vulnerable—and lawsuits do appear in which people claimed that completed contracts went against their desires. For example, the priest Cristóbal de Vargas Carvajal waged a long-running appeal before Lima's ecclesiastical authorities of a 1638 decision against him which turned on a Cuzco contract of obligation that he declared he had been forced to sign in blank. One witness testified that he had seen the Cuzco notary Luis Díez de Morales "take out a blank page or notebook, and he told the priest Cristóbal de Vargas to sign the obligation he was making, and the aforesaid [Vargas] signed his named on the blank sheet, without the terms being filled in or read back to him, which they could not have been since it wasn't written."[39] Also testifying on behalf of Vargas was another Cuzco notary, Domingo de Oro, whose matter-of-fact account of witnessing the signing of a blank page suggests that he found such things completely unexceptional.[40] The testimony implies that the notary Díez de Morales (or a penman of his) had filled in terms that acceded to the wishes of Vargas's enemies, yet no one went after the notary. Perhaps no one believed Vargas's defense—but the case certainly raises the possibility that such manipulations were not out of the ordinary.[41] Certainly the signing of a blank page was commonplace.[42]

How did people manage to exert some control, get their desires on paper? Many, it seems, had a significant amount of "preknowledge."[43] They did not appear before the notary empty-handed, but with a bit of their own penmanship in hand with instructions about what they wanted the notary to authorize. Take the above case of the priest Vargas. He claimed to have handed the notary Luis Díez de Morales a piece of paper on which he himself had written the conditions he wanted in the obligation that he had agreed—very much under duress, by his telling—to sign.[44] Traces of such prewriting, variously called *papelitos* (little slips of paper), *cédulas*, *boletas*, or *memorias*, are scattered throughout the notarial archive (figure 20), sometimes stuck as bookmarks between the pages of notarial manuals. (Tucked inside Monterroso's popular 1563 manual in Spain's national library, for example, is a handwritten note dated November 1749: someone's request for a document "including the condition that Man[ue]l

FIGURE 20. A papelito sticking up inside a protocolo, ARC-PN, Bernardo José Gamarra, protocolo 74 (1809–10). In Cuzco the practice of customizing instructions to one's notary in writing seems to have become increasingly standardized by the late colonial decades, and to have continued thereafter. Photograph by the author.

Benito will not ask Josefa for child support for the two daughters who are presently with him.")

How much care notaries and their assistants took to preserve clients' initial handwritten instructions is unclear. These bits of paper are archival rarities, but then so are draft books; just because archives today do not feature them does not mean that notaries did not keep them. A Lima lawsuit brought in 1732 by a Dominican friar suggests that notaries did routinely keep these papers (and that clients expected this). Don Gregorio José de Villalobos alleged that his notary, Diego Cayetano Vásquez, had gone against his instructions for a *renuncia*, a formal renunciation of property rights that religious men and women made before taking vows of poverty. Villalobos had wanted to leave 8,000 pesos to his niece. By his telling, however, his notary had taken advantage of his privileged insider's information to reach a different understanding about the 8,000 pesos with Villalobos's brother-in-law and contravene Villalobos's instructions. He asks that the notary Vásquez be compelled to exhibit "the draft that he made in my presence and the papelito in my own handwriting that I gave him so that in accordance with it and the draft he might draw up my renunciation."[45] Unfortunately, the case records end inconclusively, but Villalobos did succeed in compelling his notary to adduce both draft and papelito, which he did.

Such little slips of paper turn up in Cuzco across several centuries, and by the late colonial period were quite common. They add a fourth moment of writing to the drafting process as it was frequently carried out:

1. The making of abbreviated instructions on a slip of paper, probably by the client(s);

2. the making of the draft (*minuta*) of a document in a draft book, probably by a penman at his notary's dictation;

3. the completion of a fully developed draft in its proper chronological place in a register (*cuaderno, registro*) destined to be bound in a protocolo, probably by a penman under a head assistant's supervision;

4. the making of copies of the document for the client(s) by a penman, to be authorized before delivery with the notary's signature, rubric, and signo.

Merchants also employed this kind of preknowledge. Take the unusually detailed traces of a botched notarial job Francisco de la Fuente charged to one of his assistants.[46] During the inspection visit of 1597, De la Fuente deflected as much blame as he credibly could onto his subordinates, and one case of this concerned two prominent merchants of Cuzco. The licentiate Gallén de Robles and the admiral Hernando Lamero had come to De la Fuente to have him draw up an agreement between them concerning the shipping of a certain number of baskets of coca leaves. It was then the height of the coca-trading boom in the central-southern Andean highlands, and such documents were commissioned by cuzqueños constantly. These two men, according to De la Fuente, had already made and signed a cédula of the agreement they wanted, "which contained the entire substance of the said contract," and they asked him to prepare a document for them accordingly. They left, and De la Fuente also left his office to do some business in the city. At some point, however, Gallén de Robles returned and, De la Fuente testified, "begged Francisco Duarte, an assistant in my office, to make out the said document in accordance with his *memoria* because he was in a hurry, and the said Francisco

Duarte did so, and because he was a novice and not versed in the requirements, powers, and clauses that must be put in such contracts for coca, he filled out the document in the register in his own way."[47] Gallén de Robles, unconvinced, took the register elsewhere "to show some other people who said it was not done right." On returning to his office, Francisco de la Fuente explained, he had fixed the register, then had the actual contract drawn up and given to Gallén de Robles, who at that point was satisfied.

It makes sense that leading Cuzco merchants would know exactly what they wanted in a standard contract like this, to the point of being able to order notaries' assistants around and very nearly perform documentary self-service. (Almost—notice that they had to check with others to be sure the assistant's work had been done right.) These men as a group were not only literate and versed in contractual terms, but had much at stake where notarized transactions were concerned. Perhaps they owned their own copies of Monterroso and Hevia Bolaños (figure 21). Certainly, through times thick and thin, they were Cuzco notaries' best customers (table 3).[48]

The danger with merchants was that they were clever and might slip something by—like disguising interest as part of the principal of a loan.[49] Or through *mohatras*; here their malfeasance even made it into the dictionary. Covarrubias describes the mohatra as "the feigned purchase that is made when a merchant sells [on credit] at a higher than reasonable price" to someone who will sell back to him in cash at a lower price.[50] In this way people might obtain ready cash from merchants through disguised loans at interest—though as Covarrubias notes, "to fill one hole, they dig a bigger one." Notaries were supposed to be very vigilant about such things. But they might not always follow what their customers were up to. Some profit-taking schemes were quite involved, and as Victoria Hennessey Cummins notes, "it appears that ways to make unsanctioned profits were limited only by one's imagination."[51] If the notary suspected something dubious, perhaps he was tempted to overlook it in the case of an especially close or powerful client.

To ensure goodwill and reliable service, merchants and other high-volume customers might cultivate relations with a particular notary. Cuzco's convents, for instance, were in constant need of one: to formalize nuns' dowries; to certify the rentals, leases, purchases, and sales of convent properties; to document the credit extended to local borrowers through censos; and to handle any lawsuits that arose. The nuns might thus retain a trusted notary by paying him a regular salary, even though this was expressly

¶El procurador no puede hazer cócierto con la patte, de ſeguir la cauſa aſu coſta. Pre.40.c.69

¶El curador, no puede poner procurador en cauſa de menor ſuyo, ſi primeraméte el no començare el pleyto, y nolo ſiguiere haſta la conteſtacion, o el juez no le diere licencia. L.-3.tit.5.par, 3.l.9.tit.10.li, 1.del fuero.

¶Anſi miſmo ay otros poderes de mas de los eſpecificados, que llaman poderes Apudacta, eſtos ſe hazen en juyzio, diziendo el otorgante, Yo doy poder a fulano, para eſte pleyto, baſtanteméte como ſe requiere. El eſcriuano entonces baſta que lo ponga aſi por eſtas palabras formales, delante del juez, y que lo firme ſi ſu piere el otorgante, por que el tal poder es baſtante para aquella inſtancia. L.1.tit.10.li. 1.l.12.del eſtilo.

¶En dos maneras conſiſte el ſaber entender y ordenar los poderes. que eſtan dichos, eſpeciales y generales, que las partes otorgan ante los eſcriuanos, publicos. La vna es la manera que ſe ha de tener para los pleytos y cauſas, anſi ciuiles como criminales, Yla otra es para efecto de vender, y trocar, y enagenar bienes, y para deſpoſar, y hazer teſtamentos, por poderes, y otras muchas formas de poderes que no ſe an de preſentar en juyzio, mas de ſer eſpeciales, para aquel efecto que ſe otorgan. Y entendiendo bien ſu pratica dellos, por la miſma pratica, ſe podra hazer qual quier

FIGURE 21. A stylized hand, or manicule, drawn in the margin of Monterroso's manual *Pratica civil, y criminal, e instruction de scrivanos* (1563) to signal what its possessor considered a key passage. Reproduced by permission of Houghton Library, Harvard University.

forbidden. They might also give notaries preferential access to credit.[52] Or they might give them access to cells in the convent, as Santa Catalina did in 1661 for Martín López de Paredes. Two of his daughters were novices at the time, and he had remedied a labor shortage for a convent construction project by renting the nuns indigenous workers from the province of Quispicanche. The prioress Doña María de Sena Arias Dávila repaid the favor by selling him two second-floor cells in which to house his daughters, thanking him "for all that he has done for [Santa Catalina] by seeing to the collection of payments owed to it and the drawing up of all its documents."[53]

For their part, Cuzco's notaries may also have performed brokerage services for some of their closest clients, helping match those in need of a loan with those in a position to make one. After all, brokering credit was standard practice for early modern notaries in certain parts of Europe.[54] As "the use of credit grew rapidly in early modern societies," Julie Hardwick notes, French notaries' intimate knowledge of their clients' affairs, plus the legal obligation to notarize all *rentes* (comparable to Spanish censos) over a certain amount, "left notaries ideally placed not only to record loans, but also to advise and arrange them. . . . People wanting to lend or borrow knew they could turn to notaries." Notaries' archives would not reflect this

TABLE 3. Most frequently produced types of notarial documents
(sampling all remaining ARC protocolos for the years 1600, 1650, 1700)

	1600		1650		1700	
Document type	No.	% of total	No.	% of total	No.	% of total
Powers of attorney (*poderes*)	163	25	201	14.5	171	12
IOUS (*obligaciones*)	128	19.7	194	14	386	27.1
Sales (*ventas*)	76	11.7	151	11	97	6.8
Rentals (*arrendamientos*)	40	6.1	37	2.7	24	1.7
Labor contracts (*conciertos*)	14	2.2	306	22.1	45	3.2
Receipts (*recibos*)	11	1.7	61	4.4	253	17.8
Renunciations[a] (*renunciaciones*)	0	0	132	9.6	124	8.7
Other	219	33.6	300	21.7	323	22.7
Total	*651*	*100*	*1382*	*100*	*1423*	*100*

Sources (all from ARC-PN): Diego Gaitán, legajo 112 (1600); Cristóbal de Lucero, legajo 159 (1600–1601); Joan de Olave, legajo 243 (1600–1602); Antonio Sánchez, legajo 26 (1587–1600); Antonio Salas, legajo 293 (1600–1601); José Calvo, legajo 52 (1645–50); Juan Flores de Bastidas, legajo 96 (1649–51); Martín López de Paredes, legajos 134 (1649–50) and 135 (1650); Francisco Martínez de Arce, legajo 170 (1650–51); Salvador Meléndez, legajo 171 (1650–52); Lorenzo Mesa Andueza, legajo 177 (1650); Alonso de Montoya, legajo 229 (1641–61); Joan de Pineda, legajo 276 (1649–56); Gregorio Básquez Serrano, legajo 48 (1700–1701); Cristóbal de Bustamante, legajo 60 (1700); Pedro López de la Cerda, legajo 192 (1700); Escribanos de naturales, legajo 315 (1677–1705); Varios escribanos, legajo 316 (1683–1720); Varios escribanos, legajo 317 (1660–1708); Notarial folios sueltos colonia y otros, legajo 318 (1607–1782).

[a]In 1600, notaries were not yet required to live at least sixty days after renouncing their offices to a successor for the renunciation to be legally valid; once that order took effect, renunciations proliferated notably, as can be seen in the figures for 1650 and 1700. The incompleteness of ARC protocolos may account for notable changes in the frequency with which particular types of documents were produced—for example, the sharp increase in labor contracts for the year 1650 (to 22.1 percent of the total). Further research will be needed to clarify this and other changes in frequency, and whether they correspond to patterns of notarial production in other places and times.

brokerage, merely indicating that a sum had been repaid by one person and that another sum (perhaps the same amount) had gone out to another in a rente. But Hardwick shows the notary might be very much the man in the middle, even holding onto clients' money himself for a time while he found a borrower. She finds that "the lending and borrowing parties did not necessarily—perhaps not normally—meet." Many seem to have been comfortable leaving things in the hands of their notaries.[55]

This kind of brokerage would have suited Cuzco's large religious houses perfectly. By the late seventeenth century, two in particular—the cloistered convents of Santa Clara and Santa Catalina—had become the region's largest institutional sources of credit.[56] Each nun who became symbolically a bride of Christ brought a dowry to her convent's coffers. Convent communities depended for their livelihoods on the canny management of these funds, which were invested in the local economy through the contractual mechanism of the *censo consignativo*. Notarized financial dealings reflect the nuns' determination to keep their dowries gainfully invested: no sooner did one credit recipient return a dowry and cancel a censo than another approached the convent to take the money out again.[57] Nuns turned to the same trusted notaries over and over to register such transactions. Were the notaries their shadow financial advisers and brokers, helping to set up the deals they notarized? The record does not say—but the nuns' close relations with their notaries, along with the evidence from early modern Europe, make it seem quite likely.[58]

Such relationships gave rise to understandings that grew comfortable over the years. When a fiscal crisis moved Spanish officials to investigate Santa Clara's lending in the early 1800s, for example, they were surprised to uncover practices that had grown quite unorthodox. First, would-be borrowers had to obtain a notarized contract stating that a loan had been made: that they had received a particular sum of money from the nuns (even though they hadn't); that it had been handed over in the notary's witnessing presence; and so forth. Next, the borrowers would take their loan contracts to Santa Clara, at which point they would actually receive the agreed-to amount and the nuns would record the loan in the account book they kept inside their safe. Santa Clara's notaries, it seems, had grown accustomed to recording convent "loans" that had not yet been made—and might not be, should borrowers change their minds. Only the nuns' account book could be considered accurate. (Why things were done this way is not explained, but it presumably saved time for nuns and notaries, who did not have to get together for each new credit deal.) The indignant officials who uncovered this sleight of hand warned "that even if in that Monastery there is custom to the contrary," notaries should exercise their office "with greater care."[59]

These were the kinds of practical lessons a notary's apprentice learned as he worked his way up in the profession. His master might instruct him to write down that money had changed hands between parties, even though they had seen no such thing. And his master routinely asked clients to sign pages in blank—especially if they wanted long, relatively complicated documents—for him, the assistant, to fill in later. Only once in a while would anyone make an issue of it. The occasional royal inspector (*visitador*), for instance, might interrupt the normal flow of business with pointed inquiries like those that Pedro Pérez Landero prescribed in his how-to manual, *Practica de visitas* (1696):

> In documents given before the said Notaries, were the contents taken down in shorthand, and on a loose sheet of paper [*por memoria*], and the parties made to sign the documents in blank? And later, when the clients were no longer present, did they fill the documents in as they pleased, thereby causing harm and prejudice to the parties?
>
> And did the said Notaries, having been entrusted with the secrets of certain documents that passed before them, disclose them, causing harm to the parties?
>
> And did the said Notaries receive gifts, presents, or bribes of gold, silver, silks, or other things from the persons who transacted business before them, so that they might obtain friendly and favorable treatment?[60]

Inspection visits happened every few years, and depending on the rigor of the inspector, notaries might face disciplinary action. Draft books were a vital part of their archives, so their record-making shortcuts were relatively easy for inspectors to detect.[61] (Bribe taking and other infractions could more easily be hidden; no official kept books marked "Bribes and Favors.") The trouble that resulted was usually not serious—perhaps a fine of 50 or 100 pesos. Then things could go on as before. This was how early modern legality worked: by selective application in accordance with entrenched local custom. As the old saying went, "custom makes the law."[62]

If making extrajudicial records was a process shaped by custom, what about the production of lawsuits (*pleitos*)? Here, too, notaries and their assistants were called upon to insert themselves into other people's business. And here, too, they recorded words that they certified were true. Like other documents, lawsuits—with their charges, depositions, pleadings, and judicial decisions—went into a notary's archive and constituted part of the inheritance he would pass on to his buyer-successor. But this kind of notarial truth was very different in the making. A much larger cast of actors might take part in it: constables, bailiffs, and other petty officials of the justice system; the legal representatives and counsel each side might hire to advance its cause (*procuradores* and *abogados*); the judges and their legal advisors. And it was thoroughly agonistic. This was explicitly truth-in-question, produced through the legal workings of disagreement and arbitration. One side's truth challenged another's to a legal fight in which, barring a settlement, a winner and a loser would emerge.

Technically, much depended on the judge. Ultimately, he had the power to decide who had better proved his or her case.[63] In practice, however, as Tamar Herzog has argued, other judicial actors played crucial, even decisive roles—especially notaries. If judges were busy, they might delegate testimony taking to a notary, and they tended to make liberal use of the law's provisions.[64] Thus notaries had to learn specific techniques for questioning and recording, even "purifying," witnesses' testimony (as we saw in chapter 1). They had to be prepared to find and describe the wounds on an injured party's body and prepare a *fé de heridas*.[65] They also had to deliver countless subpoenas and notifications. Each such delivery earned them a fee, though on occasion the work might prove dangerous.

But who did the physical labor of writing? While notaries concentrated on breaking down the questions, "purifying" witnesses' words, and so forth, who actually wrote everything down? Juan Álvarez Posadilla is one of the rare writers to address this in his 1794 manual on criminal justice. An imaginary advocate gives lessons to his eager pupil, a notary, who has discovered to his consternation that just about everything he picked up as a small-town notary's apprentice is wrong. In one exchange the notary is in the process of unlearning the way he was taught to depose a witness. "Tell me," the advocate asks him, "as I want to know the defects that your

Master committed in the depositions he conducted: was the alcalde present at the depositions he took?"

> Not.: No, sir. The alcaldes would have been much slower if they had had the patience to attend every deposition. The witnesses went to the alcalde's house, he swore them in (and the notary was either there or he wasn't, as chance would have it), and then they went to the notary's workplace, and he examined them, and phrased their statements in different, more impressive-sounding, cultured words, and I wrote them down.
>
> Adv.: Well then, however many statements he took from witnesses without the presence of an alcalde, he committed that many falsehoods . . . and worse was changing the words the witnesses used, substituting more impressive ones as you say, because frequently those have a very different meaning from what the witness meant to say.
>
> Not.: You worry and confuse me, sir, with what you have just said. . . . [66]

Well might this imaginary pupil be worried and confused. Legally nothing had changed since Monterroso's day; notaries were supposed to record witness testimony themselves, at the moment of speech, and were not to modify witnesses' words. But the notarial literature suggests Castilian notaries had assistants do the writing at their dictation, and that while dictating they cleaned up the words of witnesses they considered uncouth and unclear—whether they were supposed to undertake such free-lance translation / "purification" or not.[67]

In the haste of deposition taking, notaries might cut corners much as they did with contracts, wills, and other records. They might have an assistant take down the essentials of a witness's deposition in draft form, to be fully developed in a clean copy later, back at the office. One of Álvarez Posadilla's contemporaries, José Marcos Gutiérrez, cautions notaries in his manual on criminal practice that "unless the urgency of a case makes it impossible," they should try to avoid this shortcut, and instead write everything down fully while witnesses are speaking. This is recommendable "both to avoid witnesses' retractions [of their statements] once they are fully filled out and ready to be signed," and "to prevent the harm and fraud that notaries may cause and commit" by keeping the draft copies around.[68]

Official inspections were supposed to check up on Spanish American notaries and assess fines to keep them in line. The one remaining Cuzco residencia, from 1596–97, indicates several of Cuzco's notaries were fined for delegating witness depositions to their assistants. Francisco de la Fuente defended himself, asserting that he was always scrupulous about being present when witnesses were deposed, except during the opening stages of some criminal cases. Then, as he put it, "I am always present for the reception and swearing-in and examination of the witnesses, and my assistants only do the writing; I do not permit them to do anything else."[69] His colleagues responded in similar fashion. They all took for granted that their assistants did the actual writing of witnesses' words, instructed by the notary as to what witnesses "said." For them this *was* writing: the notary dictated and superintended his subordinates' physical labor; his anonymous subordinates scratched out what he told them with their quills, trimming the quill's point when it dulled. A notary's place in the production of writing thus let him concentrate on the labor of phrasing and "purifying"—deleting what he judged verbiage or rustic babble, and inserting better-sounding words for the witness's own.[70]

Colonial Cuzco depositions look like they might have been made in two stages, a draft and a final form. Seldom does one come across any marked-out words or phrases. The lines are generally regular and clean. Because the final version did not have to be sized to fit into a preallotted, chronologically ordered space inside a protocolo, no squeezed or loopy handwriting gives the drafting process away. (Instead, pages were added to a lawsuit as needed, and the whole was stitched together with string. Lawsuits could thus grow to accommodate any number of pages; some stretched into the hundreds.) But the making of these records in the notarial workshop might have worked the same way extrajudicial records were made: by having an assistant sit down with a draft and develop a clean, fully worded final version for the witnesses' signatures.[71] If so, the notarial assistants perhaps honed their own skills as interpreters and "purifiers" of witnesses' words, (re)arranging them and polishing them up between draft and final copy.

But surely notaries did not simply make up witnesses' testimony and insert it into the record—or did they? This sounds like something straight out of Quevedo or *Guzmán de Alfarache*. Yet at least one Cuzco notary's career was ruined over something similarly picaresque. In 1727, Alejo Fernández Escudero had just finished acting as notary in a lawsuit against Don Francisco de Quevedo, a former magistrate of Carangas who had been absolved of two murders, when he himself was accused of certifying depositions that witnesses had allegedly signed in blank. A fresh round of testimony was ordered. The first witness, Don Manuel Venero de Valera, was asked whether in his earlier deposition he had sworn to tell the truth before testifying. Had his testimony been written down as he gave it, and had he signed it after hearing its contents read aloud, in accordance with standard procedure? Or had he signed a blank page? According to his second deposition, the witness "answered that he did not swear, nor was it written in his presence,"

> and what happened in actual fact is that one night the said Don Francisco de Quevedo had come to his house, accompanied by a friend of the witness who entreated him to sign a sheet of paper on which they said was written the declaration that the witness should make on behalf of said Don Francisco de Quevedo, and when he wanted to read it, they said he should not tire himself, that its contents only amounted to the witness's not saying that the said Don Francisco de Quevedo had killed anyone, and under that impression, and because it did not seem to him that doing so would be untruthful, he wrote his signature, because it was true that until then the witness had not heard that the said Don Francisco de Quevedo had committed such crimes, and neither a judge nor a notary was present on that occasion.[72]

When read the contents of his first deposition, Venero de Valera (according to the second one) "declared that he found it contained more than they had told him when he signed it, and that had he read it he would not have signed it."[73] Other witnesses also indicated they had signed depositions that had been prepared for them in advance without learning the contents. Nor had they sworn before the judge or notary. One witness at first maintained that his original deposition had been lawfully produced, but broke down under questioning, gave a statement like that of the other witnesses, and was sentenced to six months' exile from the city for perjury.

This looked like notarial malpractice of the most serious kind: Fernández Escudero stood accused of certifying depositions as his when they had actually been fraudulently produced by the defendant, Quevedo, and his friends. Fernández Escudero was promptly jailed and his property embargoed. In his confession he testified that he was fifty-five years old and had held his office for twenty-seven years without incident. His self-defense was that he had only obeyed his superiors' orders and acted in accordance with custom: "It was the usual practice and custom in all the tribunals for notarial assistants [*oficiales mayores*] to take witnesses' depositions on account of the busyness of judges and notaries, and to have them certified later, given the trust they all had in each other."[74] He insisted that the witnesses *had* sworn in his presence to tell the truth—he just hadn't been present when their versions were written down. But Fernández Escudero got nowhere with his petitions for release. After several months, kinsmen and friends helped an ailing Fernández Escudero break out of jail and take refuge in the nearby monastery of La Merced, where he was dead by 1730.

The loud crash of Alejo Fernández Escudero's career was an extraordinary event. But the documents of this downfall offer a textual conundrum as important as it is unusual. They disclose the relationships and pressures that might be at work in the fact-finding phase of a hotly contested case (or at least their shadowy outlines). The judge, Cuzco magistrate Don Francisco Arias de Saavedra, and the advocate who counseled him, Don Antonio de Mendoza, were also accused along with Fernández Escudero of fixing the murder case to favor Quevedo and absolve him. A petition filed by Fernández Escudero's wife argued that these men should bear responsibility; how could her husband have refused to sign when they gave him the depositions for certification? That would have been "an insult worthy of reprimand and punishment."[75] Stakes were high enough that the viceroy himself had ordered the witnesses reexamined, entrusting the task to someone powerful enough to counteract the magistrate's influence—Don Fernando de Moscoso y Venero, Marqués de Buenavista—and taking care to specify that witnesses be questioned secretly, "and with such vigilance that the partisans of the said Magistrate [Saavedra] do not frighten them [*no los Auyenten*] so that they do not give statements, as we understand they did on a previous occasion when they suspected that this reexamination would be done." Witnesses, even on secret reexamination, failed to recall living people's names and instead fingered dead people. Taking part in this case was hardly a neutral event. More than one witness's deposition indicates that they "understood that everything had been fixed up with the judges, and others who were handling this business."[76]

If this case discloses an egregious partisanship, it also contains much that was ordinary, accepted practice. Fernández Escudero insisted throughout that he had done nothing unusual. It seems from his account that his superiors did not have to force him to act as he did. Although obeying them and signing depositions he admittedly had not witnessed was clearly against the law, he defended his conduct as utterly unremarkable, in line with "practice" and "custom." By his account notaries often swore people in en masse and then let their subordinates handle the depositions.[77] There is no way to know just how common this practice was in Cuzco lawsuits. The handwriting in depositions is usually different from the notary's signature, and in different ink, but it is impossible to tell from the documents whether the notary (or for that matter, the judge) was present at the time witnesses were deposed. However, this case seems to bear out the manuals, from Monterroso to Álvarez Posadilla, that warned of routine abuse in the handling of witnesses' words. And the more spacious and unsupervised the process, the more leeway there was to manipulate it through bribes and other external forms of persuasion.

Conclusions: Materiality and Meaning

To write (*escribir*), according to Sebastián de Covarrubias's well-known dictionary, means "to form letters upon some material, using diverse instruments."[78] Yet in practice, everyone knew that many "writers" didn't physically apply pen to paper; they dictated. Notarial writing consisted largely of knowledgeable dictation to a penman, with the notary's chief contribution being to put words into the right sequences. This kind of writing was all about accurate legal formulae and good order. Doing it well required skills learned over many years of practice. And it required an instrument, or several. For Covarrubias, an *instrumento* is something we use to make something else: "A man's hands are called *instrumentum instrumentorum*, because we make use of them to carry out whatever we have to do."[79] Notaries had many young hands at their service—young men whose training was to make the records we read today in colonial Latin American archives. The archives are, in effect, a gigantic homework assignment.[80]

At this point, then, we are in position to modify the conclusion reached in chapter 1. Strictly speaking, notaries' *assistants* were the instruments of the early modern archive—certainly in the case of the colonial Andes, and perhaps in Spain as well. And the making of these archives did not proceed strictly by the book. "Custom" came into play, and the unevenness of the records themselves hints at it in countless small ways: the changes in handwriting in extrajudicial records, which show where one copyist got tired and another took his place; the gaps where names were supposed to be filled in but for some reason never were; the orphaned signatures that grace the bottom of an empty page. As for trial transcripts, their remarkable evenness seems to bespeak a drafting process whose anonymous agent(s) did their best to smooth out hasty mistakes. The materiality of the record thus complicates further our notions of agency. Words got to paper through a complicated relay process, one that might involve several people and considerable filtering and rewriting.

Young hands (and bodies) learned over the years how to perform the customary physical and intellectual labor. When young men moved to gain their own credentials as notaries, they often declared that they had grown up in notaries' offices. As José de Dueñas Palacios puts it in his 1769 petition: "From my Infancy until the present I have been raised in the office of Don Pedro José Gamarra, applying myself to all manner of documents, lawsuits, and other papers, dispatching them with vigilant promptness, faithfulness, and legality . . . and thus daily visiting the ecclesiastical and secular courts of this city."[81] Like generations of young men before him, he had learned the routes of the lettered city: its shortcuts and back alleys as well as its broad, formal avenues. He himself was all but invisible in the resulting documents. Yet his daily routines reinscribed a colonial habitus, an everyday legal world with its own rituals, phraseology, and common sense.

At the end of the day, and perhaps not until then, the notary came by to grace the finished pages of his penmen with his signature, flourish, and signo. Perhaps the penmen scurried to put away their cartoons, barbs, and verses. His would be the credit (or blame); theirs was the actual labor.

CHAPTER 4

POWER IN THE ARCHIVES

On May 19, 1629, one of the most powerful men in Cuzco, Rodrigo de Esquivel, lay in a parlor of his house "dressed in the habit of Saint Francis, and dead and gone from this present life."[1] So attested the notary who came by that evening to prepare the official death certificate, the *fé de muerte*. He also certified that he had opened Don Rodrigo's will, asking each witness who had signed it to affirm that his signature was truly his and that he had been present when the will was prepared. They declared these things to be true. What followed perhaps surprised no one. The old man had been rich and calculating, willing to do whatever was necessary to amass wealth and get his way. He had made two advantageous marriages, acquired valuable properties in the valley just south of Cuzco, and fought to retain a prized *encomienda*, a grant of Andean tributaries that enhanced his aristocratic standing. Once the notary made the terms of his will public, another of Don Rodrigo's tactics was disclosed: he forged documents.

The will is quite straightforward (albeit more than a little defensive) about his forgery. It had happened many years earlier while Don Rodrigo was in the midst of a lengthy lawsuit that sought to strip him of his encomienda. He had been advised by "the best legal minds and highest judges in this Kingdom" to hide his assets by claiming falsely that they were really the dowry goods of his first wife, Doña Petronila de Cáceres. That way they could not be seized.[2] Thus advised, Don Rodrigo moved to artificially enhance the size of his wife's dowry, "making it appear to be more than I had in truth received." How did he do it? "I took as my instrument Alonso de Paniagua, assistant to the notary public Joan de Quirós before whom I had made out the dowry letter," the will explains,

and since the said Alonso de Paniagua had written the letter in his own hand . . . he [re]wrote in the same hand the two pages that he removed, pages 741 and 742, on which he wrote falsely the . . . receipt . . . for the amount of 9,550 silver pesos, which it says I received in thirty silver bars that entered into my possession. But I declare to relieve my conscience that this receipt was false . . . and I am telling the truth in all that is recounted here.[3]

The proof was in the notary's books for the year 1583. All one had to do was look at pages 741 and 742, according to Don Rodrigo's will, and the forgery "can be seen clearly in the difference in the ink of the first two pages of the dowry letter . . . which is not like that of the third page, which is from the true, original dowry document."[4]

The ink of the first two pages of the 1583 dowry letter in Cuzco's archives is indeed a different color from that of the third page.[5] But that settled nothing for Don Rodrigo's and Doña Petronila's eldest son and heir. Don Rodrigo the younger spent years suing to prove that the version contained in the will was *not* the truth, but one more convenient story cooked up by his profligate father, who had squandered his mother's dowry. The son stood to inherit more if he could demonstrate that Doña Petronila's dowry had been truly splendid, not enhanced through forgery. He thus set out to prove his father had lied in his will. His very Christian mother would never have countenanced the deceit of a false dowry document. Moreover, it was settled "custom" among notaries public and their assistants to draw up documents on loose sheets that they later inserted into their registers. Nothing unusual about a little change of ink; it proved nothing.

So it was that the two Rodrigos, father and son, clashed sharply in their renderings of the archival evidence from 1583. A great deal hung on the making of a three-page record. Yet neither man suggested that the notary Joan de Quirós was to blame. Nor did anyone accuse his right-hand man, Juan de Paniagua, whom Don Rodrigo claimed he had taken as his "instrument" to execute the forgery. The silences here about writing and power are just as intriguing as the assertions. How difficult was it to reach inside the notarized record and tweak an inconvenient page? Did it require a potent threat or bribe (or both) from an unusually powerful figure like Don Rodrigo? Do Cuzco's colonial archives—and perhaps archives more generally—contain only the truth that powerful people found acceptable?

In this chapter, I will argue that people did not have to belong to their city's richest, most formidable clans to exert some control over the archival record. There were ways to make the documents say what one wanted. Power such as that wielded in Cuzco by the Esquivel clan certainly didn't hurt when it came to the more muscular instances of bending the rules. But less exalted people with insider's knowledge could also influence the archives' contents through a number of tactics—some applied before, some during, and some after the record was written. Timing, luck, and nerve might be involved (as well as under-the-table payments). Mostly, though, there was no special need for derring-do. Often the notary and his assistants did not even have to know they were being manipulated.

Confidence Men and Off-Record Understandings

First, we will examine the tamer methods. To get the record to say what one wanted, it helped to know how document making worked. One could, as we've seen, give the notary written instructions on a papelito, a little slip of paper. But the notary did not have to know every last detail. One might strategically hold something back. Sometimes notaries must have been aware that their clients were withholding key terms: wills, for example, might charge the executors to leave a bequest "to the person I have indicated," hiding the beneficiary's identity (perhaps to protect the honor of a lover or disguise the identity of an illegitimate child).[6] These clauses signals to the reader a secret: "You can only read to this point; here you can't come in."

But parties might also reach confidential understandings known only to them and undisclosed by anything in the record itself. These invisible riders might appear later, separately, once they had become the crux of controversy (and their precise terms might stay archivally opaque). Take the case of Doña Francisca Vela de Córdoba, who disclosed a hidden understanding several years after it backfired. In 1650 she registered a declaration that her deceased first husband, Juan de la Borda y Andía, a former city councilman of Cuzco, had arranged to sell some houses in Paucartambo to his fellow councilman Cristóbal Camberos confidentially (en confianza). Camberos had gone on record as having paid Juan de la Borda y Andía for the houses when in fact no money had changed hands. This was a bogus sale, according to Doña Francisca, and she was very explicit about the reason: it had been arranged to protect the property for Juan de la Borda's heirs by keeping it out of certain legal proceedings that had been brought against the deceased man. Yet once Juan de la Borda was conveniently dead, Camberos, the fictive buyer, had taken advantage of the contract, claiming the property in Paucartambo "as though it were true."[7]

Such confidence men only got what they deserved, according to Bartol-omé de Albornoz, whose 1573 manual *Arte de los contractos* describes such off-record understandings as gross fraud. Albornoz writes of confidential donations, but he makes clear that this sleight-of-hand might also be ap-plied to sales:

A confidential donation is a donation made on the understanding that the recipient will give back to the donor whatever is made over to him. For example, if someone wants to marry, so that he may appear wealthy, someone else may donate to him certain legacies or money, or sell them to him but release him contractually from paying for them, or claim to have received payment, or do something similar on the understanding that the recipient will give back to him everything that he has been given, once the desired effect has been achieved."[8]

The tactic might also be used to inflate the assets of would-be priests who desired ordination but lacked sufficient patrimony: "they are often given donations of real estate, so that with such title they may be ordained." Albornoz indicates both that this is commonplace and that it is wrong. The resulting contract should not be considered a donation, "but a fraud, and even manifest robbery," seriously freighting the conscience. It is a dis-guised loan made with the intent to deceive.[9]

Albornoz seems even more incensed by what he calls *Contracartas*, countercontracts, and it is worth following him deeper into the con-tractual labyrinth to see where textual manipulations might get people. These, he writes, are contracts made to repeal other contracts. For exam-ple, "say Pedro sells Martín a house for 1,000 *ducados*, and makes it over to him in a contract of sale in which he [i.e., Pedro] declares himself con-tented and paid the price, and this becomes public record." At the same time, however,

the buyer Martín makes out a contract in favor of Pedro, saying that even though he was given title to the house that was sold him . . . that the truth is he did not pay [Pedro] anything, but rather owes and promises to pay him the 1,000 pesos of the sales price by a certain date. . . . This second record is what is called a *Contra carta*, the usual effect of which is that the buyer of the house [i.e., Martín] gives everyone to understand that he is the owner of the house, and he publicly shows title to it . . . and can thus sell or otherwise make it over to a third party.[10]

Thus Pedro is protected from fraud, yet Martín is able to display as his a house that he has not "truly" bought from Pedro. But what if Martín should decide to sell the house that was not really his to begin with? Albornoz warns of what might happen next: Pedro might adduce the countercontract, revealing the fraud at the expense of the third party (presumably after Martín has skipped town with the latter's money). Albornoz concludes this convoluted passage by observing that one contract cannot be turned into two this way "unless the notary authorizes in each that he is false in the other one. In one he says that the payment has been made, and in the other that it has not: I find no agreement here." If it were up to him, Albornoz would order the notary to pay by having his thumbs chopped off. Such fraudulent contracts, he laments, "are much used in the Indies, and here," and should be remedied, "because this is complete, unvarnished falsehood."[11]

The Mexican notary Nicolás de Yrolo Calar refers frequently to "confidences" in his 1605 manual, La política de escrituras—a rare American addition to the notarial how-to literature of the day. He gives a series of templates for formal declarations (declaraciones) that notaries might be called upon to make for their clients. These reveal that other notarized documents—sales, loans, and so forth—contain the names of people who weren't the true agents, and conceal the names of those who were. Following the details is like watching a magician's shell game. "Be it known to all," begins one, "that I, Sebastián, resident of _____ , declare that, because Dionisio of _____ empowered me . . . to receive and collect from Cristóbal five hundred gold pesos . . . for a like sum that [Dionisio] confessed I had given him [in a notarized proxy or poder], I declare that the said proxy was confidential and that the said Dionisio did not receive from me the said 500 pesos nor any part of them."[12] (Sebastián goes on to promise that once he's collected the pesos from Cristóbal he will hand them over to Dionisio.) Each variation in this series asserts that a previous notarized record was mere fiction. In the next template, for example, "A." declares that because Gregorio has sold him an enslaved black man named Bernardo in a contract that passed before "so-and-so, notary, on such-and-such date, etc.," he wants to make it clear that the sale "was confidential," that no money changed hands, and that he, "A.," renounces and transfers to Gregorio all rights to Bernardo. Yrolo Calar matter-of-factly observes that "by this means other declarations can be made, of houses or other things sold in confidence."[13]

To judge from Yrolo Calar's manual—one of only a handful made in Spanish America—confidential deals were ordinary occurrences in the Indies of his day. He doesn't seem worried in the least that his (or his notarial followers') thumbs will be chopped off. But this seems to be a matter of temporality and degrees of complicity: Albornoz thunders against the notary who *simultaneously* prepares two contracts, one of which contradicts the other. Yrolo Calar merely prescribes templates for "declarations" revealing that prior contracts (perhaps by an entirely different notary) contain made-up terms. Notaries using Yrolo Calar's templates were not obviously complicit in their clients' prior confidences, though Albornoz would surely have resented the Mexican notary's matter-of-fact tone. Nothing in Yrolo Calar's manual suggests that anything is wrong with notarized confidences or the declarations that point to them.

Why might people rely on this form of documentary deception? Albornoz's examples go part of the way toward a convincing explanation: at major turning points in their lives, such as marriage or ordination, people might want to appear wealthier than they were. But why might off-record confidences have become especially commonplace "in the Indies," as well as in Spain? A more ordinary reason can be deduced from the work of economic historians: the need for credit. The Spanish American economies were perpetually cash poor.[14] This might well have led to the everyday use of creative finance through *confianzas*. For example, if Juan owed 500 pesos to his friend Diego, he might agree to cancel his debt to Diego by obligating himself to pay 500 pesos to Pedro, one of Diego's creditors in an unrelated transaction. Diego would thus be spared the effort of having a notary modify his original debt to Pedro. Instead, Juan would obligate himself formally to "repay" Pedro the amount of 500 pesos (even though Pedro had given Juan nothing). This would have seemed fair and efficient to the two friends. But the archive would reflect a deal that hadn't happened (between Pedro and Juan) and render invisible one that had (between Juan and Diego). Efficient credit, in short, might involve a significant amount of archival sleight-of-hand.

Another powerful reason for confidential deals comes through in the deceased Juan de la Borda's bogus sale of his property to Cristóbal Camberos: to protect assets from seizure. Assets were seized all the time in legal proceedings; this was the first thing a judge ordered in a lawsuit if the defendant in a civil or criminal suit appeared suspicious. A timely bogus sale could thus shelter assets for any defendant concerned about the possible embargo of his property. Merchants, who routinely engaged in risky economic activity, might suddenly become subject to creditors' claims— and this group, perhaps more than any other, would have found asset-hiding "sales" and "donations" particularly useful.[15]

A big risk for those participating in bogus contracts came at inheritance time, however. The same people who had tried to look asset poor on paper might also want to leave property to their heirs, and might encounter the same problem as Juan de la Borda (or rather, his widow): the paper trail still proved that his house belonged to someone else. They might decide to honor the contract and betray the confidence. To foreclose the possibility that bogus records might cause real harm, cuzqueños often disclosed details of their confidential dealings in their wills. A clause in the 1637 will of the Cuzco notary Alonso Calvo is a good example:

> I declare that Juan García del Corral the younger promised to pay Don Juan de Mendoza, and for him and in his name to pay Juan de Mijancas Medrano . . . five hundred or so pesos . . . and although the said Juan García del Corral promised to pay this quantity, *the truth is that I am the real, liquid debtor of it,* since the merchandise from which [this obligation] arose was for me, and the said [Juan García del Corral] entered into the agreement out of friendship, to do me a favor, and *en confianza.*[16]

Maybe Calvo wanted to appear asset poor at a particular juncture in his career to avoid sequestration of his assets. Or perhaps García del Corral owed Calvo money, and to cancel his own debt, agreed to obligate himself formally to one of Calvo's creditors. Whatever the case, Calvo protected García del Corral from the risk of having to honor a bogus obligation. Anyone who has spent time reading colonial notarial records will have noticed this relatively common kind of disclosure.[17]

Occasional traces appear of seemingly unproblematic confianzas, such as those of Alonso Díaz Dávila, a Cuzco notary who had two curious transactions put on record in July, 1652, only to cancel both a few months later. First came the sale of Díaz Dávila's inheritance to his brother Lázaro de Valencia for 2,500 pesos, registered before Martín López de Paredes. It is immediately followed by Lázaro de Valencia's donation of a furnished residence to his brother so that he might live in it with his wife and children for four years' time, since the family had just arrived from "the highland provinces where they have experienced great misfortunes and losses," and since Díaz Dávila "is poor and must behave and act with the decency that befits his person and the very public office he holds." In December 1652, however, the two brothers expressed through the medium of the same notary their desire to cancel the contracts' terms. Marginal notations (figure 22) on each of the two documents indicate that "they drew up this document *en confianza* because the said Alonso Díaz Dávila foresaw certain inconveniences at the time that it was made, and the truth is that everything contained and declared in it is and was only imaginary and made up [*supuesto y fingido*] for this reason, and not so that it might be put into effect in any way."[18] This frankly exhibited bit of fiction in the archives closes with standard protestations of truthfulness, all very matter-of-factly recorded. Whatever the "inconveniences" were, they are confined to an opaque euphemism in the margins.

This is the archive at its most textually defiant—or so it feels reading such "confidences," which can produce a hall-of-mirrors sensation of disorientation. The archive seems deliberately opaque in a case like Díaz's. Or, rather, the message is "you can't come in here." The words *en confianza* clearly might mean different things depending on the context in which they were used. They might signal that an action—the sale of a house in Paucartambo, or payment for a piece of land—did not take place even though the record certified that it had, as in the cases above. Or they might signify that an action took place but the principals were not those named in the record.[19]

The same spirit of confidentiality was at work in many deals across colonial Spanish America. People constantly needed credit for purchases large and small, yet the church prohibited the taking of interest. This gave rise to any number of subterfuges to disguise lending at interest.[20] Church authorities did what they could, but as Cummins puts it, "The need to do business and make a suitable profit transcended legal and moral scruples and was apparently tolerated, if not condoned."[21] Mid-colonial Peru seems to have been similar. In Lima, Cuzco, and elsewhere, as we've seen, people might include interest with their principal by contracting to borrow somewhat larger sums than they actually received. As with other types of confidences, the gap between what was written and what was done went undisclosed—unless a deal went bad and gave rise to litigation.[22]

What was the notary's position in the midst of all these confidences? His clients could have concealed their secret understandings from him in many cases—for example, in confidential sales or donations. He was not liable if they did; rather, they were at fault for giving him false information.

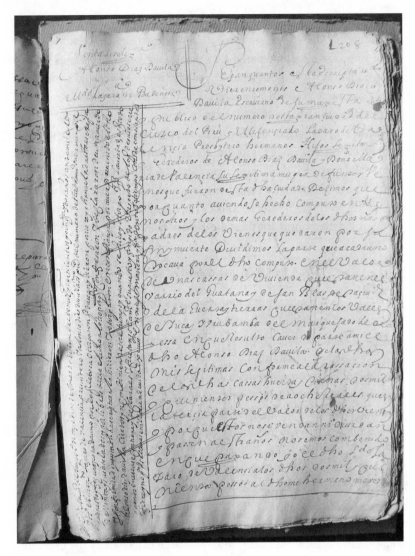

FIGURE 22. The Cuzco notary Alonso Díaz Dávila and his brother
Lázaro de Valencia declare in the margin that the entire content of this
1652 sales contract was made up ("es y fue tan solam[en]te supuesto y
fingido") in order to get around certain unspecified "inconveniences."
ARC-PN, Martín López de Paredes, protocolo 137 (1652), fol. 1208.
Photograph by the author.

(The technical name for this form of fraud was *subrepción*.)[23] Yet it seems likely notaries knew about or suspected some of their clients' subterfuges. Form language often stipulated that the notary was a witness as money changed hands: that it was counted out in front of him, and so forth. If clients contracted to borrow a larger amount than they actually received, for instance, the notary should have been in a good position to notice. Given the ample margins of custom, however, it is easy to imagine notaries signing off on exchanges without seeing each and every peso handed over.[24] The parties to deals with secret terms did not sue notaries over this kind of thing (although they might sue each other). The archives thus leave the impression that notaries either did not know what their clients were doing or did not consider it their business to stand in the way.[25]

Exclamations: Forms of Protest

Thus through literacy, money, and the right kind of familiarity, cuzqueños might exert a reassuring amount of control over the truth that notaries produced for them in writing. They might even get the notary's page to reflect transactions that never took place and attribute agency to the people they found most convenient. But what about those less experienced with notaries and poorly equipped (or unequipped) with legal knowledge? The 1704 will of Doña Clara de Montoya suggests that the very circumstances of notarial draft-making might be used to intimidate someone into agreeing to something she did not want. Doña Clara was a *beata*, a woman who had professed simple religious vows and lived much like a nun, and a descendent of Cuzco's indigenous elite. She had inherited property in the parish of San Cristóbal on her mother's death. According to her will, Doña Clara, "being a poor maiden beata with no knowledge about how to bring a lawsuit to ask for what I deserved," had been exploited by the executors of her mother's estate into covering expenses that they were supposed to pay. Thereafter, her will declares, she had been sent for by the priest Pedro de Oyardo, her spiritual confessor. When she went to see him, she found him in the company of the Cuzco notary Pedro López de la Cerda and other people. And in that context, Oyardo had asked her to donate her house to the parish priests of San Cristóbal. In response (according to her will), "because I did not understand what was happening since I am a woman and not versed in such things," she gave in:

I agreed to make the donation, though I had no other assets to support myself or settle my funeral expenses and debts, and thus I was completely tricked into this transaction, as it went against me and was done against my will, and because . . . there were a lot of people there and the aforesaid Doctor Don Pedro de Oyardo was my father confessor, I was embarrassed to contest anything in what was drawn up. And I did not understand it fully until I had asked my confessors and other people . . . when I finally understood my error and the fraud I had suffered.[26]

The assembled authorities, including the notary, seemingly cowed Doña Clara into obeying their wishes. But later she discovered that she, too, could use a notary to try to reverse the damage. According to her 1704 will, she first consulted others, then had her notary embed in her will a protest clause—a kind of counterwriting. It probably did not work. Her executors would have had to bring suit to reverse the donation, and Doña Clara did not leave enough resources for a legal battle. Yet people did not have to wait until they were near death to do what she did. They might commission a notary to register an "exclamation" (*exclamación*), a type of notarial record that was literally a form of protest. These formalized outbursts mark the rare archival occasions on which notaries registered discord.

In mid-colonial Cuzco, this type of document was commissioned most often by women.[27] Take, as a case in point, the 1642 exclamation registered by the Cuzco notary Alonso Beltrán Lucero for Doña Micaela Palomino. According to this brief record, Doña Micaela was under pressure from her husband—a Cuzco notary named Juan Flores de Bastidas—to cosign with him a 2,000-peso loan from his brother-in-law. He wanted her to put up her dowry as collateral. "Because I have refused," her exclamation declares, "saying that I do not want to do it and thus compromise my dowry, he has shown me great anger and has threatened me, saying he will kill me, and he has mistreated and beaten me and otherwise been physically and verbally abusive, and to stop this I have said I will do it."[28] The document goes on to register Doña Micaela's desire not to be bound by any note she may cosign, because she will have done so "thoroughly against my will and forced and frightened by my husband," and in order to "avoid further difficulties and violence." She claims the legal protections granted women under the terms of Roman and Castilian law, indicating that these should remain in full force even if she should explicitly sign them away.

The exclamation is thus both a protest and a kind of notarial skeleton key to release someone from the terms of other documents she may be forced to sign. Note that Doña Micaela's is lodged preemptively against the notarial record itself. Its construction does not directly pit wife against husband, but paper against paper—in this case, a loan she has not cosigned yet but believes she will soon be forced to. As the 1642 document phrases it, "I hereby claim and exclaim against the said document of indebtedness one, two, three, and more times, as many as the law concedes, and protest that entering into the said contract of indebtedness shall not harm me nor compromise my dowry goods because it will not have been done with a desire to compromise them."[29] The direct concern here is release from future obligations. Gaining release from Juan Flores de Bastidas himself would have required the much more complicated, dishonorable, and expensive legal maneuverings of divorce.[30]

Just six months later, on January 14, 1643, the same Cuzco notary registered the exclamación of Doña Luisa Laso de la Vega in very similar terms. Her husband, Don Mateo de Valer Melgarejo, according to this document, had been attempting to persuade her through a combination of cajolery and threats to enter with him into a 2,000-peso *censo*, a contract similar to a mortgage that would have required annual payments of 5 percent of the principal (100 pesos per year) until such time as the principal was repaid in full. Such contracts were almost always secured with real estate. Don Mateo wanted her to secure this one by putting up her dowry as collateral, and he also wanted her to enter into other kinds of agreements using her dowry funds as security: land sales, loans, and other censos. Her protest declares:

> Because she has not agreed to one or the other because it would compromise her dowry goods, he has scowled at her, and has threatened to kill her and has attempted to lay hands on her and otherwise mistreated her in both words and deeds, and because she is a noblewoman she does not want to expose herself to such risks, and out of the just fear and respect in which she holds him she has promised to enter into the obligations and sales to which she has referred and anything else that he may ask of her.[31]

This time the formal protest is registered in the third person, as though Doña Luisa were keeping these unpleasant disclosures at a noblewoman's arm's length. But she was moving to gain herself and her dowry the same legal protection that Doña Micaela was seeking. She likewise exclaims "one, two, three and more times" against any contract to which she may formally agree, saying that she will have done so against her will, forced by her husband's threats. And this document is similarly a protest within a protest. Its direct concern is release from future contractual obligations, but it also puts on record a wife's disclosures about her husband's violence.

The legal basis for this form of protest lay in the concept of "just" or "reverential fear" (*miedo justo*; *miedo reverencial*): fear so strong that it would move even the most steadfast man. According to the *Siete Partidas*, contracts were not legally valid if made by people whose consent had been forced.[32] They were not obeying their own free will. Doña Micaela and Doña Luisa thus drew, through their notary, on an old legal concept designed to be a "weapon of the weak"—or at least a shield, a means for those who had been frightened and manipulated by others to avoid harm.

Exclamations like these are not hard to find in colonial Andean archives, and to come across one is something of a textual jolt. Their wording contrasts vividly with the routine form language all around them: they puncture the mold of seemingly mutual agreements, insisting that textual "agreement" might paper over deep disagreement, even death threats. Yet exclamations are at once curiously disobedient and obedient. The regularity of phrasing suggests that they, too, conformed to a preexisting template—and for the most part, they did. Bartolomé de Carvajal, in his *Instruction y memorial para escrivanos y juezes executores* (1585), provides the form for what he calls the "protest (*reclamación*) of a married woman whose husband wants to obligate her by force." The detailed hypothetical parties bear a striking resemblance to the two couples from mid-colonial Cuzco:

> In such-and-such a place on such-and-such a day, month, and year . . . in the presence of me, the notary, and of the witnesses . . . so-and-so, wife of so-and-so, citizen of such-and-such place, appeared and declared that during their marriage, and before the wedding took place, her husband had contracted many debts, both on his own and as guarantor of others, on account of which he is broke, and for quite some time her husband has been asking and demanding of her that she permit him to obligate her contractually to pay his creditors, jointly and in *mancomún* [common legal action] with him . . . and he has also tried to persuade her to sell her dowry goods to pay off his debts.[33]

As the form language continues, it constructs a hypothetical broke husband who turns violent at his hypothetical wife's refusal to accede to his demands: "He has beaten her many times, and has caused her much fear, seriously threatening her."[34] Fearing for her life, this hypothetical wife promises him to do whatever he wants, but then protests in documentary fashion that she has gone against her will.

This form of protest, then, is modeled on a hypothetical husband's violent coercion of his wife in order to exercise control through her over her dowry. Doña Micaela and Doña Luisa were resorting quite literally, by means of their notary, to form language.[35] Others were out to protect dowry too, representing themselves as fearful, "compulsa y apremiada," while challenging husbands as far as they dared. In a random sample of thirty-seven exclamations registered in Cuzco between 1565 and 1731, twenty-two were by women (59 percent); of these, fifteen were protesting their husbands' attempts to force them to compromise their dowries. For example, Doña Constanza de Esquivel y Alvarado protested in 1661 that her husband Captain Gaspar Jaimes Ramírez de Zavala had become so deeply indebted that he was constantly casting around for fresh loans, and that she might be forced to compromise her dowry even further than she already had. The exclamation she registered by means of the Cuzco notary Lorenzo de Mesa Andueza expressed her desire to resist her husband's demands, "because he has already dissipated much of my dowry and what little remains I do not want to compromise [as collateral for her husband's debts] so as not to be left without any dowry [*indotada*]."[36]

If the typical exclamation was based on form language, might it hide off-record understandings? After all, the typical "exclaimer"—like the parties engaged in confidential sales, loans, and donations—was trying to shelter assets from possible seizure. On the face of it, the threat was her husband's poor handling of the couple's property (including her dowry, legally hers but under her husband's control). But perhaps one or both spouses were legally savvy enough to foresee potential difficulties and opt for the exclamation as a convenient fiction. It could always remain in the notary's care, unused—or it might be brought before a judge in the event of a financial disaster to preserve at least some of the couple's property.[37]

There is no way to be sure whether or not the brief narratives contained in exclamations are so much fiction in the archives, to borrow Natalie Zemon Davis's resonant phrase. It seems quite possible that Doña Micaela Palomino's protest was a convenient fabrication designed to shelter 2,000 pesos' worth of family assets: after all, her husband was a notary.[38] However, this form of protest was much more versatile in practice than we might imagine from these examples and Carvajal's model. Many cuzqueños whose circumstances did not coincide with those of the hypothetical people in the template still sought this notarial recourse. The emphatic phrase *contra toda su voluntad* (entirely against his or her will) was commissioned of notaries by both married and unmarried cuzqueños, and by both women and men, along with other key words and phrases: "one, two, three times," and so forth. Each tells a heavily scripted story of fearful defiance, of resistance-in-capitulation. And each indirectly denounces "bad patriarchy" —whether husbands' profligacy with dowries or something else.

No two exclamations are exactly alike. In their subtle differences, we can glimpse varying strategies of self-representation and self-defense. For instance, Doña Mariana García del Corral, a woman whose marital status was in the process of changing, registered two spirited exclamations in less than three months in the year 1684, calling on the Cuzco notary Pedro de Cáceres to adapt this form of protest to suit her specific needs. In neither case was defense of dowry the issue. In the first document, dated September 6, she appears as the lawfully married wife of Captain Diego de Raya. By the second, dated November 25, she is described as being "presently in pending separation proceedings" with her husband. The first exclamation indicates that she felt herself under considerable pressure, not only from her husband but from the region's highest Spanish authority, the Cuzco corregidor, Don Pedro Balbín. Her husband was attempting to force her to join him in adopting a boy named José as the couple's legitimate son:

> She said that because her husband brought suit against her to have a boy named José, abandoned on their doorstep, declared their legitimate son although he is not, she has faced growing unpleasantness and vexations and her husband has threatened her urging her to make the said declaration, and because of the closeness and friendship he has with General Don Pedro Balbín, Corregidor . . . she is afraid that the said Corregidor may cause her harm by imprisoning her or mistreating her in deeds or words.[39]

In this case physical violence is not aimed directly at the wife, but at the boy, according to Doña Mariana's exclamation. Her husband "violently kicked the boy out of the house," and because she cared about José, "having raised him from a very tender age," she agreed to sign a declaration, "saying that the boy is her son and that of her husband, not because he is, but because, as she has said, he was abandoned on their doorstep"—all in order to get the boy back and prevent further troubles.

This curious case resists easy interpretation. Why did the couple disagree about adopting José? Doña Mariana might well have wanted to protect the couple's property for their legitimate children to inherit. Perhaps she knew or suspected that the boy was her husband's son by another woman. Whatever the case, Doña Mariana figures textually more as a responsible protector than as someone in need of protection. Interestingly, although the overall goal of her actions was to *prevent* the boy from becoming their son and having a claim on their inheritance, she represents herself as a loving, devoted mother to José and her husband as cruel and coercive. Her exclamation mentions fear, and in it some formulae of fear are mobilized, yet the archival record makes her comes across as unusually unbowed.

Is this Doña Mariana's determined independence or just the notary's frugality with form language? Her second protest suggests someone unusually active on her own behalf. In November 1684 Doña Mariana registered a fresh exclamation, this time against her son-in-law, Don Felipe de la Puente, "who has urged her many times" to incur a 2,700-peso debt (*obligación*) to Captain Blas Pérez. On seeing her refusal, this document declares, "he has told her that if she does not enter into this obligación he will leave this City and not return and will abandon his wife [i.e., Doña Mariana's daughter] and he has made many other threats that she might come to some harm." Doña Mariana was moved to commission another protest from Pedro de Cáceres, saying that if she were to sign a note of obligación on behalf of Captain Blas Pérez it would be against her will, done solely to protect her daughter. This time fear is not on record even in stock expressions, only Doña Mariana's will and its contravention. Her protest registers in formulaic terms that any debt she may incur should be considered totally invalid, "because her will is not to obligate herself."[40]

The relative assertiveness of Doña Mariana's exclamations comes across as well when they are compared to others notarized by Pedro de Cáceres. On January 2, 1696, the wife of a local Spanish authority registered an unusually lengthy exclamation in which the language of fear and respect is salient, with enough additional detail that one has the impression of reading about a woman who is seriously scared. Doña María Josefa de Losada y Castilla is depicted as young, timid ("de condición tímida"), and an orphan with no kin to defend her; her husband, Don José de Silva y Obando, chief constable of Cuzco, as violent, difficult, and frightening ("de muy áspera y mala condición").[41] This exclamation, not Doña María Josefa's first, reiterates a previous protest. It closes with an unusual passage indicating her desire that its contents be kept secret.

Even more abject is the exclamation commissioned of Cáceres two months later by Tomás Rodríguez de Villegas, which suggests the circumstances in which this form of protest might be adapted for men's self-defense. Tomás was not out to defend his dowry, of course. In March 1696 he was seeking what he considered his rightful inheritance, "some property" left him by Pedro Rodríguez de la Bandera ("who raised me from birth") plus half of the estate the deceased man had acquired during his marriage to Doña Sebastiana Maldonado y Álvares (*bienes gananciales*). According to the exclamation, Tomás had been in conflict with his benefactor's widow because Doña Sebastiana was offering him only 423 pesos, less than half of the 1,000 pesos he believed he stood to inherit. Through the mediation of Cáceres, he declares:

> Because I have not wanted to accept her offer she has used Field Marshall Don Pedro de Eraso and Don Juan Arias de Lira priest of the said pueblo of Yucay and Lorenzo Durán . . . very respectable persons whose requests of me I cannot refuse, being as I am a poor, helpless, pusillanimous man . . . and thus any document . . . that I may sign in favor of the aforesaid [Doña Sebastiana] . . . I will have signed completely against my will, forced, induced and frightened.

This first-person exclamation goes out of its way to represent Tomás as cowardly and at the mercy of other men. He dares not go against them "out of fear and respect."[42]

Tomás's case underscores the gender asymmetries of the exclamation, a form of protest that expressed fear and worked by deferral, dissimulation, and indirection. Men could employ the same defensive textual strategy as women, but they had to be willing to go on record as dominated, fearful, and weak. In mid-colonial Cuzco, men seem to have employed this device infrequently; when they did, they typically expressed fear and reverence toward a father or religious superior. Yet in men's exclamations, too, we can read significant variations in self-representation. A far less "pusillanimous" tack than Tomás's was taken in 1705 by Don Pablo de Orna Alvarado, who protested that he should have been given a particular benefice after Cuzco's bishop-elect named someone else and ordered the head diocesan counsel not to admit any appeal of the decision. Don Pablo's exclamation indicates that he protests "on finding himself subjected and so as not to experience the violence and vexations he has been experiencing."[43] Having been denied his right to the benefice and then his right to appeal the bishop-elect's move, he has no further recourse—at least for the moment—but to put on record his desire to appeal at a future date. Don Pablo does so without registering any formulaic fearfulness or respect for his superiors. Like Doña Mariana García del Corral, Don Pablo comes across as a relatively bold defender of rights and property, "subjected" but still active on his own behalf. However, her assertiveness is markedly maternal; he appears textually defending his own rights and property, not protecting other people's.

Thus men, too, might invoke the legitimating powers of the notary to clear spaces of possibility for undoing the archive's textual efficacy. Those with enough resources might register their protests with more than one notary: this appears to be the tactic adopted by Juan de Loyola in 1686. Among Joan de Saldaña's notarized records is a "ratification" document dated June 8, 1686, which indicates that earlier that day Loyola had registered some sort of protest before another notary named Juan de Samalvide. The ratification before Saldaña indicates that it has been made to reinforce the earlier document ("para que tenga más fuerza"). It remits the reader for further details to the first protest, which is no longer in Cuzco's archives. Loyola seems to have moved from one notarial workshop to another to be sure his protest would stick.[44]

For all its constraints and mediations, then, the notarial record gave people access to a form of protest against patriarchal violence and coercion. The protester had to be willing to publicize her grievances to the point of making them known to several people, at the very least the notary, his penmen, and witnesses. Notaries were supposed to keep their clients' business a secret, but they were certainly well positioned to serve as information brokers if their clients wanted them to.[45] They had excellent access to leading local families' business. Through them word could easily get around. In some cases, that might have been the whole idea: the exclamation might have worked as a kind of restraining order.[46] (Perhaps for that reason Doña María Josefa de Losada y Castilla asked specifically for her exclamation's contents to be kept secret.) Commissioning one was far less complicated, expensive, and damaging to an honorable person's reputation than divorce. Perhaps some "exclaimers" never sought remedy through lawsuits at all, relying instead on channels of rumor, ties of family loyalty, and other forms of pressure and suasion that word of an exclamation might mobilize. The intended audience for an exclamation might have been one's local kin group and its defenders, rather than a judge.

Whatever the case, women position themselves in these documents well within accepted gender norms—as good mothers, obedient daughters, reverent wives.[47] In other contexts their self-representations are much less conventionally feminine. When a wealthy Cuzco widow named Doña Bárbara Antonia de Carrión y Mogrovejo petitioned in 1714 for a grace period in making annual payments on her hacienda, for example, she (or her amanuensis) described the floods that had ruined her irrigation system. Next comes her claim "I have rebuilt it completely"—which surely represents a crew of indigenous workers' labor as her own.[48] Yet when availing themselves of legal forms of protest against "bad patriarchs," women (through their chosen notaries) seem to have gone in for a saturated femininity, the most concentrated possible version. Nancy van Deusen's work indicates that women of mid-colonial Lima did likewise when taking the more difficult, costly step of seeking divorce.[49]

Clearly we are not simply hearing women's voices through these exclamations. The mediations are too significant, the scripts too obtrusive for that. While we can speculatively read fear and defiance between the lines, it's also quite likely—given cuzqueños' creative use of notarized "confidences"—that some exclaimers were acting on a joint marital strategy to shelter potentially endangered assets. But in any case, the fascination of these protests is their refusal to fit any simple categorization. However submissive the exclaimer's textual self-representation may be, the very act of commissioning such a document complicates this image, suggesting a counterimage: that of someone who knew how to be active and purposeful in her own self-defense.

After the Fact

Certain kinds of documents worked, in effect, as cover-ups or preemptive strikes, to prevent a different version of events from gaining the status of official, notarized truth. But what to do when a record was already made? How could one change it or contest its validity? Don Rodrigo de Esquivel had the clout to make a Cuzco notary's chief assistant rewrite the record the way he wanted it, but such a thing was probably rare. (To find obvious changes of ink *between* pages of a document is not common.)[50] What other recourse did people have?

Changing one's mind, or heart, was certainly possible. Records might be revoked or canceled by other records registered at a later date. The *distrato* is a good example: this form existed to undo previously agreed-to contractual bargains.[51] The parties were then free to rewrite a deal, or drop it altogether. Wills, too, could be revoked and remade. The testator's preferences might have shifted significantly over time: bequests might have multiplied (or dwindled); the desired recipients might have changed, and so forth. The same person might leave multiple wills as long as each new one carried a clause invalidating all previous versions.[52] Alternatively, a testator might embed a distinctive phrase in a will to prevent it from being revoked—a kind of early modern password, such as a bit of Latin psalm (figure 23). Monterroso notes that women might do this to frustrate those who would force or frighten them into changing their wills. "Such a will may not be revoked by any subsequent ones," he explains, "even if they say that they revoke the first one . . . unless the same psalm is inserted in it."

In theory, no will was ironclad if the testator herself wanted to change it. But in practice, others might try to foreclose the possibility of such changes. The 1633 Cuzco will of Doña Isabel de Soto is a case in point that illustrates a vindictive variation on the use of Latin passwords. It indicates that some forty years earlier, in Lima, Doña Isabel defied her father in her choice of a marriage partner but agreed to make out her last will and testament to placate him and other relatives. In that prior Lima will, "by order of Dr. Carrasco, my brother-in-law, they made me insert a clause that repealed and prohibited any other will I might subsequently leave," specifying lines of Christian scripture in Latin that she would have to repeat word for word in order for any later revocation to be valid. Doña Isabel thus found herself unable to remake her own will, "being a woman with no knowledge or understanding of Latin, nor the ability to remember [the words] after so long a time." Her family members boasted that the document was irrevocable. They hid it from her so that she could not memorize the mysterious Latin words she would need in order to undo it. She eventually filed suit with the viceroyalty's highest ecclesiastical authorities to frustrate this dubious use of scriptural code.[53]

What about contesting the validity of documents? One could sue on a technicality, if one could be found—and colonial Peruvian archives are full of lawsuits alleging documents' invalidity (*nulidad*; *insustancia*) on tech-

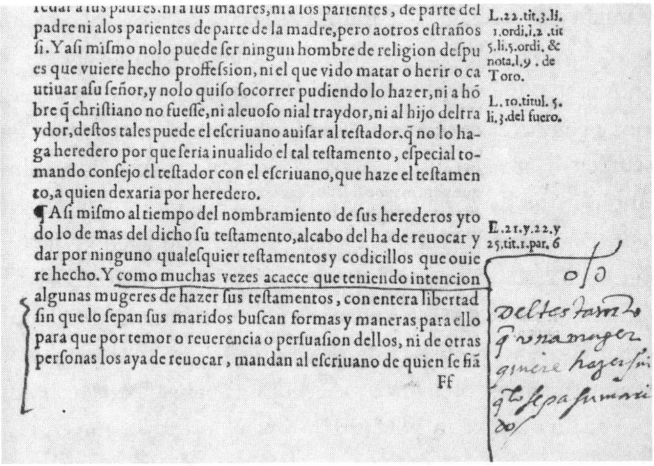

icuai a ius paures. ni a ius madres,ni a los parientes , de parte del   L.22.tit.3.li.
padre ni a los parientes de parte de la madre,pero a otros eſtraños   1.ordi,i.2 .tit
ſi.Y aſi miſmo no lo puede ſer ningun hombre de religion deſpu   5.li.5.ordi, &
es que vuiere hecho proffeſsion, ni el que vido matar o herir o ca   nota.l.9 . de   Toro.
utiuar aſu ſeñor, y no lo quiſo ſocorrer pudiendo lo hazer,ni a hó
bre q̃ chriſtiano no fueſſe,ni aleuoſo ni al traydor,ni al hijo deltra   L.10.titul. 5.   li.3.del fuero.
ydor,deſtos tales puede el eſcriuano auiſar al teſtador.q̃ no lo ha-
ga heredero por que ſeria inualido el tal teſtamento, eſpecial to-
mando conſejo el teſtador con el eſcriuano,que haze el teſtamen
to,a quien dexaria por heredero.

¶Aſi miſmo al tiempo del nombramiento de ſus herederos y to   E.21.y.22.y   25.tit.1.par. 6
do lo de mas del dicho ſu teſtamento,alcabo del ha de reuocar y
dar por ninguno qualeſquier teſtamentos y codicillos que ouie
re hecho.Y como muchas vezes acaece que teniendo intencion
algunas mugeres de hazer ſus teſtamentos , con entera libertad
ſin que lo ſepan ſus maridos buſcan formas y maneras para ello
para que por temor o reuerencia o perſuaſion dellos, ni de otras
perſonas los aya de reuocar , mandan al eſcriuano de quien ſe fia
Ff

FIGURE 23. Marginal annotation in Monterroso's manual *Pratica civil, y criminal, e instruction de scrivanos* (1563), highlighting a passage about women's wills. The marginal notation draws attention to a passage "about the will a woman wants to make without her husband's knowledge." Reproduced by permission of Houghton Library, Harvard University.

nicalities. If the notary had not done his job properly, there might be grounds for a suit. In 1680, for example, Don Pedro Gutiérrez de Quintanilla y Sotomayor and his wife, Doña Luisa Cano Velarde de Santillana, charged that a Huamanga notary by the occupationally appropriate name of Francisco Blanco had altered the draft of a credit deal they had made with a local convent, inserting a clause that pledged more property as collateral than they had wanted. They obtained a judgment barring the notary from completing the contract until matters were better sorted out. Blanco was made to produce his draft book for inspection. It was seen to contain a number of marginal annotations of added clauses. According to the nuns, however, the notary had advised Don Pedro and Doña Luisa about the marginal clause in question: "What happened for a true fact was just what is contained in the margin of the draft, as they were advised at the time it was made." From that point the legal attack waged by Don Pedro and Doña Luisa wilted. Their legal representative had to admit that the notary *had* read the draft agreement to them, adding rather lamely that when people "are read things in the midst of a crowd of people who are engaged in conversation, they may be distracted, as in the present case."[54]

POWER IN THE ARCHIVES   115

One might also question the status of the parties: a married woman, for example, could not enter into contractual dealings without the permission of her husband. Unless she sought special permission from a judge, she could not legally act alone, even if her husband had disappeared for years or had landed in jail. The Lima notary Diego Sánchez Vadillo and his client found this out the hard way. In 1625, Doña Elena de Aguiar y Acuña had obtained viceregal permission to transfer rights to indigenous labor to her daughter, Doña María, and had commissioned a notarized transfer (*dejación*) without first consulting her second husband—Don Gerónimo Hurtado de Salcedo, a former corregidor who was in jail for his debts.[55] Doña Elena was in the midst of divorce proceedings against Don Gerónimo, and Sánchez Vadillo mistakenly believed they were already divorced. The irate husband promptly sued the notary for damages of 12,300 pesos.

There was also a kind of insanity defense: people could not make valid contracts and wills if they were not in their right mind. Thus in 1660, Don Melchor del Junco contested his recently deceased father's sale of a valuable sugar estate in the Cuzco region for what Don Melchor claimed was an outrageously low price. His father had been sick at the time, and suffering from dementia. That was why he had agreed to sell Casinchigua for only 18,000 pesos, "when the just price and value of the said estate at that time was commonly estimated to be at least 60,000 pesos."[56] In 1691, relatives of the deceased Antonio Daza contested the will he left in Cuzco in similar terms. Daza's sister indicated that at the time his will was made, her brother was "not in his right mind because of the serious circumstances that aggravated his illness, which were so violent that they hastened his death."[57]

A document was also invalid if it could be shown that the client had expired before signing it. Thus in 1742, the royal notary Alejo Gonzáles Peñaloza was sued in Cuzco for allegedly drawing up an invalid *poder para testar*, a document authorizing a third party to make out a will, for an elderly widow named Doña Francisca Calvo Justiniano. Witnesses testified he had indeed finished the document as she lay on her deathbed. (Called in haste, Gonzáles Peñaloza seems not to have brought along any assistants for the job.) The notary had then read its terms to her and asked her to sign. Helping hands raised Doña Francisca to a sitting position, but at that critical moment, according to witnesses, she had "suffered a seizure, and immediately died." The notary disputed this version, testifying that Doña Francisca *had* managed to ask that a witness sign for her. The judge absolved him of the crime of falsifying (*falsedad*), but declared the document invalid and ordered that it be remade.[58]

None of these ways of contesting the record was new or distinctively colonial. All had deep roots in Castilian legal practice—as did the notion that the use of force rendered contracts invalid. Alleging use of force was popular, as we have seen, in colonial Cuzco, where propertied people seem to have been quite adept at commissioning exclamations to defend themselves and their assets. Whether these documents were sincere cries for help or cooked-up stories is impossible to tell at several centuries' remove; probably some of both. The exclamation embedded by Doña Clara the beata in her 1704 will is a relatively convincing example. The rest of the will indicates that she was (as she claimed) not very well-to-do or well connected. The 1701 donation of her house to the priests of San Cristóbal gives nothing away, but the brief 1704 narrative of how she was manipulated by her father confessor is entirely plausible.

The exclamation and supporting narrative are much less convincing in the case of a far wealthier cuzqueña, Doña Josefa López de Paredes. In 1707, Doña Josefa declared through the Cuzco notary Francisco Maldonado that a year earlier she had signed away her hacienda, Vicho, because she had been "ignorant of her rights and forced and compelled" to [donate] it to the Jesuits by the rector of a local Jesuit school.[59] According to Doña Josefa, the rector had taken advantage of her in a moment of weakness. Her second husband had died, leaving her with considerable debt, and the Jesuit had promised that if she donated Vicho to his order, they would defend her from financial ruin.[60] He pressured her so doggedly that she finally gave in—curiously, on the very day of her marriage to a third husband—and signed a blank page, where the rector later had a notary draw up terms she had not approved. She had meant to register an exclamation, but had not done so at the time. Numerous details of her convoluted narrative raise doubts about Doña Josefa's timing and motives. Why would she sign a blank page for the rector on the day she was to be married to a third husband and legal protector? (Her father, Martín López de Paredes, had been one of Cuzco's wealthiest and most calculating colonial notaries; didn't she know better?) And why did she wait a year to protest the alleged manipulation of her desires? Perhaps she was elderly and distracted; by 1709 Doña Josefa was dead, leaving her widower to carry on the lawsuit. But the whole thing could have been a ploy instigated by him, after he learned of the donation, so he could attempt to gain control of a valuable asset.

Whatever the case, compared to others' use of the language of exclamation, Doña Josefa's seems concocted (a bit improbably) as a last-ditch legal defense.

Did these documents work, when presented before a judge? In Cuzco, far more often than not, this isn't clear. Judges did not give lengthy explanations of the legal reasoning behind their verdicts, and their decisions are often on the very last page (or near the end) of a lawsuit. Unfortunately, these pages are the most likely to have been stripped away over time in the anonymous handling of the record. Working in Cuzco's archives thus means cultivating a tolerance, if not a taste, for the mysterious—the plausible outcome, rather than the definitive one.[61] As for extrajudicial exclamations, gauging their effectiveness would require a systematic search of the available lawsuits and appeals of the years subsequent to their making—a search likely to be time consuming and fruitless in Cuzco's archives.[62] So it is much easier to know what people *thought* might convince Cuzco's judges than to know what actually did. Still, we can know what they thought was plausible, and justified.[63]

Disappearing the Documents

One could only sue if there were documents to show a judge. Keeping track of one's records was not always easy, however. The archives hold plenty of cases in which people claim to have lost their documents and seek justice once they turn up. In 1682, for example, three Inca nobles of Cuzco —Don Florián Carlos, Don Lázaro Carlos Ynquiltopa, and Don Lucas Carlos Ynquiltopa—sued Diego de la Coba over the right to cultivate certain potato fields just above the Inca fortress of Sacsayhuamán. The plaintiffs indicated that their ancestors had cultivated these *papacanchas*, but title to them had been lost at the time of their grandfather's death. Their father's efforts to find the title had been fruitless. In 1682, however, it unexpectedly reappeared among the possessions of a dead man, Don Martín Quispe Topa. (How it got there is not explained.) Don Florián, Don Lázaro, and Don Lucas adduced the document to sue De la Coba for back payments for his use of the land.[64] Around the same time, Don Gerónimo Valladares was waging legal battle with the indigenous parishioners of San Gerónimo over plots he claimed to have received as his wife's dowry goods. By his account, "because the title to said lands could not be found, the Indians took over a portion of [the land], until recently due to the efforts of my father-in-law [the title] reappeared and I hereby present it . . . and it proves that the lands they took over belong to me."[65] The outcomes of these cases are unclear, but they hinged on the putative recovery of valid records.

Residences were not necessarily safe places for storing important papers. Thieves might break into the house and steal them; this was what the widowed Doña Leonor María, an indigenous property owner in the Cuzco parish of the Hospital de los Naturales, claimed had happened to her around 1690. Years later, she went before a judge to register that she owned two urban lots, "one of which," according to her petition, "I bought from Don Francisco Vicho in a contract drawn up before Don Bartolomé Roque Inga, notary [escribano de cabildo] in the said parish," and an adjoining lot, donated to her and her husband, deceased master hat-maker Don Juan Guaman, by his mother. The couple had held these lots for over thirty years, notes Doña Leonor María's petition, "and as it was our property we had built walls around it." She requested that the judge order witness testimony that she was indeed the owner of the lots.[66]

Such theft might be part of a deliberate effort to handicap an adversary by disappearing his documents. This was what befell Don Juan Costilla, according to the deathbed declaration of his former overseer (mayordomo), Miguel Bejarano y Castilla. In 1691, the dying Bejarano, through the notary Joan de Saldaña, disclosed that Costilla had fired him years earlier from his job running Tamboconga, Costilla's hacienda in the nearby province of Abancay. To "avenge this injury," Bejarano had cultivated the friendship of Costilla's brother, Don Gerónimo Costilla, the powerful Marqués de Buenavista, and told him that he knew where his brother Juan kept his land titles: he had pawned them with Lorenzo de Contreras, a petty shopkeeper just off Cuzco's Plaza de Armas. The two struck a bargain, and the Marqués gave Bejarano thirteen pesos to redeem the titles from the shopkeeper, plus an additional fifty pesos for his trouble and a new suit of clothes. Bejarano then went to Lorenzo de Contreras with the thirteen pesos, pretending to act on behalf of Juan Costilla,

> and giving him the payment [recaudo] in his name, took the aforesaid titles and other papers and brought them to the said Marqués de Buenavista and put them in his hands, and seeing that he held title . . . [the Marqués] seized the hacienda without giving [Bejarano] any portion of what he had promised him. It has weighed on his conscience that he was

unable to make restitution of the titles to Don Juan Costilla, and his confessor refused to absolve him unless he first made a judicial declaration, or declared before a notary the truth of this case.[67]

Bejarano might not have lived to see the outcome, but with his deathbed disclosure in hand, the elderly Costilla was able to get a judge to restore his rights to Tamboconga.[68]

Was *any* place secure for the storage of documents? None was entirely reliable, but the offices of Cuzco's numerary notaries seem to have been considered relatively safe. The archives thus contain cuzqueños' occasional requests that a numerary notary public "protocol" records for them in his registers. Yet even the archives of a city's numerary notaries might be breached. In 1676, for example, a ten-page viceregal order (*provisión*) was stolen from the archives of the Cuzco notary Juan Flores de Bastidas "during the days when there were bullfights in the Plaza del Regocijo" to celebrate a particular fiesta.[69]

A less risky approach was the one Don Rodrigo de Esquivel claimed to have used: that of getting a notary's apprentice to be an "instrument." This form of instrumentation might enable an outsider to filch as well as rewrite part of the record. Apprentices were not (yet) royal officials sworn to serve their sovereign's justice; they were young and inexperienced, and might like the idea of some extra income. These things seem to have been the undoing of the longtime Cuzco notary Bartolomé López Barnuevo in 1672. Though old and infirm, he had been serving as the designated notary public in a hard-fought contest between two elite families—the Berrios and the Silva Córdoba y Guzmáns—over a valuable entail (*mayorazgo*). One day in October 1672, the corregidor dispatched him to his office to fetch the copy his assistants had made of the case record (the originals of which had been sent to the Real Audiencia in Lima). It comprised over 400 pages at that point, yet López Barnuevo could not find it. When the corregidor sent him to look again, the anxious notary lost consciousness and collapsed, convincing onlookers that he might be dying. He was carried to his house and placed under house arrest.[70]

The subsequent inquiry into the documents' disappearance led to López Barnuevo's assistants, on whom he had been relying heavily. By 1672, López Barnuevo was not only blind but so ill that, by his own testimony, he often had to retreat to bed, "leaving the assistants at work and staying in bed for three or four days and sometimes more, judging my assistants to be upright and trustworthy; they kept the office open so that business would not come to a halt."[71] He had fired one of them for improper conduct, he admitted. And he thought he had seen his former head assistant Agustín de Hinojosa in frequent conversation with Don Bernardino Silva Córdoba y Guzmán, whose side in the case, according to López Barnuevo, was clearly losing. Hinojosa had also experienced a curious change in status; while he had entered the notary's office poor, "today he has many fine clothes and has bought himself the office of procurador." All this was enough to convince the notary of Hinojosa's guilt. Once the assistants themselves were interrogated, they began turning on one another. Agustín de Hinojosa refuted his former boss's version, casting suspicion instead on his successor, the head assistant Martín de la Borda. Another penman also testified that he had seen Martín de la Borda act suspiciously, taking document bundles (legajos) out of the office along with one of the new apprentices. He reckoned that together they had stolen and sold off eight bundles of criminal and civil cases.[72] When his turn came, Martín de la Borda denied everything.

The testimony in this case fails to clarify the thief's (or thieves') identity. But it underlines once again that notaries might be absentee owners of their workshops, leaving them to the care (or mishandling) of their assistants. And these young men might prove to be the weak point in the notarial archives' security. If left to their own devices, they might be open to inducements—or intimated by threats. It's easy to imagine that if one of the Berrios or Don Bernardino Silva Córdoba y Guzmán had sent a henchman to make a threat, a young assistant would have felt (to borrow from notaries' own lexicon) "compelled and forced" and in a state of "just fear."[73]

Conclusions

Cuzco's archives are full of references to powerful people, and the references go, in apt synecdoche, to their hands. A local potentate is someone "with a powerful hand" (con mano poderosa), or simply mucha mano.[74] He might use his sway to make others obey his desires, even do things that might get them in trouble. Inside households and relationships, too, people might be known for exercising a lax hand or a strong, even violent hand (manos violentas). Sometimes notaries were accused of this. In nearby Huamanga, for example, an indigenous nobleman named Don Andrés Cutiporras charged the local cabildo notary, Andrés López de Rivera, with attempting to swindle him out of his land by making him enter into a rigged writ of obligation. Cutiporras testified that he had gone along at first, in view of "the great power and influence that the aforesaid [notary] Andrés López enjoys in all the tribunals of the city, due to the office that he holds."[75]

Yet the possibilities of the notarial record itself cannot be simply characterized. It might become an extension of someone's powerful hands, as in the case of Don Rodrigo de Esquivel or the Huamanga notary López. At the same time, the notarial archive might offer a kind of shield against the powerful. Cuzqueños could not take advantage of these offensive or defensive possibilities for free: notaries' services did cost money. But if people could pay them, notaries were not supposed to turn them away.[76]

The creativity of cuzqueños when it came to the official record was considerable. They might even pawn their titles as surety for a loan, as did a beata named Bartola Ignacia Sisa. In 1702, she used the title to her modest tract of land to borrow 100 pesos from a petty trader to enable four siblings to cover the funeral expenses of their mother.[77] (As with many creative tactics, this one only showed up in the record because it didn't work out: the siblings never repaid her, so two years later, she sued them.) Cuzqueños also used notaries' archives to disguise the identities of those who owed debts, sold merchandise, and controlled property. And they seem to have been specialists in using dowry records to shelter assets. When his assets were threatened in the 1580s with a lawsuit, Don Rodrigo de Esquivel had consulted the best legal minds of the viceroyalty, "the greatest letrados and judges of this Kingdom, who studied and weighed the said lawsuit with all possible care and told me it was unjust and a notorious wrong." Thus fortified in his sense of injury, Don Rodrigo seems to have felt no qualms about manipulating the documentation of his wife's dowry. The available record supports his story: that he took his notary's penman as his instrument to reach inside the archive and rewrite its contents.[78]

Ironically, Don Rodrigo himself seems to have died in the midst of yet another manipulation of his fortune's paper trail. For years he had tried to reach a formal understanding about the care of his youngest children, Doña Leonor and Doña Antonia Gregoria, with his eldest son and namesake. At last, the two men had reached a negotiated settlement in October, 1628, ratified in the elder Don Rodrigo's will four months later. It stipulated that the younger Don Rodrigo would inherit his father's estate in exchange for carrying out specific obligations, such as making generous payments to his two half sisters. But Doña Leonor died just as the deal was being struck.

The seven-year-old Doña Antonia Gregoria's legal defenders then began vigorously contesting the arrangement.[79] They argued that the girl was being shortchanged (even thought she would have received at least 7,000 pesos annually for ten years). Witnesses testified that Don Rodrigo had been coerced while on his deathbed into signing an agreement he had never wanted. As one put it, the old man "was not in his right mind, nor could he tell if what they were proposing was acceptable to him, because the said transaction, and the draft [*minuta*] of it, were not drawn up in his presence, but outside the bedroom where he lay; and he agreed to what was read to him . . . responding YES to everything they proposed, pressed by the seriousness of his illness."[80] A doctor testified that the deceased had had "*parba frenitis*, which causes delirium in those afflicted from time to time, [meaning] sometimes they are in their right mind and other times they are not, and that was what afflicted Don Rodrigo de Esquivel." And a priest testified that Don Rodrigo had spoken in a way that was hard to understand, answering yes to everything "without pronouncing it clearly, as if his tongue did not work."[81] At the end, then, one of Cuzco's master manipulators of the notarial archive had no more power left in hands or tongue, and the same tactics he once used on others were used upon him.

How are we to read an archive so susceptible to manipulation? Some of the most common tactics are not disclosed by anything in the record itself, such as confidential understandings. Things might not be what they appear to be. What is a historian (several centuries later) to do?

CHAPTER 5

ARCHIVES AS CHESSBOARDS

The durable metaphor of the archive as a window on the past is still with us—though historians increasingly see archives as murky, clouded windows.[1] After all, how else are we to go into archives if not through our senses? Metaphors of the visual, or the aural, predominate: we see the past through a window, or in a mirror; we hear voices. We let our mind's ear enjoy the seduction of the archival first person, the "I" created through notarial mediation: "Be it known to all who see this document that I, *fulano*, do grant the following. . . ."

The preceding chapters suggest a different metaphor. Examined closely, the archives of colonial Cuzco are full of small inconsistencies that hint at a productive tension between *teoría* and *práctica*: between the way documents were supposed to be made and the ways they were made in practice. And practice, as we've seen, mobilized relationships—often very unequal ones—between clients and notaries, and notaries and penmen. The resulting documents are dialogic, made with an eye to the potentially litigious future (or, in the case of judicial records, an eye on the litigious present).[2] The overall point was not transparency. Rather, the point was to prevail, should one's version of what was right and just be legally challenged. To draw on an old Mediterranean passion that captures nicely the elements of competition and strategy, document making was like chess: full of gambits, scripted moves, and countermoves. Archives are less like mirrors than like chessboards.[3]

To get the most from our sources, then, we need to go into the archive —not just literally, but figuratively, getting into the rules and gambits that contoured the ways people made documents. Happily, the rules aren't hard to find. They are hidden in plain sight, in the modern editions of legal codes and classics. Both rules and gambits are also treated extensively in the literature of diplomatics, the study of the forms and techniques through which documents were produced. This literature has been out of fashion for some time, as Randolph Starn points out, yet has much to offer us.[4] Then there are the lessons to be gained from what James Lockhart calls "reading between the lines": the insights we get from "being immersed in the material, with all antennae active," sensitive to its regularities and irregularities, material and textual patterns, small slippages, and sleights of hand.[5] This is where we see traces of the chess masters in action—always in accordance with specific local custom.

I'm suggesting, in short, that we make our archives and sources part of our research, looking *at* them as well as through them. This approach doesn't diminish the possibilities for historical understanding. To the contrary, I argue, it expands them. Whatever we may lose in the way of certainty (and, to be sure, definitive meaning can become more elusive if we study our sources' ambiguities) is compensated by what we gain: many new, often unsuspected avenues of interpretation. To demonstrate—and to bring home the importance of viewing archives as subjects of inquiry, as historical artifacts in their own right—this chapter unfolds a series of close readings, drawn once more from the rich archives of colonial Cuzco.

Of Intertexts and Agency

The case of Doña Clara de Montoya is worth reprising here. On December 1, 1701, according to the records of the Cuzco notary Pedro López de la Cerda, the unmarried Doña Clara donated property to the priest of her parish church of San Cristóbal. First, she declared the specifics: the property was a residence at the foot of the bell tower of the church; Doña Clara had inherited it in accordance with the 1694 will of Doña Isabel Ñucay, a member of Cuzco's Inca nobility.[6] Next, Doña Clara declared, "because I have no legitimate children or heirs, to attend to the good of my soul and that of [her sister] Doña Inés Ñucay and those of my parents and ancestors . . . I want and it is my wish to make a donation . . . to Doctor Don Pedro de Oyardo Aramburu, priest of the said parish of San Cristóbal, and to those who come after him . . . [of] the aforesaid house." The arrangement was to take effect after her death, and in return the priests of San Cristóbal would say a dozen masses annually on behalf of her soul, that of Doña Isabel Ñucay, and for anyone else Doña Clara should designate. The priest Don Pedro de Oyardo went on record as accepting the donation gratefully. A witness signed for Doña Clara, who did not know how to write.

This was legal ventriloquy of the most standard kind. The notary Pedro López de la Cerda did for Doña Clara what countless other cuzqueños had their notaries do for them: create a first-person subject, an "I," who carries out an action in accordance with his or her will (*voluntad*). One did not have to be able to read or write to participate in document making. Witnesses signed for people all the time. (Literacy rates have not been calculated for colonial Cuzco, but must have been quite low.) Doña Clara's 1701 donation appears to be a straightforward case of what Armando Petrucci calls "delegated writing." This was how the lettered city came to be much larger, its terms more far-reaching, than one might suppose.

But as we have seen, a later document puts Doña Clara's donation in a very different light. Her will, registered in March 1704 by the Cuzco notary Gregorio Básquez Serrano, discloses more about the principals in the 1701 donation (including Doña Clara herself), and insists that it was her father confessor's idea, not hers. She was a *beata*, a woman living under simple religious vows. The deceased Doña Isabel Ñucay, from whom she had inherited her residence, was her mother. And her father confessor was none other than the chief beneficiary of her donation, the priest Don Pedro de Oyardo. In 1701, according to Doña Clara's will, he had called her to his house, "where I found the aforesaid [Oyardo] and Pedro López de la Cerda, notary public, and other people, where the said Doctor Don Pedro de Oyardo told me to donate my house to him and the priests who would succeed him in the said parish of San Cristóbal." He had laid out the terms for her, "and because I did not understand it all, being a woman and not versed in such things, and as there were many people in the said house . . . I agreed to the making of the document of donation." Her 1704 will asserted that she had been "completely defrauded" into a deal that went against her own best interests.[7]

What did Doña Clara really want? Should the more detailed 1704 will be taken as the truth? Or did she make the 1701 donation willingly but then change her mind (perhaps under the pressure of financial need), take a new notary as her instrument in 1704, and register a convenient, document-revoking fiction? There is no way to know for sure. But Doña Clara's will is unusually revealing about the setting in which a document might be made. "As I have said," it repeats, "because of the large number of people present [at the 1701 donation], and because the said Doctor Don Pedro de Oyardo was my confessor, I was ashamed to contest anything that was done." We're reminded that document making did not take place in a social vacuum. Documents were made by people in relationships—perhaps relations of very unequal power. The result was what William Hanks has called "an intertext," an object whose meaning emerges in the dialogic details of its making and circulation.[8]

What about the original notary, Pedro López de la Cerda? His template for a donation was a rigid stencil for tracing out and registering agreement, not ambivalence or disagreement. Indeed, with his tool kit of extrajudicial templates, he could *only* represent accord, except in the case of a formal exclamation. (No contract ever reads, "She thought it was a terrible idea, but reluctantly decided to go along.") The notary thus occupied a strategic pressure point at which a powerful man such as Don Pedro de Oyardo might work the system in his favor. In a case like this in which a priest seems to have proposed a deal to an illiterate spiritual dependent, very much putting her on the spot, what option did the notary have? Doña Clara had agreed without protesting. Technically nothing was amiss. Pedro López de la Cerda couldn't refuse to do his job—certainly not if he wanted to stay in Oyardo's good graces and profit from his business.[9]

A close reading of Doña Clara's two documents is especially useful for understanding subaltern agency. Notarial records do not necessarily disclose unequal power relations between the parties involved. But we need to keep in mind that, as Hanks puts it, "one of the central empirical and methodological problems in working with colonial materials is *the sheer partiality of what was written*"—its striking incompleteness, as well as the "power asymmetries" inherent in it.[10] The notary could create the legal fiction of an "I" with clear, decisive agency where perhaps none existed. His representation of dealings between parties of unequal standing might thus be (witting or unwitting) *mis*representation.

Some basic methodological points emerge here. First, as Lockhart notes, we must learn to read between the lines, and beware of overreading any one document; "one of the primary skills of the document detective is to feel when one is on unsure ground and step back." Establishing context is crucial.[11] From Doña Clara's 1701 donation alone, we can gather that an indigenous beata of colonial Cuzco made over her house to her father confessor and his companions, but given the likely power asymmetry of the parties, we can also wonder whether the notary's template reflected the donor's intentions. Actions are one thing; intentions are another—and "I want and it is my wish" is form language. The notary's formulae could be used to disguise ambivalence or disagreement.

Clearly the more context we can piece together—and the more we know about document production and form language—the better. The notary's words cannot simply be taken at face value. But neither should we be too quick to assume that they cover up devious manipulations. As our next cases suggest, indigenous cuzqueños were not necessarily at the mercy of the high-ranking criollos and Spaniards with whom they had formal dealings.

Reading the Gap between Theory and Practice

On January 13, 1714, the Cuzco notary Francisco de Unzueta made a house call, probably with a penman in tow. Bernardo de Benavente was sick in bed and sought to unburden his conscience about an incident that had occurred "about forty years ago more or less." Benavente had himself worked as penman to the notary Joan de Saldaña, and one day he had accompanied Saldaña, "carrying the draft book and the inkwell," to the residence of an Inca nobleman named Don Cristóbal Paullo Topa Inca. They had gone there "along with Don Agustín Jara the elder, Don Agustín Jara the younger, Doña Josefa de Valer his wife, and other gentlemen . . . to propose to said Don Cristóbal Paullo Topa that he sell the land called Chamancalla with its highlands, to which said Don Cristóbal Paullo Topa said yes, in accordance with which [Benavente] began writing the draft dictated by said Joan de Saldaña and it was in the amount of 500 pesos." Fifteen years later, however, Benavente had been approached by another Inca nobleman, Don Lorenzo Carlos Inca, and told that the sale of Chamancalla "had been in confidence, and that he should declare what he knew about the case because [Don Lorenzo] had sought general censures and they had been posted in the churches of this city."[12]

What was going on? At first I was convinced the Jara de la Cerdas—a powerful criollo clan then on the rise in Cuzco—had bullied Don Cristóbal into accepting an offer he dared not refuse. Benavente's declaration indicated that although the price was 500 pesos, no money had changed hands that day. Eventually I located the notarized 1685 sale of Chamancalla in Saldaña's records. It attested that Don Cristóbal *was* paid 450 pesos in cash at the time of the sale, with the remaining 50 pesos to be paid to him later. So this discrepancy seemed to be at the root of Don Lorenzo's complaint: Don Cristóbal must not have received anything, even though everyone signed in 1685 to attest that he had.[13] The sales contract was not simply an agreement, but (like Doña Clara's donation) the result of a colonial power play. Benavente had kept quiet about it to protect both himself and Saldaña.

Gradually, though, I pieced together the meaning of those curious words "in confidence" (*en confianza*). Confidence is a bit slippery. In both English and Spanish, it can denote trust, certainty: the person in whom you confide your deepest secrets has your confidence. Yet the same word can point to swindling and falsehood, as in the figure of the "con man." Both senses come into play in the legal definition of *confianza*. The Spanish jurist Joaquín Escriche gives a very specific rendering in his 1837 legal dictionary: a confianza is "the pact or agreement made secretly between two or more persons, especially if they are traders or involved in commerce."[14] This kind of confidence was used to conceal assets. The royal treasury was swindled out of the income it would otherwise have received through the sales tax, and the whole thing depended on the parties' trust in each other not to disclose a secret.

Did Don Cristóbal Paullo Topa and the Jara de la Cerdas have a secret pact? This was what Don Lorenzo, probably a kinsman of the Inca noble, later claimed. The contract itself betrays nothing—but that was how confidences worked. The bogus sale of Chamancalla to the Jara de la Cerdas might have been arranged to help Don Cristóbal hide property with which he never really intended to part. Maybe he faced a lawsuit and the potential sequestration of his assets. Key details are still missing if we are to make sense of the allegedly bogus sale; perhaps someday Cuzco's archives will clarify the principals' motives. But if the Jara de la Cerdas later tried to pass off Chamancalla as their own, betraying the confidence of 1685, that would explain why Don Lorenzo Carlos Inca moved to obtain a form of censure.

Here, as in the case of Doña Clara, one document unsettles interpretation of an earlier one. From the 1685 contract alone, the sale of Chamancalla appears straightforward: an Inca nobleman made over a piece of his land to a prominent local family. Yet Benavente's deathbed declaration of 1714 suggests that something was irregular about the sale. I initially thought the Jara de la Cerdas had made a heavy-handed power play, bullying Don Cristóbal into a deal in 1685 and somehow getting the notary Saldaña to register a payment they did not actually make. Little by little, though, another possibility came into view. The sale might have been entirely bogus—the result of a secret understanding reached between Don Cristóbal and the Jara de la Cerdas. Maybe Saldaña and his assistant witnessed a "payment" that Benavente later learned had been a mere act of stagecraft.

The second interpretation, based on Benavente's disclosure and the way confidences worked, completely recasts the parties' relationships. No longer is the indigenous nobleman Don Cristóbal the rather stereotypical victim of a dastardly criollo clan (in league with a complicit notary). Instead, Don Cristóbal and the Jara de la Cerdas appear as allies in a secret bargain, and we glimpse a clique of elite Cuzco insiders working a deal, perhaps without their notary's knowledge, for reasons we cannot know. Benavente kept their secret almost to the end.

On the Archives that Aren't

Among the criminal cases heard by Cuzco's seventeenth-century magistrates is one that looks different from the others: attached to the front is a cover letter. It is addressed to Don Pedro de Olivares, "protector general por su mages[ta]d"—the royal defender of natives. This brief letter, which covers the front and most of the back of one small sheet, is dated November 23, 1650, and signed by Don Diego Gualpa Nina, a cacique who lived just south of Cuzco in the town of Oropesa. He begins with a salutation: "Amo y Señor" (Master and Lord). The letter continues,

> May God grant that this letter find Your Grace in good health, as this your most humble servant desires. My master, what I need to ask of Your Grace in support and defense of all the poor Indians, which you are, second only to God, and on behalf of Our Majesty, is . . . that Francisco Alarcón is holding an Indian by force on his estate [*hacienda*], shut up in his storeroom . . . ignoring the orders of the corregidor . . . and thus for the love of God I ask Your Grace to make a petition on behalf of this Indian, reporting what I have told Your Grace.[15]

The request worked. Two days later, on November 25, 1650, Cuzco's official protector of natives brought a petition before the city's magistrate on behalf of Bartolomé Atao, "an elderly Indian more than seventy years old" who lived in Oropesa and belonged to the Yanamanchi ayllu. Before long, Francisco de Alarcón, a local Spaniard, was being held inside the Cuzco city jail and examined by a notary about the abduction and forced labor of Bartolomé Atao.

Personal letters are rare in Cuzco's colonial archives, especially missives from indigenous leaders such as Don Diego Gualpa Nina.[16] Yet we know some (perhaps many) caciques knew how to write. By the 1620s the Jesuits were running a school in Cuzco specifically for the sons of caciques. And indigenous notaries, the *escribanos de cabildo*, were active in the region as early as the 1580s. Unfortunately, the paper trail these men generated was not gathered into state-sanctioned repositories, but allowed to remain at the local level, and much (if not most) of it has been lost.[17] Indigenous notaries' work is visible today mostly in the occasional, fleeting mention of it by urban Spanish notaries.

This scarcity, as we've seen, can also be traced back to Viceroy Toledo's late sixteenth-century judicial reforms. Local indigenous officials might exercise jurisdiction over local disputes, civil and criminal, as long as the stakes were not large.[18] However, Toledo restricted the written judicial records that Andean mayors and notaries could generate: "They shall not write, because they are to [administer justice] summarily."[19] Summary justice meant deciding cases on the basis of oral arguments rather than written petitions.[20] The paper trail would have been minimal.[21]

Enormous amounts of activity thus never made it into colonial archives at all. The paradox is striking to anyone who enters Andean archives today in search of indigenous agency: although Spanish authorities constantly complained of Andeans' litigiousness, the record of it is surprisingly thin. The records we do have are strikingly skewed toward Spanish business of all kinds. Occasionally, they invoke quipu literacy as confirmation—for example, in a 1614 lawsuit in which the stewards of a Cuzco estate were consulted about the estate's productivity. Several of them responded by citing their quipu records from the years in question.[22] Such archival evidence is quite rare, however. Viceroy Toledo and other Spanish authorities generally wanted to "reduce" quipu literacy to writing, and to keep Andeans' writing to a minimum.[23]

Yet the 1650 lawsuit from Oropesa reminds us that colonial archive-making had its own curious borderlands, "contact zones," and agents such as Don Pedro de Olivares, royal protector of natives.[24] His job was to represent indigenous agency. Most of the lawsuits that he and others like him put forward contained no cover letters explaining their provenance (or if they did, these were stripped away over time). The 1650 lawsuit he filed on behalf of the seventy-year-old Bartolomé Atao is different, even unique. It contained a back story, and by its telling, the lawsuit's agent was not Don Pedro de Olivares, but Don Diego Gualpa Nina. The cacique acted as a kind of ventriloquist who got Olivares to articulate his community member's grievance.

This Oropesa lawsuit, like Doña Clara's will and the contested sale of Chamancalla, points to the collaborative forms of agency so characteristic of record making in the colonial Andes. Stripped of its cover letter, the suit would appear to be motivated by the zeal of a Spanish official, Olivares, the protector of natives. But the letter discloses the hand that a cacique, Don Diego Gualpa Nina, had in the matter. It also suggests how Olivares might do his job for the region even though he resided in Cuzco. Perhaps he received a constant stream of correspondence such as Gualpa Nina's. Without such tip-offs, and with a limited term of office, the protector of natives probably would have had neither the details nor the local knowledge necessary to interpret them and initiate legal proceedings. His ability to act could well have depended on the activism of men such as Don Diego Gualpa Nina.[25]

To locate indigenous agency, we often have to read the archive's silences.[26] We also have to understand, as much as possible, who collaborated with whom, what was "customarily" done, and what the record was built to exclude.[27] One cover letter from 1650 hints at any number of pregnant silences in the lawsuits waged by the men who were official protectors of natives. Many of them across Spanish America might have acted at the behest of caciques like Gualpa Nina. Perhaps other Spanish officials who brought suit on behalf of indigenous subjects were likewise activated not by their own sense of injustice, but by others' urgings. What appears to be Spanish agency, in short, may turn out to be a form of indigenous ventriloquy.[28]

On Hearing Voices at Trial

For a lawsuit to begin, then, there had to be writing. And much depended on the opening petition, the *libelo* or *pedimento*, asking a judge to do something. It was typically a one-page narrative of events, followed by a formulaic plea for justice and an offer to adduce proof. If the case went forward, questioning of the accused and witnesses would be based on its contents (*según el tenor del pedimento*). Cuzco's petitions are overwhelmingly civil suits: requests for the return of disputed property, the settling of overdue contractual obligations, the delineation of property boundaries, and the like. This was one kind of writing that notaries were explicitly barred from doing. Their job was to take plaintiffs' petitions to judges, not to write them. But if notaries did not draw up civil and criminal petitions, who did? The legal literature prescribed advocates (*abogados*): various manuals urged litigants to seek their counsel before petitioning. These men had formal legal training and could frame the best legal approach.[29]

Once more, though, cuzqueños seem to have diverged from recommended best practices. When in 1733 the city council ordered judges not to accept petitions that had not been signed by an advocate, the city's justice system was plunged into confusion. Councilmen investigated complaints that the new order was causing "notable harm to the poor, Indians as well as those of other classes, who cannot afford to pay an abogado." Cuzco's notaries confirmed that lawsuits by the poor—both Indians and Spaniards—had dried up entirely. One testified that Cuzco's abogados (all five or six of them, he wasn't sure) were busy with one large debt prosecution against the sugar estate of Sicllabamba. Another testified that before the 1733 order, poor people had "made their cases as best they could . . . and since many do not know the Spanish language, and the Judges do not know that of the Incas, to ask for justice and make allegations they had to make their cases through writing, which they can easily obtain, but now without the required signature these [documents] are not admitted, and they lose their rights."[30]

It is unclear how the 1733 impasse was resolved, but very few petitions before (or after) that date carry the name of an abogado, or of anyone else beside the parties to the suit. Clearly cuzqueños knew how to bypass abogados and find cheaper alternatives.[31] Perhaps they turned to *procuradores*, who knew the judicial system well; they might have drawn up petitions for a lower cost than local abogados. Moonlighting penmen were perhaps an even cheaper option. Any conclusions can only be speculative; we still know very little about the various actors in the Andean judicial system and the things it was considered customary for them to do.[32] How did cases come to trial before a particular judge? Did litigants "shop" for a favorable judicial arena, as Richard Kagan indicates they did in early modern Spain? Was it rare for judges to order torture (or the threat of it) to force the "truth" out of defendants and witnesses?[33] How often did litigants appeal judges' decisions, and were such appeals likely to succeed?[34] About these issues and many others, we still have much to learn.

This has not kept trial records, particularly criminal ones, from becoming popular sources for scholars, in Cuzco as well as elsewhere. They often present a rare subaltern perspective, even the voices of people otherwise unable to represent themselves in writing. But these voices do not come to us unmediated. Take the opening petition in a 1699 case from Cuzco. The plaintiff Asencia Sisa narrates in the first person, but with a good deal of legalese—frequent "aforesaids" and formulaic passages such as "in keeping with the law"—as well as words and phrases she might well have uttered herself:

> [I,] Asencia Sisa, Indian, legitimate spouse of Isidro Chalco, in keeping with the law appear before Your Majesty and declare that I bring civil and criminal charges against a Spaniard whose name I do not know except that he is the son of someone named Medina and is currently in jail by order of Your Majesty, and stating the circumstances of my complaint: I declare that last Sunday night, between about seven and eight at night . . . the aforesaid, with little fear of God or of the justice Your Majesty administers, in the alley of San Agustín stole the *ñañaca* I was carrying . . . and a *lliclla*, upon which an Indian named Antonio came up to me and because he defended me against the aforesaid assault the aforesaid prisoner Medina gave him a stab that went through his thigh and he fell to the ground . . . committing a serious crime that deserves severe punishment.[35]

Like all other petitions, this one continues with a formulaic plea for justice. The only signature on it is Asencia Sisa's. No doubt some of the terms were hers; she might have been returning from a Sunday at the market when she was assaulted. (The Quechua term *ñañaca* refers to a headdress, and a *lliclla* is a woman's shawl.) But the language and handwriting of her petition indicate that Sisa made her complaint through an undisclosed collaborator, who composed it with her input and penned all of it, including her signature (figure 24). Ghostwritten "signatures" do not seem to have troubled anyone in colonial Cuzco, even when those in the same lawsuit clearly do not match. This seems to have been an accepted part of legal representation. Putting everything succinctly and clearly was crucial in an opening petition; the plaintiff's own words (and hand) were not.[36]

The lettered city thus had its back alleys and shortcuts: ways in which someone like Asencia Sisa could put on record her story, albeit not necessarily in her own words. Sisa's petition offers another excellent example of delegated writing. She did not need to know all the Spanish legal formulae to bring suit. Indeed, she did not need to know Spanish at all. It would be a mistake to attribute too much pure "voice" or legal savvy to petitioners. Such interpretations not only overstate agency but neglect the framework

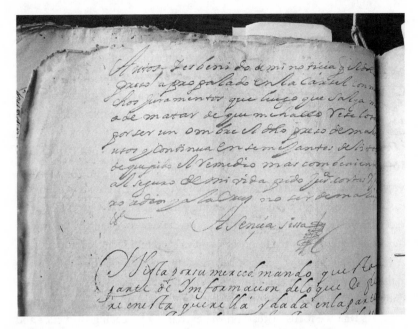

FIGURE 24. Asencia Sisa's petition, presented on her behalf on October 9, 1699. ARC, Cabildo, Justicia Ordinaria, Causas Criminales, legajo 92 (1600–1697). Photograph by the author.

within which petitioners acted: they wanted to have the greatest possible effect on the judge. If they might "easily obtain" effective legal writing from others, why risk putting it in their own words? We may deeply desire to see their unique, individual agency, but what they wanted was justice.

Hearing Voices, Part Two

Criminal trial records are undeniably rich, in Cuzco and elsewhere—and the more we know about the way they were co-produced by plaintiffs, defendants, witnesses, and legal personnel, the better we can interpret them. Judges might well give most credit to testimony taken in the initial investigation or *sumaria*. This material was the freshest and least scripted (and was often gathered by notaries working "in the field," so to speak, rather than in the judge's presence). Witnesses were supposed to tell with relatively little interference what they had seen or heard.[37] Yet there was built-in bias at work. Sumaria fact-finding was guided by the allegations in the plaintiff's petition, and because the point of it was to enable the judge to decide whether there was good cause to proceed, it tended to feature witnesses who could confirm the plaintiff's charges (and the defendant's guilt). If a case proceeded to an additional stage of proof, the *plenaria*, each side could produce further witnesses to support its version of events. Using this material as historical evidence also requires care since the record is so often incomplete, even fragmentary. Whose side, the plaintiff's or the defendant's, are we getting?

Only rarely in Cuzco's archives is a criminal case record complete.[38] When one is, the effect can be disconcerting: dueling witnesses may give very different accounts of the same events. The more we read in a lengthy case, the *less* certain we may feel about what happened. Cynthia Herrup recommends that we entertain this uncertainty as a fruitful source of questions rather than try to push past it in search of something definitive. A verdict, she cautions, often "obscures as much as it clarifies, reinforcing rather than upsetting the notion of a trial as a story with an objective ending." Herrup, drawing on her work with early modern English trials, suggests that we focus instead on the exchanges preceding verdicts, "and see the enforcement of the law for what it is—a forum of cultural interaction."[39] What insights does dueling, contradictory testimony give us into the witnesses' world?

Take one of the few complete criminal cases that remain from seventeenth-century Cuzco.[40] On the night of May 15, 1699, witnesses agreed, a lively, well-lubricated party took place inside the home of cacique Don Gabriel Tupa Yupanqui in the Cuzco parish of San Blas long after he and his wife, Doña Inés Ocllo, had retired to bed. A tailor's apprentice named Cristóbal Pillco, a harpist named Francisco, and Magdalena Sisa, the indigenous overseer of Don Gabriel's larder, were all involved, as well as other indigenous women who worked for Don Gabriel and Doña Inés. Tipped off by one of their servants, the couple discovered a few days later that they were missing several valuable items. They questioned everyone, especially Magdalena Sisa—who turned out to have some of the items in her possession, and who later fled. Then they filed a lawsuit accusing Cristóbal Pillco, Francisco the harpist, and Magdalena Sisa of theft.

Cristóbal Pillco was eventually convicted and sentenced to a year's hard labor in a local sweatshop. Eyewitnesses who had given sumaria testimony against Pillco ratified it in the plenaria stage, placing him at the scene of the theft. Yet Pillco maintained his innocence, and the witnesses presented on his behalf by the protector of natives raised significant doubts about the extent of his involvement. They were asked a number of leading questions: Did they know that Don Gabriel was "a bad-natured Indian" accustomed to overreacting and to "fomenting damaging lawsuits bolstered by the wealth that he possesses?" Did witnesses know that Don Gabriel had "induced witnesses to make declarations contrary to their truth [*contra su verdad*]," and that the women who testified in the sumaria (i.e., his domestic servants) had made this known? Witnesses affirmed the charges, including an indigenous nobleman from a different Cuzco parish, Don José Poma Inca of San Cristóbal, who testified that Don Gabriel was indeed "a bad-natured Indian accustomed to filing unjust petitions based on false suppositions." Yes, he had heard "at the bars of the jail" that Don Gabriel had "induced witnesses and solicited and coached them to declare in the sumaria of this case, coercing them, and that it was Indians from his household and service, accomplices in the theft."[41]

The finding of Cristóbal Pillco's guilt is arguably much less interesting than other aspects of this case. Pillco came from the Cuzco parish of San Cristóbal; according to the protector of natives, he was "of known nobility among the Indians," and of higher rank than his accuser.[42] The main witness on his behalf—Don José Poma Inca, who testified that he had known Pillco "since a very young age"—was likewise from San Cristóbal.[43] Don Gabriel, on the other hand, was a nobleman from the parish of San Blas, and the young women who worked for him were all San Blas natives. The case thus raises interesting questions about the rivalries and divisions within Cuzco's complex indigenous society. Certainly "Indian" parishes such as San Blas and San Cristóbal competed ritually on occasions, notably during the annual Corpus Christi festivities. (Friendly interparish rivalry goes on within Corpus Christi to this day.) This case seems to point to a more quotidian, perhaps more serious kind of interparish rivalry. It also provides a sense of the everyday lives of Cuzco's Inca nobles. Don Gabriel and his wife, according to one of their servants, had left Cuzco for about a week in late May, 1699, to pick potatoes.[44] This hardly seems like aristocratic activity, but the telling detail helps flesh out our sense of what it meant to belong to Cuzco's Inca nobility at the time.

Moreover, the echo effect in the witnesses' statements is far from unusual, due to the way questioning worked. The interrogator, often a notary, asked witnesses to respond to items from a questionnaire prepared in advance by the plaintiff's or defendant's representative(s). The questions were often long, detailed, and (by modern standards) extremely leading.[45]

Bartolomé de Carvajal warned in his manual that such phrasing was quite deliberate: "They put at the start two or three things that are the hardest to prove, and finish the question with something well-known and highly probable. Because as notaries are accustomed to read the [entire] question to the witness, once it has been read it does not stay in the memory, except for the last part, to which the witness answers 'yes sir, I am sure of it.' "[46] Witnesses might thus be led to perjure themselves without even knowing it. Carvajal, Monterroso, and others thus urged notaries to go over every item carefully in advance, to be prepared to rephrase difficult terms in language the witness could understand, and to break questions down into smaller parts as necessary.[47] We have no way of knowing if they did. In any event, witness responses from Cuzco often closely resemble the items in the questionnaires used to elicit them.

Reading trial testimony is thus a curious and sensitive business, just as eliciting it was. If we dip into testimony for evidence without regard to the questionnaires used to shape it, or to the opposing side's counterarguments, we may miss things that would add nuance to our interpretations— perhaps change them altogether. And if we put too much store by the verdict, we may miss much more interesting cultural statements about guilt and innocence, coercion, "good credit," and everyday rivalry.

What Is Colonial about This Picture?

Deep inside the Casa de la Contratación, in Seville—the majestic "house of trade," built in the sixteenth century to house the burgeoning administration of Spain's transatlantic commerce—are many miles' worth of shelved records, the bulky bundles of business of every description. This, fittingly, is the Archivo General de Indias, or General Archive of the Indies. Its astounding diversity overflows the categories within which archivists have labored over the years to contain it—including Patronato (literally "patronage"), Escribanía (concerning the credentialing and conduct of notaries of all kinds), Justicia (justice), and the mysterious, seemingly unconcerned Indiferente General, a miscellaneous category for documents not readily classified elsewhere.

In its glory days as the House of Trade, the Casa housed many different kinds of activities, including mapmaking (known at the time as *cosmografía*, world graphing, and its practitioners as "cosmographers") and the licensing of ships' masters and pilots.[48] Like other officials in Spain's increasingly far-flung empire, the cosmographers, ships' masters, and pilots of the Casa underwent inspections for quality control. Sometimes these inquiries gave rise to lengthy lawsuits. That was exactly what happened in late 1551, when the inspector Dr. Hernán Pérez of the Council of the Indies charged several key personnel of the Casa de la Contratación—including the outgoing interim head (*piloto mayor*), Diego Sánchez Colchero; the cosmographers Diego Gutiérrez and Pedro de Medina; and the notary Juan Díez—with accepting bribes. The stakes were not small, according to witnesses. One pilot, Francisco Hernández Moreno, testified that everything at the Casa happened through "favors and gifts," and that it was notorious among ships' masters and pilots in Seville that some "twenty-five to thirty ships loaded with merchandise, gold, and silver [had] been lost while sailing to the Indies" due to the improper licensing of pilots and masters. The Casa had licensed foreigners and people whose genealogies were suspect. He had even heard that a local shoemaker had paid Diego Gutiérrez to teach him the arts of navigation, then passed his exam and set sail for the Indies.[49]

The notary Juan Díez was in the thick of the malpractice, according to witnesses for the prosecution. It was his job to administer the requisite battery of questions to those seeking a pilot's or master's license regarding their background and their experience, and to take down their responses and those of the supporting witnesses they presented.[50] (The result was known as the candidate's *información*.) Aspiring pilots and masters were to pay him a standardized fee. Rather than question people himself, however, Díez allegedly entrusted the job to his young son-in-law, Gonzalo de Ribera, who was not a notary. Various witnesses testified that they had seen Ribera conduct these interrogations while Díez was not present. Moreover, they attested, they had had to pay *both* men, not just the notary—an abuse one witness characterized as "great thievery and wickedness."[51]

Thus Juan Díez, in mid-sixteenth-century Seville, had to defend himself against the same charges most often lodged against contemporary Andean notaries: procedural sloppiness and overcharging. And Díez invoked the same marvelously flexible defense of his conduct that they did: custom. His fees were no greater than those of his predecessors, he argued. Indeed, the rate had been the same for fifty years, ever since the Casa was founded, and no one had ever objected, "hence the aforesaid custom has been used and kept without contradiction."[52] As for the way he did background checks on prospective pilots and masters, he asserted that (despite allegations to the contrary) he conducted the questioning personally: "He said that yes, [he] had examined [the candidates and supporting witnesses] and written in his handwriting [the responses of] some witnesses, and others were written in his presence by his assistant named Gonzalo de Ribera, with [Díez] dictating to him and asking the questions."[53] No one seemed to mind that Díez had had his assistant do some of the manual labor. This went unremarked, and appears to have been taken for granted. At issue was whether or not Díez had been present, "ordering" the version Ribera wrote down.[54] To leave a young assistant to examine witnesses on his own would have gone beyond the bounds of what a notary could responsibly delegate.

This insistence on the notary's presence went beyond legalistic nitpicking. The case neatly illustrates one of the notary's filtering responsibilities: he was supposed to recognize witnesses, to be able to tell whether or not they were who they said they were. A raw, inexperienced youth could not be expected to do this. As one witness put it, "The youth [Ribera] does not know any of the witnesses, whether or not they are qualified pilots" able to vouch convincingly for a candidate.[55] The final outcome of Juan Díez's case is not clear. But the stakes emerge clearly enough: if Díez had routinely left Ribera to his own devices, the Casa's overarching mission of quality control could have been seriously compromised.

Around the same time, another Seville notary found himself facing more dramatic and unusual charges. As he awaited trial in 1547 in his city's notorious jail, the notary Cristóbal de Aguilar—"of middling stature, brown of face, with a stringy beard and missing two front teeth"—did not exactly cut an imposing figure.[56] But some months previously, he had denounced Don Alonso Luis de Lugo, governor of the province of Santa Marta, for evading taxation by smuggling gold, silver, and precious stones to the Canary Islands. The royal prosecutor had sent Aguilar to substantiate the allegations by having the witnesses who had testified in the case's initial phase (the sumaria) ratify and expand upon their original testimony against Lugo. Instead, the prosecutor charged, Aguilar had "prevaricated and allowed himself to be bribed" to disappear the documents and abandon the case.[57]

Thus Aguilar, like some of his Andean counterparts, found himself caught between the duties of his job and the desires of powerful people—those with "manos poderosas," powerful hands. The prosecution asserted that Aguilar had been specifically warned by Lugo's people "that the said *adelantado* [Alonso Luis de Lugo] was much in favor, and married to the sister of Doña María de Mendoza, and that if [Aguilar] pursued his denunciation he would anger the Comendador Mayor de León." Better for him to take 400 or 500 ducados and go in peace, Aguilar was allegedly told, than pursue the case and make potent enemies. Unlike his counterpart in Cuzco, Francisco de la Fuente, Aguilar lacked the backers and resources to put up much of a fight. He chose to flee instead. The prosecution charged that he had taken the money, bought merchandise, and set sail for the Indies "secretly . . . without license from Your Highness," abandoning his wife and children in Madrid.[58]

Examples like these could go on, thanks to the efficient Boolean searching now possible among the digitalized records of the Archivo General de Indias.[59] But the point is clear: some of the same flexible strategies we have seen in the Andes can be found on the other side of the Atlantic as well. Seville and its House of Trade were the very heart of Spanish empire by the late sixteenth century and throughout the seventeenth. Legendary riches flowed through the city. And as historians have known for years, money talked. Arguably this was less "corruption" than an accepted way of doing business.[60] Not surprisingly, notaries and archives were not exempt from the pressures and inducements.

Yet record-making practice was not exactly the same in all times and places, as I could see in the notarial archives in the Archivo Histórico de Sevilla. On my first visit, I was struck by the similarities: the binding, the forms, even the handwriting of the sixteenth- and seventeenth-century notaries of Seville looked just like those of their Andean counterparts. After a while, though, this archive began to seem very different from the ones I was used to. There had been twenty-four numerary notaries in Seville (four times the number in colonial Cuzco), and while most were concentrated in the central business district, about a third were located in neighborhoods around the city: San Juan de la Palma, Santa Catalina, Barrio del Duque, Barrio de Triana, and so forth.[61] A notary's records might vary significantly according to his office's location. The forms in use seemed more diverse than those I had encountered in Cuzco: there were the usual credit instruments, proxies, donations, sales, and wills, but also revocations of wills, *resguardos*, *desistimientos*, and other kinds of records I had seldom or never seen before, plus numerous sales and rentals of *olivares*, olive groves. Descriptions of people of African descent seemed unusually detailed: Francisca Paula, for example, an enslaved woman freed by her owner in 1687, was "the color of cooked quince."[62] I did not see any exclamations, though, and a local academic with whom I struck up a conversation said he had never seen such a thing—nor could he recall seeing any doodles.

I could only wonder about the notaries themselves: how much did those in Seville (or Madrid, or Granada, or elsewhere) resemble those in Cuzco, Lima, or Quito? Certainly there were more of them. In general, Spanish cities—like other medieval and early modern European cities—seem to have had significantly more notaries than did Spanish American cities. Notarial workplaces might be dispersed among different parts of a city, as in Seville. Urban Spanish American, by contrast, tended to concentrate notaries in the administrative and judicial heart of things—alongside the cabildo, or very close by. And I thought I glimpsed another contrast in Seville's notarial archives: many notaries seemed to have passed their offices along to a son or other relative.[63] (This kind of thing happened in Cuzco, too, but less frequently in the early years.)[64] Just how these contrasts might have contoured a distinctively metropolitan notarial culture was not immediately apparent. Did notaries face more competition for clients in the Old World? What kinds of social networks did they belong to, and whose interests did they serve? Did they perhaps rely less than their Spanish American contemporaries on a battery of assistants, performing more of the labor of writing themselves? I couldn't tell from my limited exposure to their records.

There I was in the heartland of the picaresque—home to Cervantes and Alemán, and the stomping grounds of the fictional Guzmán de Alfarache—and as usual, it was impossible to gauge the accuracy of authors' acid (and hilarious) renderings of the Castilian notary. Was he a walking stereotype, venal and corrupt? That had been one of my foremost questions years ago. But the only reasonable answer seemed to be a vague "yes and no." Some notaries did seem to fit the picture. Whether they were in the majority, though—or somehow worse than the judges, aldermen, abogados, procuradores, bailiffs, and constables around them—was always going to be impossible to tell. Gradually I had become more interested in the writing process itself: its conventions and practical shortcuts; what it was good for. And I could see that on both sides of the Atlantic, record making was not a straightforward, by-the-book matter. Local interests and customs bulked much too large. The archives themselves were part of this history, marked by the intervention of "powerful hands"—and this much was clearly not just colonial.

The point of these readings, and this book, is to enrich the way we read our sources. If we know how archives were made, and the ways people might use them to further their own ends, then our interpretations can go further. We can see a case like that of Bernardo de Benavente's deathbed confession about the sale of land in Cuzco and *not* default too readily to the interpretation that, once again, an overbearing Spaniard forced the will of an indigenous man. We can imagine, instead, the possibility of an intraelite alliance between two local nobles who decided to register a piece of archival fiction. The possibilities get much more interesting if we understand how "confidences" worked. Certainly many people at the time, including those incapable of writing themselves, knew how records were made and how they might use this knowledge to their advantage: by fixing it in various ways, exclaiming against it, and so forth. If we are to trace people's histories, we need to know, as much as we can, what *they* knew—the myriad ways they found to register the details (or keep them off the books).[65]

This means taking on our archives anthropologically, as part of our fieldwork. Obviously we cannot quiz seventeenth-century subjects or live among them. But we can still read the legal and notarial literature some of them used—manuals such as Monterroso's, which circulated so widely that it became a transatlantic bestseller, and a traveling priest in the 1580s found a copy in a remote Andean village.[66] We can keep an eye out for the inspection reports, such as *visitas* and *residencias*, which assessed the job performance of notaries and other officials, and the lawsuits that occasionally resulted.[67] And we can look closely at the materiality of the documents themselves as well as the words of their formulae.[68] It does not take long to see in the records of a given Cuzco notary, for example, that more than one writer was involved, and that the process of making a document took several stages: the signs are there in the changes of ink and handwriting, the things left blank or crossed out. Just how did such practices, and people, shape a particular archive (figure 25)?

This approach—what Ann Laura Stoler calls "ethnography of the archive"—does not invalidate the methods of social and cultural history; instead, it makes them more precise. Social historians tend to cast a wide

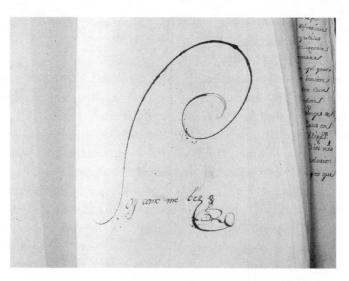

FIGURE 25. "Soy como me bez" (I am as you see me): this doodler's
claim can be taken as a challenge to read between the archival lines.
ARC-PN, Juan Bautista Gamarra, protocolo 133 (1746–81), registro 3.
Photograph by the author.

net, to create databases, and to identify patterns in past societies. Take
James Lockhart, whose pioneering scholarship initially focused on Spaniards in sixteenth-century Peru.[69] Prior to the 1970s, he observes in *The
Nahuas After the Conquest*, "The gods of the disciplines seemed to have
decreed that historians should study Indians indirectly, leaving it to others,
mainly anthropologists, to approach them through their own language."[70]
Since then, Lockhart and other historians have embarked on a "New Philology" that approaches indigenous Mesoamericans through their own
languages: the Nahuas through Nahuatl, the Yucatec Mayas through Yucatec Maya, and the Mixtecs through Mixtec (or Ñudzahui). The source base,
Lockhart writes, "only rarely allows us to track a single person through a
variety of documents." Thus Lockhart and the New Philologists do not
study indigenous career patterns, but patterned language: "the categories
that the person and his peers used to classify himself and his thoughts and
actions, as well as the phenomena surrounding him. . . . Only in *the original
language* can the categories be detected, for in a translation one sees the
categories of the translator's language instead."[71]

Using the categories found in Nahua notarial records, Lockhart has
proposed a three-stage process of Nahua cultural and linguistic change.

Stage 1 (from 1519 to around 1545 or 1550) saw relatively little change in Nahua "concepts, techniques, or modes of organization," whereas in Stage 2 (from then to about 1640 or 1650), "Spanish elements came to pervade every aspect of Nahua life, but with limitations, often as discrete additions within a relatively unchanged indigenous framework." By Stage 3 (from 1640 or 1650 until today), "as the rapprochement between the two cultures advanced," the Nahua were increasingly open to adopting elements of Spanish culture even when these bore little or no resemblance to Nahua traditions. Lockhart concedes that "not all dimensions of Nahua life reflected the three-stage evolution with equal clarity." Nevertheless, he asserts, "The stages represent a major secular trend for indigenous life in central Mexico and by extension for the whole of postconquest central Mexican society, Hispanic as well as Indian."[72]

The New Philologists thus move readily from the patterned details of the notarized page to "culture" writ large. Their work has had a major impact on the field of Latin American studies. Yet as Eric Van Young notes, "The axis is philology rather than power. There is an inclination, in fact, to feel that the work is done when the philology is done."[73] For one thing, Lockhart and others tend to assume that indigenous notaries spoke for their communities, faithfully representing their language and desires.[74] At the same time, however, they seem to point toward further analytical possibilities. They note that indigenous notaries tended to be nobles—a group that took pains to set its members apart from commoners and prided itself on speaking more exalted language.[75] After the Spaniards invaded in 1519, Mesoamerican nobles were privileged by the Spanish crown and exposed (albeit unevenly) to Spanish culture.[76] Those who became notaries clearly based their work to some extent on Spanish templates.[77]

All this seems to suggest that indigenous notaries, too, were translators of a kind: they were in a position to translate people's desires and their categories into the new Hispano-Nahua (or Hispano-Maya, or Hispano-Mixtec) forms. If we ask after their everyday practices, the notion of "the original language" of native-language sources becomes less transparent and all the more interesting. Did indigenous notaries put words in people's mouths the way their Spanish counterparts did? Were these words inflected by Franciscan missionary discourse and Castilian legalese as well as by indigenous concepts and categories? Did indigenous notaries' language and culture change at the same rate and in the same ways as those of commoners? Unless we can feel sure that they did, Lockhart's Stages 1–3 may trace changes more prevalent among Nahua notaries (or elites) than among the Nahua more generally.

For those of us who focus more on deeply researched cases than on broad patterns, the making of the record may be even more crucial to take into account. Writing of anthropologists who have taken the "archival turn," Ann Laura Stoler notes that their "archival labour tends to remain an extractive enterprise more than an ethnographic one." In other words, "students of the colonial experience 'mine' the *content* of government commissions and reports, but rarely attend to their peculiar *form* or *context*. We look at exemplary documents rather than at the sociology of copies, or what claims to truth are lodged in the rote and redundant. . . . We are just now critically reflecting on the making of documents and how we choose to use them, on archives not as sites of knowledge retrieval but of knowledge production."[78] The same can be said for historians. Cultural historians in particular look for meaning in the telling archival anecdote, the revealing turn of phrase, the pregnant silence. Given our goals and method, we need to know what the documents we're reading were carefully constructed to "say" or suppress.

The temptation, particularly with extrajudicial documents of the most formulaic sort, is to ignore formulae entirely and concentrate on what seems unique (such as names or place descriptions).[79] But this creates a blind spot: without some working knowledge of basic templates, how to tease the formulae from the specifics in a given document? Some consist of a great deal more "officialese" than others. A typical power of attorney (*poder*), for example, is brief—one page, front and back—and opaque: one person simply delegates to another the authority to act on his or her behalf.[80] Wills occupy the opposite end of the spectrum; they may run to a dozen pages or more, and are among the most revealing of extrajudicial documents. Yet as Monterroso and others make clear in their manuals, testators' reasons—even their emotions toward their heirs and legatees— may be glossed in form language (e.g., "because of the love I have for them").[81] Thus knowing something about the formulae one encounters in the archive is as useful as having some insight into the relations between the parties involved. Fortunately, good modern editions of manuals by Nicolás de Yrolo Calar, Tomás de Mercado, and others are now available, and offer us a way to gain a sense of context and confidence before going into the archive.

As for judicial records, whose "voices" are registered in the testimony of witnesses brought before colonial authorities to tell the sworn truth? That depends on many things, as we've seen, including which stage of the case one is reading (sumaria or plenaria), the degree of notarial "purification" of the testimony, and the relations between interrogators and witnesses. It may not be possible to tell about all these things, especially when the records are incomplete. But as Stoler notes, it is important to be able to think in these terms—and "to pause at, rather than bypass," the archive's constitution, "its conventions, those practices that make up its unspoken order."[82] This means finding out as much as one can about the trial situation: how criminal cases were initiated and moved forward, decided, and appealed, a subject researched in depth by Alonso Romero, Kagan, and others for Castile (and extensively commented upon in early modern legal literature). It also means noticing when something about a manuscript page —perhaps marginal notations or marks, rips or crosshatching, changes in handwriting in mid-page—seems to pull us in the direction of a new interpretation.

This is what Rebecca Scott calls "making the documents speak"—making their forms as well as their content meaningful.[83] These forms mattered tremendously to the inhabitants of Spanish America. In theory, all of the crown's vassals could act through them: a Spaniard, Nahua, or Inca could file a lawsuit, make a will, donate the house left to her by her deceased mother, and so forth. The archives of colonial Cuzco remind us, as does Guaman Poma's eloquent chronicle, that everyday practice in the colonial Andes was often wrested to serve the interests of those with "powerful hands." So it went across Spanish America, and well beyond. But the more we go into the archive and learn about our sources and their subjects, the less any simplistic generalization is possible, and the richer our story lines become.

EPILOGUE

After the archivist tried to sell me a document that day in Cuzco's archives, a drama started to unfold, or something that had the potential for drama. His immediate superior (over whom the mantle of political protection did not extend) began to worry about his job. If things went missing, he could be held responsible for what the other man had done. We came up with a solution that both put his mind at ease and made me very excited: I would draw up a *constancia* explaining exactly what had happened that day in the archives, in case it was ever needed. Then I would get it notarized.

The thought of entering a twenty-first-century Cuzco *notaría* got me up early the next day, with my one-page document—my best stab at a concise, formal explanation. "To whom it may concern: Let the record show the following, so that responsibility will not be attributed to other people who perform their duties in the Archivo Regional with all honesty. *Atentamente*," and my signature. Then I went off to see the notary, an elderly gentleman who had been in business for over fifty years. Behind the front counter, the large, golden number "50" was still affixed to the wall from what must have been the big fiftieth anniversary office party. People were coming in and out with various kinds of papers to be notarized: parental permission slips, and so on. Various assistants were attending to the clients: three (sometimes four) men and women with work tunics over their clothes and a reassuring air of professional competence, moving back and forth between two old, clattering typewriters and the large front counter that dominated the room. Sometimes they slipped into the back office for a signature. I'm sure I must have sighed with contentment as I settled into a chair to take it all in.

Eventually I made bold to approach the counter myself and express my desire to meet the notary. This must have struck the notary's assistants as novel—foreigners didn't usually ask to see a notary—but they politely relayed my request to the inner office. I did not have long to sit musing on the similarities between notaries' offices and convent visitors' parlors before I was escorted to the back, where the notary greeted me kindly. And for the next half hour or so, I listened with fascination as he described to me the everyday routines of his workplace. Each of the assistants had been with him for years (an understandable source of pride). One was his own daughter. If he needed them, he just rang a little bell—which he demonstrated—the exact number of times for the person he needed. Each of them knew his or her special ring: one long, two short; short-long-short; and the like. Most of the time, though, this wasn't necessary, as the assistants knew exactly how to handle the most routine kinds of business and needed little correction or instruction from him. When his signature was required, they popped in and set the papers down in front of him, indicating the right spot for it. And he quickly but, I thought, ceremoniously drew his signature. It looked exactly like the drawing in Antoine de Saint-Exupéry's *The Little Prince* of the boa constrictor digesting an elephant.

Nothing ever came of my constancia, as far as I know. But I was delighted that it gave me the opportunity to ask a twenty-first-century Cuzco notary all my seventeenth-century-derived questions. Did he have much contact with the city's other notaries? Not really; there was a kind of friendly rivalry between them, but almost no contact. Was there a limit to their numbers? Yes, the city of Cuzco had an allotted number of notarial offices, just like Lima or any other city. Training to become a notary or notarial assistant used to require no professional education, but now most of them had a law degree. And so on. On the way home, I passed another notary's office—very sleek and modern, glass and chrome, displaying not typewriters but computer terminals—and decided to look inside for comparison's sake. There was the same busy front counter, with the same professional-looking assistants (only younger). The notary, a woman, was out of sight, in her own inner sanctum.

Documents have certainly changed over the years, and so has the notary's job. Cuzco's notariate now includes women as well as men, and they respond to the procedural mandates of the Peruvian state. The job is diminished, compared to the powers of the colonial notary, that workhorse of the legal system. But having official papers is every bit as important to cuzqueños now as it was several centuries ago. They go to notaries constantly. The prominently displayed signs of notarías are easy to find in the city's main business district (figure 26). Indeed, business couldn't function without them: in Peru, as legal historian M. C. Mirow observes of Latin American countries more generally, "almost all important civil and

FIGURE 26. Outside a Cuzco notary's office (2004), typists await
clients' requests to prepare standard documents for notarization.
Photograph by the author.

commercial transactions or property rights require notarial drafting and
recording to have full legal effect."[1] Revealingly, the common expression
for losing control is "to lose one's papers" (*perder los papeles*).

Cuzqueños go into local archives as needed, too, in search of documents they require and once possessed but can no longer locate: land titles,
wills, the parish records of marriages, births, and deaths, and more. For a
fee, the archivists will photocopy relevant pages of the old case records and
bulky *protocolos*. Sometimes old colonial titles are found, copied, and adduced to uphold modern claims. Indeed, this gave me a calling card years
ago with the nuns of Santa Clara, Cuzco's oldest convent: I could tran-
scribe old titles. The nuns wanted a modern copy of a sixteenth-century
record from their archive so they could to use it to bolster their claim to a
storefront on Cuzco's Plaza de Armas.

Thus the colonial Andean archive is not dead; it's continuously being
remade. Old forms may turn up at the center of social movements, as in
modern Bolivia.[2] (When caciques of the 1920s and '30s fought to retain
communal lands, for instance, colonial titles were crucial to their success.)[3]
Extraordinary bits of the colonial archive seem to surface every few years
in unexpected places, along with new interpretations.[4] And the coming of

the Internet has thrown open a once-unthinkable range of possibilities of access and interpretation. Increasingly, the colonial archive is at our fingertips, thanks to "a new type of collaboration in the scholarly world between the archive and the academy" that Rolena Adorno calls "the electronic research center."[5] All the more reason to go into the archive curious about the way its particular kinds of truths were made—and whose interests they serve.

NOTES

Unless otherwise noted, all translations are my own; I have left some passages in Spanish in both main text and notes to give the sense and flavor of the original. Proper names have been modernized in both places as well as in the list of works consulted (e.g., "José" for "Joseph"). Titles and transcribed passages of old Spanish works are not modernized, except where "v" appears in place of "u" (e.g., "segvir," "qve") and vice versa (e.g., "escriuano"). Where "v" follows a page number, it signifies "verso"; all other pagination refers to conventional pages or recto pages.

Preface

1. See Boone and Mignolo, *Writing Without Words*. On the work of an international assortment of epigraphers, archaeologists, and anthropologists, see Coe, *Breaking the Maya Code*. Rather dramatic re-readings of the history of Mesoamerican peoples are now being written as a result (surely with much more revision to come). Thanks to the work of Gary Urton and others, Andean quipus can now be seen as a strikingly original form of literacy, with sophisticated record-keeping capabilities all their own. Nor did quipus simply succumb to Spanish conquest, as was once thought. See Salomon, *The Cord Keepers*; Quilter and Urton, *Narrative Threads*. On "prejudice in favour of [alphabetic] literacy," see Clanchy, *From Memory to Written Record*, 7, 11. Derrida, *Of Grammatology*, 109, comes at the problem of ethnocentrism differently: "If writing is no longer understood in the narrow sense of linear and phonetic notation, it should be possible to say that all societies capable of producing, that is to say of obliterating, their proper names, and of bringing classificatory difference into play, practice writing in general. No reality or concept would therefore correspond to the expression 'society without writing.'"

2. González Echevarría, *Myth and Archive*, 44–45.

Introduction

1. Columbus, *The* Diario *of Christopher Columbus's First Voyage to America 1492–1493*, 63.

2. Ibid., 63–65. The document no longer exists, but the journal's brief excursus into form language has a distinctly notarial ring to it. On the journal's reconstruction by Bartolomé de Las Casas, see Zamora, *Reading Columbus*, 39–62.

3. Morales Padrón, "Descubrimiento y toma de posesión," 337, citing *Colección de documentos inéditos de Ultramar*, tomo VII, pleitos de Colón, p. 107; Paria refers to a peninsula on Venezuela's northern coast.

4. Morales Padrón, "Descubrimiento y toma de posesión," 331, citing AGI, Patronato, legajo 20, ramo 4.

5. Morales Padrón, "Descubrimiento y toma de posesión," 342–44. Centuries later, Spaniards would continue claiming land in much the same form. See AGI, Estado, 38A, n. 6–9, regarding possession ceremonies carried out along the coast of California in 1775, discussed in Morales Padrón, "Descubrimiento y toma de posesión," 50–55.

6. See Zamora, *Reading Columbus*, 95–151, on Columbus's influences and his first voyage as "an *imitatio Christi*" and "the figurative first step in a millenarian journey" (97), and Roland Greene, *Unrequited Conquests*, on Petrarchism's long reach.

7. A royal decree (*real cédula*) of 1504 ordered that people "who want to go make discoveries, if they are trustworthy and provide the required guarantees, be given license in the royal name, with the conditions considered appropriate, placing in each ship . . . a notary and someone who will keep account for his sovereigns of everything that happens and witness everything, so that no one commits fraud." AGI, Indiferente, 418, legajo 1, fols. 120–120v.

8. See Morales Padrón, "Descubrimiento y toma de posesión"; see also Seed, *Ceremonies of Possession in Europe's Conquest of the New World, 1492–1640*, 69–99, on the infamous Requerimiento, an ultimatum to Indians to capitulate, which became "the principal means by which Spaniards enacted political authority over the New World" after 1512.

9. The focus here and throughout this study is on Spanish America, but contemporary Portuguese notaries (*tabeliães, escrivãos*) played an analogous role, in Brazil and elsewhere. See *Regimento que os tabaliaens das notas, e do iudicial ham de ter*; and on the administrative history of colonial Brazil, Schwartz, *Sovereignty and Society in Colonial Brazil*.

10. According to Nicholas, *An Introduction to Roman Law*, 60, "Justinian's Institutes declare that 'the whole of our law relates either to persons or to things or to actions' "; he goes on to specify that "in the Institutes the second part of the law—and by far the largest—relates to things (*res*)." On the intricacies of possession, see ibid., 107–16.

11. R. I. Burns, *Jews in the Notarial Culture*, draws on medieval Hebrew wills, which might also be registered in Latin. For an influential Muslim notarial manual from tenth-century Córdoba, see Ibn al-'Attar, *Formulario notarial y judicial andalusí del alfaquí y notario cordobés m. 399 / 1099*.

12. Clanchy, *From Memory to Written Record*, 3. That shift had taken medieval Europeans hundreds of years. Written title was once rare, mainly for monarchs, popes, bishops, and nobles. Mundane possession had relied instead on spoken words and gestures and the living memory of their performance.

13. Morales Padrón, "Descubrimiento y toma de posesión," 327–32, notes the deep Roman and Germanic legal roots of these possession-taking practices.

14. Nussdorfer, "Writing and the Power of Speech," 111. The literature on medieval and early modern European notaries is immense, with rich new additions all the time. See, e.g., Hardwick's work on the notaries of Nantes, *The Practice of Patriarchy*; Ian F. McNeely's study of the scribes and *Schreiberei* of Württemberg, *The Emancipation of Writing*, esp. chap. 2, "The Tutelage of the Scribes"; and Nussdorfer's study of Rome's Capitoline notaries, *Brokers of Public Trust*. I am very grateful to Laurie Nussdorfer for sharing her manuscript with me when it was still a work in progress.

15. González Echevarría, *Myth and Archive*, acknowledging the influence of Bakhtin (8–9), notes the dialogic quality of the (legal) archive: "No utterance can occur in legal proceedings without assuming a question or a response, in short, a dialogue of texts." The most routine notarial record, for instance, is framed for potential presentation in court before a judge.

16. Spanish American notaries' archives contained much more than the records we tend to think of as "notarial records": extrajudicial papers such as contracts and wills. As we will see in subsequent chapters, notaries were also the keepers of judicial records of all kinds.

17. González Echevarría, *Myth and Archive*, 45.

18. Ibid., chap. 1.

19. See Covarrubias's influential 1611 dictionary *Tesoro de la lengua castellana*, 763: "Letrado, el que professa letras, y hanse alçado con este nombre los juristas abogados." *Abogado* is defined as "el letrado que defiende o acusa a alguno en juyzio" (29).

20. Rama, *The Lettered City*, 16. Rama's suggestive concept unfolds across his essay's initial chapters: see esp. chaps. 2 and 3 (16–49).

21. See Petrucci, *Prima lezione di paleografia*, 25, on "il fenomeno della 'delega di scrittura.' " Clanchy, in *From Memory to Written Record*, 2, also advances this wider notion of literacy: "Those who used writing participated in literacy, even if they had not mastered the skills of a clerk." By around 1300 in England, "literary modes were familiar even to serfs, who used charters for conveying property to each other and whose rights and obligations were beginning to be regularly recorded in manorial rolls."

22. Lockhart, *Spanish Peru 1532–1560*, 68.

23. Nussdorfer, *Brokers of Public Trust*, 3.

24. Ibid., 4. Nussdorfer makes especially clear the paradox of *scriptura publica*, or "public writing": "The notaries who produced it sold it to make a living and held various degrees of proprietary rights over the records they had penned. They combined aspects of public officials and, at the same time, self-employed professionals." Her study traces (among other things) the coming of venality to the offices of Rome's Capitoline notaries.

25. Columbus, *The Diario of Christopher Columbus's First Voyage to America 1492–1493*, 65, 139; they are additionally described as "quite lacking in evil and not warlike."

26. See Tomlinson, *The Singing of the New World*, and Lockhart, *The Nahuas after the Conquest*, chaps. 8 and 9.

27. The essays in Boone and Mignolo, *Writing without Words*, counter centuries of condescension toward Americans' ways of writing: see esp. Boone, "Introduction: Writing and Recording Knowledge," 3–26.

28. Motolinia [Toribio de Benavente], *Historia de los indios de la Nueva España*, 2; I am adapting Boone's translation of this passage in "Aztec Pictorial Histories: Records without Words," in Boone and Mignolo, *Writing without Words*, 50.

29. For names and details, see Guajardo-Fajardo Carmona, *Escribanos en Indias durante la primera mitad del siglo XVI*, 1:284–334.

30. Gruzinski, *The Conquest of Mexico*, 15.

31. Landa, *Relación de las cosas de Yucatán*, 105. On Landa's notorious pursuit of "idolatry" among the Maya in the 1560s, see Clendinnen's excellent study, *Ambivalent Conquests*.

32. Mignolo, *The Darker Side of the Renaissance*, xv and pt. 2. On the Philippine extension of this vast colonizing project, see Rafael, *Contracting Colonialism*.

33. Scholarship that draws on Mesoamericans' alphabetic literacies has been growing rapidly: in English, see esp. the broadly gauged studies of Lockhart, *The Nahuas after Conquest*; Restall, *The Maya World*; and Terraciano, *The Mixtecs of Colonial Oaxaca*. Sell and Burkhart have edited a remarkable collection of Nahuatl dramas in translation: see their *Nahuatl Theater*, vol. 1, *Death and Life in Colonial Nahua Mexico*.

34. The appendices in Lockhart, *The Nahuas after Conquest*, 455–74, are fascinating cultural composites, and include a model Nahuatl will from the Franciscan friar Alonso de Molina's 1565 confessional manual. See also the documentary appendices in Restall, *The Maya World*, 323–31; and Terraciano, *The Mixtecs of Colonial Oaxaca*, 369–95.

35. Writes Lockhart in *The Nahuas after Conquest*, 434, "I have the impression that the time around 1580–1610 represents an absolute peak in postconquest Nahuatl alphabetic writing in a great many respects—expressiveness, aesthetic

quality, range." The rise of a Nahua notariate accompanied the establishment of town councils, or *cabildos*, a Spanish institution of governance refashioned on colonial ground: see Gibson, *Tlaxcala in the Sixteenth Century*.

36. Restall, "A History of the New Philology and the New Philology in History," 113–34.

37. See Cook, *Demographic Collapse*, and *Born to Die*.

38. T. Cummins, *Toasts with the Inca*. On *quipus* (or *khipus*), which predated the Inca empire of Tawantinsuyu by hundreds of years, see Urton's work, especially Urton and Quilter, *Narrative Threads*.

39. Acosta, *Natural and Moral History of the Indies*, 342–43.

40. Murúa, *Códice Murúa*, fol. 77v.

41. Durston, *Pastoral Quechua*; see also Mannheim, *The Language of the Inka since the European Invasion*.

42. Spaniards felt great ambivalence toward them, and the feeling was mutual. See Adorno, "Images of Indios Ladinos in Early Colonial Peru," 232–70; and Charles, "Indios Ladinos."

43. T. Cummins, "Representation in the Sixteenth Century and the Colonial Image of the Inca," in Boone and Mignolo, *Writing without Words*, 194–95.

44. These men were known as *escribanos de cabildo*, "council notaries," because of their connection to the indigenous town councils (*cabildos*) ordered by Viceroy Francisco de Toledo. See K. Burns, "Making Indigenous Archives."

45. By far the best-known indio ladino, Guaman Poma spent much of his life accompanying Murúa and others who preached Christianity and tried to suppress the worship of Andean deities. Sometime after 1600, Guaman Poma began his extraordinary magnum opus: a profusely illustrated 1,200-page chronicle for his king, Philip III of Spain. The result, *El primer nueva corónica y buen gobierno* (1615), has become famous for its strong denunciation of Spanish abuse.

46. K. Burns, "Making Indigenous Archives." Local justice in the indigenous settlements mandated by Toledo (*reducciones*) was also to proceed summarily.

47. See Salomon's remarkable study, *The Cord Keepers*, on the changing use of quipus in Tupicocha, near Huarochirí. Villagers now use quipus to mark the investiture of new village authorities.

48. See, e.g., Steedman, *Dust*; Hamilton et al., *Refiguring the Archive*. On the enormous diversity of archives, see Blouin and Rosenberg, *Archives, Documentation, and Institutions of Social Memory*; and Burton, *Archive Stories*.

49. Especially provocative of dialogue was (and is) the work of Michel Foucault, Edward Said, and the Subaltern Studies collective. See, e.g., Foucault, *The Archaeology of Knowledge and the Discourse on Language*, and *Power / Knowledge*; Said, *Orientalism*; and Guha and Spivak, *Selected Subaltern Studies*. Axel examines some of these fruitful conversations in his introduction to *From the Margins*, 1–44.

50. Davis, *Fiction in the Archives*, 3; see also White, *The Content of the Form*.

Anthropologists and literary scholars, meanwhile, have been taking what Stoler calls "the archival turn": "Colonial Archives and the Arts of Governance," 94.

51. Dirks, "Annals of the Archive," 58; see also Stoler, "Colonial Archives and the Arts of Governance."

52. Generally the nineteenth- and twentieth-century imperial state, figured as a Foucauldian panopticon amassing colonial data: see, e.g., the essays in Burton, *Archive Stories*. See also projects as different as those of Richards, *The Imperial Archive*; Hevia, "The Archive State and the Fear of Pollution," 234–64; and Stoler, "Colonial Archives and the Arts of Governance."

53. Dirks, "Annals of the Archive," 61. Eighteenth-century French peasants in revolt attacked not just nobles but the documents that had guaranteed their privileges; the new government, for its part, supported "state-sponsored bonfires" that "consigned papers of the nobility, orders of knighthood, and other documents of the old regime to ashes in the years between 1789 and 1793" (62).

54. Steedman, *Dust*, 13n2.

55. On the panopticon, Jeremy Bentham's contribution to efficient prison design, see Foucault, *Discipline and Punish*, 195–228; and Latour, "Drawing Things Together," 19–68.

56. Scott, in *Seeing like a State*, 6, is concerned mainly with "the *imperialism* of high-modernist, planned social order."

57. Pagden, *Lords of All the World*; Headley, *Church, Empire, and World*.

58. Guajardo-Fajardo Carmona, *Escribanos en Indias durante la primera mitad del siglo XVI*, 1:285n1041, cites portions of Columbus's testimony of his 1494 efforts to discover Tierra Firme: "No había hallado persona en la costa . . . que le supiese dar relación cierta dello, porque eran todos gente desnuda que no tiene bienes propios, ni tratan, ni van fuera de sus casas, ni otros vienen a ellos, según de ellos mismos supo." For Columbus, Americans' barbarism is manifested by their lack of property and trading relations.

59. This is the project eloquently traced in Rama, *The Lettered City*. On relations of resemblance, the underlying episteme of what Foucault calls "the Classical age," see *The Order of Things*, esp. xv–xxiv, 17–45. Mörner, in his analysis of the Spanish monarchs' efforts to implant "good examples" in the Americas of the early 1500s, depicts this philosophy in action in *La corona española y los foráneos en los pueblos de indios de América*. See also K. Burns, *Colonial Habits*, chap. 1.

60. The state works at this level too—"For the sixteenth-century Spanish state," as Abercrombie puts it in *Pathways of Memory and Power*, 246–47, "rule in Castile as well as in the Indies meant the extension of the techniques of surveillance and discipline into the most intimate corners of subject peoples' lives"— but not in a way that can simply be deduced from studying its ordering intentions and mandates.

61. Herzog, *Upholding Justice*, 8. Brooks, in *Pettyfoggers and Vipers of the Common-*

wealth, 16, highlights "the extremely personal nature of legal office holding": "The major office holders enjoyed almost complete freedom to exercise their posts more or less as they pleased. In most instances, this meant the creation of a small empire. . . . [T]he basic unit of organization was the household of the official" (15). Litigants might have to make their way past clotheslines and laundry to get there.

62. Compare Anderson's analysis in *Lineages of the Absolutist State*, 52, or Waquet's in *Corruption*, with Herzog's, *Upholding Justice*, 8, in which "auxiliary staff . . . played an important role in the resolution of conflicts . . . the division between professional and nonprofessional justice was unclear and . . . there was a similarly blurred division of labor between different institutions, instances, and people." Tomás y Valiente, "La Venta de Oficios en Indias, y en particular la de Escribanías," 102, argues that the sale of offices probably produced a better judiciary than would otherwise have resulted. On the sale of offices and the legal profession in England at that time, see Brooks, *Pettyfoggers and Vipers of the Commonwealth*, 121–24: he similarly finds that "at least up until the 1630s, the sale of offices does not appear . . . to have resulted in a drastic reduction of standards in the courts." That didn't prevent an Elizabethan-era spike in public unhappiness with members of the legal profession: ibid., 132–50.

63. If harmony at the grass roots was not the result, royal magistrates were there to provide justice. Herzog, *Upholding Justice*, 10, argues that justice, not strict legality, was the judiciary's goal.

64. The classic study in English is Parry, *The Sale of Public Office in the Spanish Indies under the Hapsburgs*. See also Tomás y Valiente, *La venta de oficios en Indias (1492–1606)*; and for a wealth of details, Guajardo-Fajardo Carmona, *Escribanos en Indias durante la primera mitad del siglo XVI*.

65. Both kinds were *escribanos públicos*, as Guajardo-Fajardo Carmona notes in *Escribanos en Indias durante la primera mitad del siglo XVI*, 1:427, although royal notaries tended to identify themselves simply as *escribanos de Su Majestad*. On the remarkable variety of other Spanish American notaries, including *notarios eclesiásticos*, see ibid., vol. 2.

66. See ibid., 1:229–45. In addition to their fees (*derechos*), Spanish American *escribanos de concejo* received a salary, with which they had to buy paper and ink for themselves and their assistants (1:244).

67. Hardwick, *The Practice of Patriarchy*, xiii n10.

68. *Las Siete Partidas*, 1:21 (Partida 2, Título 9, ley 2). This passage pertains to notaries in the monarch's service, but reflects well the social location envisioned for all notaries. It begins by alluding to Aristotle's counsel to Alexander—a recommendation of moderation, the ideal of "omes [hombres] medianos." Portuguese notaries were similarly situated; see Homem Correa Telles, *Manual do Tabellião*, 15.

69. Carvajal, *Instruction y memorial para escrivanos y juezes executores, assi en lo criminal como cevil, y escripturas publicas*, fol. 1.

70. Between 1500 and 1700, as Kagan has shown, Castile was experiencing a "legal revolution": "a sharp increase in the overall volume of civil litigation, accompanied by a widespread interest in legal study, the development of a sophisticated legal profession, and the expansion of the royal judiciary." Kagan, *Lawsuits and Litigants in Castile, 1500–1700,* xxii.

71. Cervantes, *Exemplary Stories,* trans. Lesley Lipson (New York: Oxford University Press, 1998), 126.

72. This is my interpretation of a particular passage; for more on the popular Cervantine tale of the Licenciado Vidriera, see George A. Shipley, "Garbage In, Garbage Out," 5–41, and his "Vidriera's Blather," 49–124.

73. Ecclesiastical notaries were supposed to be laymen and, wherever possible, royal notaries (*escribanos reales*): *Recopilación de leyes de los Reynos de las Indias,* 2:153 (Libro 5, Título 8, ley 37). The training of ecclesiastical and public notaries would thus have been the same, at least in theory, and ecclesiastical notaries were supposed to charge the same fees as royal notaries (ibid., 2:152, Libro 5, Título 8, ley 32). Restricted hours at the Archivo Arzobispal de Cuzco made it difficult for me to do sustained research there. However, the more accessible, well-organized Archivo Arzobispal de Lima (AAL) holds much Cuzco material, and Apelaciones del Cuzco documents reflect the activities of several Cuzco *notarios,* in divorce cases, lawsuits against priests, and more. Pedro Carrillo de Guzmán, an ecclesiastical notary active in Cuzco during the late seventeenth century (AAL, Apelaciones del Cuzco, XXIV:7 [1674]), also appears in AGI, Lima, 194, n. 19 (1680), among those seeking to succeed Cuzco notary public Martín López de Paredes in 1675. Carrillo's training thus prepared him to take his career in either direction, into the ecclesiastical realm or public notarial service.

74. Spivak, "Can the Subaltern Speak?," and *A Critique of Postcolonial Reason,* chapter 3.

75. See Dean, *Inka Bodies and the Body of Christ*; Garrett, *Shadows of Empire*; and De la Cadena, *Indigenous Mestizos.*

76. K. Burns, *Colonial Habits,* chap. 2.

77. For instance, the Archivo Regional de Cusco (hereafter ARC) records of Cristóbal de Lucero from 1623–24: to judge from the table of contents of this protocolo, from a quarter to a third of its contents have disappeared.

78. Monterroso, *Pratica civil, y criminal, e instruction de scrivanos.* Monterroso was granted privileges to sell his manual overseas, and it quickly became a staple of the Spanish American book trade: see Leonard, *Books of the Brave,* 221.

79. See Kirshner, "Some Problems in the Interpretation of Legal Texts *re* the Italian City-States," 16–27.

80. Stern, *Peru's Indian Peoples and the Challenge of Spanish Conquest,* 95.

81. Moreover, as Van Young puts it in "The Cuautla Lazarus," 7, "We must

make space for a double subjectivity . . . that of our objects [of study] and that of ourselves."

82. Stoler, "Colonial Archives and the Arts of Governance," 91. See also Mallon, "The Promise and Dilemma of Subaltern Studies," 1491–1515.

83. How Bourbon, Pombaline, and republican notaries handled their notarial offices and interacted with the power groups of their day would be well worth exploring. By the mid-1800s, the city of Cuzco had numerary notaries with indigenous surnames, a notable departure from colonial practice. See ARC-PN, siglo XIX, Julián Tupayachi, protocolo 221 (1827–31); and Luis Ramos Tituatauchi, protocolo 191 (1833–35). Interestingly, Ramos Tituatauchi's registers still segregate indigenous cuzqueños' business (as "registros de indígenas" rather than "registros de indios"), a practice that began in the mid-1600s.

1. Of Notaries, Templates, and Truth

1. Pagden, *Lords of All the World*. The Siglo de Oro extends roughly from 1500 to the 1650s. For some the endpoint is the Treaty of the Pyrenees (1659); for those who focus on arts and letters, it tends to be the year the playwright Pedro Calderón de la Barca died (1681).

2. The literature on this period is vast and rich: see, e.g., the work of Domínguez Ortiz, including *La sociedad española en el siglo XVII*, and *The Golden Age of Spain, 1516–1659*; J. H. Elliott, *Imperial Spain, 1469–1716* (New York: New American Library, 1963); and John Lynch, *Spain, 1516–1598*, and *The Hispanic World in Crisis and Change, 1598–1700*. On the Escorial, see George Kubler, *Building the Escorial* (Princeton: Princeton University Press, 1982). On increased litigiousness, see Kagan, *Lawsuits and Litigants in Castile, 1500–1700*. The phrase "religious racism" is Sicroff's: "Spanish Anti-Judaism"; see also Nirenberg, *Communities of Violence*; and Domínguez Ortiz, *Historia de los moriscos*.

3. These are the main characters in Lazarillo's sequence of masters in *Lazarillo de Tormes*; for an English translation, see *Two Spanish Picaresque Novels*.

4. Literature on the picaresque, too, is vast. See, e.g., Maiorino, *The Picaresque*; Sieber, "Literary Continuity, Social Order, and the Invention of the Picaresque," 143–64; and A. Cruz, *Discourses of Poverty*.

5. Alemán, *Guzmán de Alfarache*.

6. *Guzmán* is saliently about merchants, money, and trade: see Michel, *Pícaros y mercaderes en el Guzmán de Alfarache*.

7. Alemán, *Guzmán de Alfarache*, 1:136.

8. In its day *Guzmán* was as popular as the perennial bestseller *Don Quijote* (and in Spanish America, even more popular): see Leonard, *Books of the Brave*, 258–59. The stereotype of the notary was neither new nor restricted to Spanish letters.

Reyerson and Salata, *Medieval Notaries and Their Acts*, 10, note that Dante, Boccaccio, and Chaucer "all portrayed the medieval notary, invariably in a very negative light." See also Hardwick, *The Practice of Patriarchy*, 22–24.

9. Quevedo, *La vida del buscón llamado don Pablos*, 244; I have modified Alpert's translation in *Two Spanish Picaresque Novels*, 175.

10. Alpert, *Two Spanish Picaresque Novels*, 181; I have modified Alpert's translation of *escribano* as "lawyer."

11. Ibid., 182, translation lightly modified. Eventually Pablos's friends come to the rescue, but not before the notary gives him another working over and reprehends him for thieving—something that "he knew plenty about."

12. Gonzalo Correas, *Vocabulario de refranes y frases proverbiales (1627)*, 344, 639. Correas gives many more such sayings: "Papel y tinta, dinero cuesta" (620); "Papel y tinta, y poca justicia" (620); "Tintero y escribanías, lanza y dardo" (774). See also Martínez Kleiser, *Refranero general ideológico español*, which has a lengthy entry for "Escribanos" (244–45).

13. Also lampooned were lawyers, doctors, apothecaries, priests, and others who held delicate, vital matters in their hands. Regarding lawyers or advocates, see Kagan, *Lawsuits and Litigants in Castile, 1500–1700*, 69–73. But cf. the length of the entry "Escribanos" in Martínez Kleiser, *Refranero general ideológico español*, with that of the entries for "Abogados."

14. Navarro, *Favores de el Rey de el Cielo, hechos a su esposa la Santa Juana de la Cruz, Religiosa de la Orden tercera de Penitencia de N.P.S. Francisco*, 429. See also Matienzo, who in *Gobierno del Perú*, 321–22, tells of a clergyman named Martínez who caused trouble in the province of Tucumán by forcing witnesses to make declarations about things of which they knew nothing. I borrow the concept of the narrative annex from Keen, *Victorian Renovations of the Novel*.

15. Tamar Herzog makes this point regarding the notaries of Quito: *Mediación, archivos y ejercicio*, 51–53.

16. On this increase in litigation, see Kagan, *Lawsuits and Litigants in Castile, 1500–1700*, esp. 3–20, 79–127. Brooks shows a very similar situation in Elizabethan England: see *Pettyfoggers and Vipers of the Commonwealth*, 132–50, on popular distaste for the "lower branch" of the legal profession, exacerbated by rapid growth in litigation.

17. Kagan, *Lawsuits and Litigants in Castile, 1500–1700*, 12–13, notes that ordinary people might frequently be found in court in Golden Age Spain. Brooks similarly finds that English litigiousness of this period was not restricted to the wealthy: see *Pettyfoggers and Vipers of the Commonwealth*, 59–63.

18. Kagan, *Lawsuits and Litigants in Castile, 1500–1700*, 139: "Organized into 'colleges' in 1502, the [notarial] profession flourished in the sixteenth century owing to the spread of written contracts and other legal documents they themselves helped introduce." Meanwhile, as litigation flourished, judges increasingly

relied on notaries to depose witnesses and otherwise move litigation forward. As a result, according to Alonso Romero, *El proceso penal en Castilla*, 195, "with enormous frequency, those who in reality handled the [criminal justice] process were not the judges so much as the notaries themselves."

19. Herzog, *Mediación, archivos y ejercicio*, 5.

20. See Pedro de León, *Grandeza y miseria en Andalucía*, 390; and Domínguez Ortiz, *Crisis y decadencia de la España de los Austrias*.

21. Herzog, in *Mediación, archivos y ejercicio*, 4, stresses the notary's transforming power: "En ningún caso los redactores eran simples ejecutores: aunque de manera sutil, lenta, anónima y callada, *los escribanos iban transformando el mundo con el que entraban en contacto*; no sólo daban otro carácter—nuevo y 'público'—a los textos, sino que iban modificando su lengua, su estilo y su contenido" (italics mine).

22. Mijares Ramírez, in *Escribanos y escrituras públicas en el siglo XVI*, begins with the cuneiform contracts of ancient Sumeria: see her chap. 1, "Antecedentes históricos" (13–43). See also José Bono, *Historia del derecho notarial español*, vol. 1, which traces Spanish notarial history from Roman times to the fifteenth century.

23. For abundant detail, see Zimmermann, *The Law of Obligations*.

24. Berger, *Encyclopedic Dictionary of Roman Law*, 727–28, provides this job description: "Tabellio. A private, professional person who drew up written documents for private individuals. . . . The *tabelliones* exercised their profession in public places (*fora*, markets) or in offices (*stationes*) assisted by clerks and secretaries (*scribae, notarii*). Their activity was controlled by governmental officials who were authorized to inflict penalties for fraud or negligence or for cooperation in illicit transactions. Justinian required every *tabellio* to obtain official permission (*auctoritas*), and settled rules about the formalities to be observed by a *tabellio* in his work. . . . The ceiling-price schedule issued by Diocletian . . . fixed the fees to be paid to a *tabellio*, by the lines of the written document."

25. See Berger, *Encyclopedic Dictionary of Roman Law*, 352: "The *advocatus* assisted his clients (*clientes*) with juristic advice before and during the trial, in both civil and criminal matters, and pleaded for them in court"; 523: "Iurisconsultus . . . alludes to the activity of the jurists as *qui consuluntur*, i.e. who are consulted for an opinion in a legal matter and who give *responsa* to the consultants (*consultator*). . . . The jurists 'enjoyed the highest esteem among the Roman people'" (Cic. *de orat.* 1.45.198).

26. *Tabelliones* were not exalted figures in the Roman legal system; Jones goes so far as to call them "barely literate hacks," inferior to jurists and advocates: *The Later Roman Empire*, 284–602. But their influence is profound in Mediterranean legal cultures and in those of Europeans' colonies. For instance, Spanish American contracts often mention the *senatus consultum velleianum*: this refers to a decision by the Roman senate regarding women's rights. See *The Digest of Justinian*, bk. 16.

27. This is pointed out by Morales Padrón in "Descubrimiento y toma de posesión," 327–32. See Bono on Germanic peoples' influence on the legal cultures of Mediterranean Europe in *Historia del derecho notarial español*, 1:64–92.

28. See Hoenerbach, "Some Notes on the Legal Language of Christian and Islamic Deeds."

29. See *The Function of Documents in Islamic Law*. Wakin, in her introduction, mentions the Arabic forms' roots in pre-Islamic Near Eastern practice.

30. See Ibn al-'Attar, *Formulario notarial y judicial andalusí*; and Al-Tulaytuli, *Formulario notarial*. Such works would later influence the well-known Bologna school: see Flórez de Quiñones y Tomé, "Formularios notariales hispano-musulmanes," 179–226. Islamic, Jewish, and Christian notaries all worked under Islamic rule in medieval Spanish cities such as Córdoba and Toledo. "We . . . find in Spain Islamic documents in Christian official language and Christian documents in Islamic official language," according to Hoenerbach, "Some Notes on the Legal Language of Christian and Islamic Deeds," 38.

31. The recovered *Corpus Juris Civilis* that had been codified under Byzantine emperor Justinian stimulated such landmark works of Italian legal scholarship as Rolandino's *Summa totius artis notariae*, and Salatiel's *Ars notariae*. See Bono, *Historia del derecho notarial español*, 1:165–220; and Nussdorfer, *Brokers of Public Trust*, chap. 1: "The Jurists."

32. For details, see Bono, *Historia del derecho notarial español*, 1:245–56; he notes that "La difusión teórica de [las Partidas] . . . fue grande, siendo traducida al portugués, gallego y catalán" (256). The thirteenth century marks a watershed in the development of notarial culture in Spain as well as legal culture more generally. See R. Burns, *Jews in the Notarial Culture*, 39; Bono, *Historia del derecho notarial español*, 1:231.

33. On the training and job performance of *abogados* or "advocates," see Kagan, *Lawsuits and Litigants in Castile, 1500–1700*, 60–70.

34. On *procuradores* or "attorneys," see ibid., 57–60. Cf. the Roman *procurator*: Berger, *Encyclopedic Dictionary of Roman Law*, 653–54. There is little scholarship on these men, and not much prescriptive literature was designed for them. However, the manual by Juan Muñoz (whose prologue extensively plagiarizes Monterroso's) was popular enough to go into multiple editions and printings: *Pratica de procuradores para seguir pleytos civiles, y criminales*. Still more obscure is the role of the *solicitador*, whose activities seem to have merged in Spanish America with those of the procurador: see Kagan, *Lawsuits and Litigants in Castile, 1500–1700*, 52–57.

35. Bono, *Historia del derecho notarial español*, 1:148–50. These numbers might change over time (148–49): in Toledo, for example, the number was fixed at twenty in 1295, later augmented to thirty in 1348, and to thirty-three in 1445. In Valladolid, where in the fourteenth century there had been as many as eighty

notaries, the number was reduced and fixed at thirty in 1396, then further reduced to twenty at the end of the fifteenth century.

36. As mentioned in the introduction, the church had its own notarial corps, the *notarios eclesiásticos*, about whom much less is known: see Guajardo-Fajardo Carmona, *Escribanos en Indias durante la primera mitad del siglo XVI*, 2:481–98.

37. On the notaries of Seville, see Hoffman, "The Archivo de Protocolos de Sevilla," 29–32, a condensed version of a piece he published in *Itinerario* 5, no. 1 (1981): 39–45.

38. See the illustration included in Núñez Lagos, *El documento medieval y Rolandino (notas de historia)*. See also Cruz Coelho, "Os tabeliães em Portugal," 11–51.

39. *Las Siete Partidas*, 2:122 (Partida 3, Título 19): "Lealtança es una bondad que esta bien en todo ome [hombre]. E señaladamente en los escrivanos. . . ."

40. According to Bono, *Historia del derecho notarial español*, 2:315, this professional reserve was expressed in the Castilian term *poridad*. See *Las Siete Partidas*, 2:122 (Partida 3, Título 19, ley 2): "Deven ser omes [hombres] de poridad, de guisa q[ue] los testamentos, e las otras cosas q[ue] les fueren mandadas escrevir en poridad q[ue] las non descubran en ninguna manera."

41. *Las Siete Partidas*, 1:21 (Partida 2, Título 9, ley 2); see also Guajardo-Fajardo Carmona, *Escribanos en Indias durante la primera mitad del siglo XVI*, 1:438.

42. Bono, *Historia del derecho notarial español*, 2:286–87. On the various forms of transmission of notarial offices, see ibid., 2:281–86.

43. As quoted in Rodríguez Adrados, "El derecho notarial castellano trasplantado a Indias," 59.

44. Bono, *Historia del derecho notarial español*, 2:291–95. According to Bono, the point was to prevent officeholders from gaining control over notarial offices in perpetuity.

45. Rodríguez Adrados, "La Pragmática de Alcalá, entre Las Partidas y la Ley del Notariado."

46. *Libro de las bulas y pragmáticas de los Reyes Católicos*, vol. 2, fol. 362: "declarando las personas que la otorgan, y el dia, y el mes, y el año, y el lugar o casa donde se otorga, y lo que se otorga: especificando todas las condiciones, y pactos, y clausulas." These had to be passed along to the notary's successor. Similar requirements were imposed on Rome's Capitoline notaries after 1580: see Nussdorfer, *Brokers of Public Trust*, chap. 3: "The Laws."

47. According to Rodríguez Adrados, "El derecho notarial castellano trasplantado a Indias," 68–69, "Se abandona [a partir de la Pragmática de 1503] toda referencia a la cuantía del negocio . . . y se acude solamente a la extensión del escrito: 'diez maravedís por cada tyra,' por cada hoja, que fueron 'acrecentados' a quince por Pragmática de Felipe II en 1564; en todo caso, remuneración 'por fojas.' "

48. See Rogelio Pérez-Bustamante, "Los documentos de Cristóbal Colón y la práctica notarial," 27.

49. For detailed studies of various parts of Andalusia, see Ostos Salcedo and Pardo Rodríguez, *El notariado andaluz en el tránsito de la edad media a la edad moderna*.

50. Ostos Salcedo, "Los escribanos públicos de Córdoba en el tránsito de la edad media a la edad moderna," in Ostos Salcedo and Pardo Rodríguez, *El notariado andaluz en el tránsito de la edad media a la edad moderna*, 180–87.

51. See Obra Sierra, "Aproximación al estudio de los escribanos públicos del número en Granada (1497–1520)," 147.

52. According to Bono, "La nueva literatura notarial castellana en el Reinado de Felipe II," "Los libros del oficio notarial—literatura notarial—castellanos aparecen por primera vez, en el reinado de Felipe II (1556–1598), con el nuevo carácter de manual práctico y no de simple formulario" (23). Ribera's and Monterroso's manuals were the most important works, and of these two, writes Bono, Monterroso's "es superior" (33).

53. Monterroso, *Pratica civil, y criminal, e instruction de scrivanos*, fol. i verso.

54. Ibid., fol. ii.

55. Ibid.

56. Ibid., fol. 7.

57. Of course, Monterroso was also out to sell books, and in this he was notably successful. The *Pratica* went into multiple printings and editions, and circulated widely; it was still used in the eighteenth century. For a manual aimed at ecclesiastical notaries, see Cristóbal Escudero, *Estilo y pratica eclesiastica, y civil de procuradores, generalmente para todos los tribunales eclesiasticos, y seglares destos reynos*. Such works were part of a broader judicial how-to literature that included general procedural manuals such as Villadiego Vascuñana y Montoya, *Instruccion politica, y práctica judicial, conforme al estilo de los consejos, audiencias, y tribunales de corte, y otros ordinarios del reyno, utilissima para los governadores, y corregidores, y otros jueces ordinarios, y de comission, y para los abogados, escrivanos, procuradores, y litigantes*; and Hevia Bolaños, *Curia filipica donde se trata de los iuizios forenses, eclesiasticos, y seculares, dividida en cinco partes*. Many of these works enjoyed transatlantic success: see Leonard, *Books of the Brave*, 207, 221.

58. These were known variously as *demandas, libelos, pedimentos,* or (when a plaintiff made criminal charges) *querellas*. Technically, notaries were not to prepare such petitions for clients; that would put too much of the proceedings in their hands. The wording was very important. According to Villadiego Vascuñana, *Instruccion politica*, 340, "En el libelo bien hecho consiste casi toda la fuerza del Juicio, y determinacion de los pleytos, y causas, y porque el Juez debe juzgar conforme a lo pedido en el libelo; y assi, podrá dañar mucho a la Parte, siendo mal hecho."

59. Assuming, that is, the judge did not begin the case himself, which he might do on behalf of an injured party or parties; on cases brought *de oficio*, see Alonso Romero, *El proceso penal en Castilla, siglos XIII–XVIII*.

60. Merryman, *The Civil Law Tradition*, 111–23.

61. In criminal cases, oral argumentation happened only at the end, according to Alonso Romero, *El proceso penal en Castilla, siglos XIII–XVIII*, 145: "Después de la conclusión para sentencia, en la vista oral del proceso . . . las partes o sus abogados informaban de palabra al juez sobre sus respectivas posiciones y las razones que las apoyaban. Por eso se les llamaba 'lengua,' porque eran los que llevaban la palabra en el juicio." See also Navas, *La abogacía en el Siglo de Oro*.

62. Castilian law stipulated that judges should be present at depositions in criminal cases and in "arduous," important civil ones: *Recopilación de las leyes destos reynos*, 1:262v (Libro 3, Título VI, ley 28) and 1:266 (ibid., ley 43).

63. Villadiego Vascuñana, *Instruccion politica*, 65, adds that judges should have notaries write these expressions down in the deposition as well, "para que conste al Juez, al qual es arbitrario el discernir quanta fé se les debe dar."

64. "It often happens," writes Monterroso, *Pratica civil, y criminal, e instruction de scrivanos*, fol. 14v, "that the judge entrusts to the notary the reception and examination of witnesses, for him to depose them." Juan y Colom, in *Instruccion de escribanos en orden a lo judicial*, 175, says much the same, noting that judges should not delegate such activities in "grave" cases, those serious enough to merit consideration of the death penalty. Alonso Romero's findings, in *El proceso penal en Castilla*, 194–95, support the legal literature's assertions that judges delegated a great deal to notaries and their assistants.

65. Monterroso, *Pratica civil, y criminal, e instruction de scrivanos*, fol. 16v.

66. In an ordinary civil suit, the judge would first order the defendant (*reo*) to testify; the notary would deliver a summons. When the defendant appeared, the notary would swear him (or her) in before the judge, read the plaintiff's petition aloud to him, and then record his response: did he admit or deny the allegations were true? The accused was not allowed to contest the plaintiff's version at this point. His statement would be read back to him by the notary, and if he felt the contents reflected his responses, he would sign it. Then there might be further back and forth between the parties, often through legal representatives. Things might end there if proof was considered sufficient; if not, things might proceed to the stage of witness depositions.

67. In a criminal suit, defendants came last. First the judge ordered testimony from the injured party and from witnesses. This was known as the *sumaria información*, the preliminary, "summary" investigation. According to Carvajal, *Instruction y memorial para escrivanos y juezes executores*, fol. 1, judges tended to place most credit in the testimony of the *sumaria* because that was when witnesses' memories were fresh. If it gave sufficient grounds, the judge might order the defendant apprehended and his or her assets seized. Then the defendant would be heard and his or her "confession" taken. On Castilian-style penal process, see Alonso Romero, *El proceso penal en Castilla, siglos XIII–XVIII*; see also

Herzog, *Upholding Justice*, 24–42; Cutter, *The Legal Culture of Northern New Spain*, part 3.

68. Carvajal, *Instruction y memorial para escrivanos y juezes executores*, fol. 4v. The inducements to which his go-between role might expose him are easy enough to imagine.

69. Ibid., fol. 2.

70. Ibid., fol. 2v; Monterroso, *Pratica civil, y criminal, e instruction de scrivanos*, fol. 17.

71. Carvajal, *Instruction y memorial para escrivanos y juezes executores*, fol. 1v. This meant carefully questioning the witness about the allegations contained in the initial petition ("según el tenor del pedimento")—hence the importance of those opening documents.

72. Monterroso, *Pratica civil, y criminal, e instruction de scrivanos*, fol. 16v.

73. Ibid. While the notary's questioning had to proceed in accordance with the initial petition in a case, Carvajal urges the notary to be prepared to make as many follow-up questions ("preguntas y repreguntas") as necessary to get at the truth—*Instruction y memorial para escrivanos y juezes executores*, fol. 1v—even if it should contradict the plaintiff's allegations.

74. González de Torneo, *Pratica de escrivanos que contiene la judicial, y orden de examinar testigos en causas civiles, y hidalguias, y causas criminales, y escrituras en estilo estenso, y quentas, y particiones de bienes, y execuciones de cartas executorias*, fol. 4

75. González de Torneo, *Pratica de escrivanos que contiene la judicial*, fols. 147–147v.

76. Juan y Colom, *Instruccion de escribanos en orden a lo judicial*, 33. This entry is under "juicio civil ordinario," but Juan y Colom affirms this for criminal lawsuits as well (178).

77. Monterroso, *Pratica civil, y criminal, e instruction de scrivanos*, fol. 7v.

78. González de Torneo, *Pratica de escrivanos que contiene la judicial*, fols. 148–148v; see also *Recopilación de las leyes destos reynos*, 1:267 (Libro 3, Título 7, Ley 11). Perhaps they do this, he speculates, because the lawsuit is in an early stage and the accused can always clear himself in the next one (*en plenario*). In any case, he avers, this practice is wrong, "because the law orders [the witness] to swear to tell what he knows, whether it favors one party or the other." If notaries did their job properly, accused parties might be able to clear themselves of suspicion earlier and at much less cost. Note that here González de Torneo discloses an economic incentive for notaries where we might not expect to find one. If they strategically suppressed words at this introductory stage of a lawsuit, notaries might produce more defendants cooling their heels in jail—and generate more judicial business for themselves.

79. How much shaping or polishing is of course impossible to gauge, but the effect might well be to enhance the guilt of the accused. Carvajal, *Instruction y* *memorial para escrivanos y juezes executores*, 1 v, also instructs notaries to adopt the practice of registering "with great care" what took place, "even if [the witness's testimony] goes against the plaintiff." In his *Instruccion de escribanos en orden a lo judicial*, Juan y Colom agrees: witnesses' testimony should be admitted in full whether it supports a guilty verdict or not (fols. 178–79).

80. To claim this privilege, one might take refuge in a convent or monastery, or touch the door of a church and cry, "I call on the church!" or "Church! Church!" See, for example, the picaresque adventures of Catalina de Erauso, *Lieutenant Nun: Memoir of a Basque Transvestite in the New World* (Boston: Beacon Press, 1997), for whom this becomes a crucial means of escape.

81. According to Peters, in *Torture*, 79, "Torture was to be employed only in those cases in which full proof was lacking for the conviction of a defendant for a crime whose punishment was death or mutilation; lesser crimes, *delicta levia*, were not involved." In theory it could only be used on certain kinds of people; nobles, for instance, were supposed to be exempt. On the early modern convictions that formed the epistemological basis for torture, see Silverman, *Tortured Subjects*.

82. Monterroso, *Pratica civil, y criminal, e instruction de scrivanos*, fol. 56: "Aveys de saber que el escrivano, es la execucion del tormento."

83. Ibid., fol. 56. Likewise, he adds, the notary is in position to notice if the judge is a friend of the defendant and lets him off lightly; Monterroso thus wants the notary to act as a check on higher authority.

84. See Tomás y Valiente, *La tortura en España*.

85. Gonzalo Correas, *Vocabulario de refranes y frases proverbiales* (1627), 33: "A quien mal quieras, pleito le veas; y a quien más mal, pleito y orinal (médico)." For an enlightenment-era critique of torture in Spain, see Forner, *Discurso sobre la tortura*. See also Peters, *Torture*; Enders, *The Medieval Theater of Cruelty*.

86. J. M. Gutiérrez, *Practica criminal de España*, 280.

87. The Spanish verbs and phrases expressing agreement vary, but important keywords are *otorgar* and *concertar* (often used together, e.g. "otorgamos y concertamos"). Covarrubias, *Tesoro de la lengua castellana o española*, gives for the former "To grant / concede [*conceder*] what is requested or respond truthfully [*confessar*] to what one is asked" (842). *Concertar* means to come to terms, to agree; Covarrubias gives as synonyms *componer, ajustar, acordar* (346).

88. Not the truth of the scientific fact; for comparisons' sake, see Shapin, *A Social History of Truth*.

89. Covarrubias, *Tesoro de la lengua castellana o española*, 587, notes that "fé" has various meanings: it can indicate a promise, or willingness to believe; it can also signify authentic testimony, "like the *fé* a notary gives."

90. The notary had to know the parties well enough to vouch for their identities in his document; if he did not, they had to bring witnesses who could vouch

for them. As Siguenza warns, in his *Tratado de clausulas instrumentales, util, y necessario para Iuezes, abogados, y escrivanos destos reynos, procuradores, partidores, y confessores, en lo de justicia, y derecho*, 10v, "Ha de tener especial cuidado el Escrivano en conocer las partes otorgantes, porque de no hazerlo assi, le haran que con facilidad incurra y caya en una falsedad."

91. On rates stipulated by the 1503 Pragmática, see Guajardo-Fajardo Carmona, *Escribanos en Indias durante la primera mitad del siglo XVI*, 1:231.

92. As mentioned earlier in this chapter, after 1503, notaries were required to keep bound registers (*protocolos*) with completely filled-out, orderly records of the transactions they had drawn up, signed by the parties. From 1525 the notary was required to sign too: Guajardo-Fajardo Carmona, *Escribanos en Indias durante la primera mitad del siglo XVI*, 1:144–45. At the end of the year the notary had someone create a table of contents (*abecedario*) for the year's records, and he affixed a statement to the protocolo with his unique *signo*, indicating it was complete.

93. Guajardo-Fajardo Carmona, *Escribanos en Indias durante la primera mitad del siglo XVI*, 1:145–46.

94. Monterroso, *Pratica civil, y criminal, e instruction de scrivanos*, fol. 7.

95. Mercado published a second edition of this influential work two years later, expanding upon certain points. For a modern edition, see *Suma de tratos y contratos*.

96. De la Ripia, *Practica de testamentos, y modos de subceder*, fols. 2–19.

97. Bono [Huertas], *Breve introducción a la diplomática notarial española*, 45. See, e.g., AHS-PN, Bernardo García, libro primero del año 1687 (1 enero–7 julio), signatura 642, fols. 373–93v, a series of printed dowry agreements for young women from the Casa de Misericordia, all enacted on March 28, 1687. I have not encountered preprinted forms in Peruvian archives, but for early Chilean examples, see *Protocolos de los escribanos de Santiago*, 1:121–22, 129–30, 138, 140.

98. Guajardo-Fajardo Carmona, *Escribanos en Indias durante la primera mitad del siglo XVI*, 1:229–30.

99. Ibid., 1:231.

100. Rodríguez Adrados, "El derecho notarial castellano trasplantado a Indias," 68–69, notes that Philip II raised the rate from ten to fifteen maravedis per page in 1564, and notaries were permitted to charge this rate for both draft and final copies. This did not satisfy Spanish notaries, who succeeded in obtaining an additional raise in 1569: see Ribera, *Primera parte de escrituras, y orden de particion y cuenta, y de residencia judicial, civil y criminal*, fols. III–III v.

101. Making acceptable rates was particularly problematic for faraway Spanish America: see Guajardo-Fajardo Carmona, *Escribanos en Indias durante la primera mitad del siglo XVI* , 1:229–44.

102. Bono [Huertas], *Breve introducción a la diplomática notarial española*, 45; see

also Arguello, *Tratado de escrituras y contratos publicos, con sus anotaciones,* whose prologue laments that ignorant notaries create documents "con tanta prolixidad y verbosidad de razones, que muchas se confunden y prevarican con otras," causing doubt and harm to their clients.

103. Leonard, *Books of the Brave.*

104. Bartolomé Álvarez, *De las costumbres y conversión de los indios del Perú,* 267.

105. Álvarez, *De las costumbres y conversión de los indios del Perú,* 268: "Un indio ladino de un pueblo llamado Andamarca, en la provincia de Carangas, compró un Monterroso, y en otro pueblo llamado Corquemarca otro ladino compró *Las Partidas* del rey don Alonso, que le costaron 40 pesos." Álvarez did not approve, opining that these men's ignorance would lead them to mangle Monterroso: "Trastornará [a] Monterroso y las leyes de *La[s] Partida[s]* para sólo hacer mal" (269).

106. His treasury went bankrupt in 1557, not for the last time. See Kamen, *Philip of Spain.*

107. Philip II and his advisors did not invent this expedient; they were doing what contemporary monarchs also did. According to J. H. Parry, *The Sale of Public Office in the Spanish Indies under the Hapsburgs,* 3, "The Spanish Crown in the sixteenth century sold offices more openly than the English but less freely than the French." On England, see Brooks, *Pettyfoggers and Vipers of the Commonwealth,* 121–31; and on France, the classic study is Mousnier, *La vénalité des offices sous Henri IV et Louis XIII.* See also Doyle, *Venality;* K. W. Swart, *Sale of Offices in the Seventeenth Century.*

108. Tomás y Valiente, *La venta de oficios en Indias (1492–1606),* 42–71, gives important historical context and documentary detail for the measures taken in 1558–59.

109. Tomás y Valiente, *La venta de oficios en Indias (1492–1606),* 93–94, 106. Those buying notarial offices could begin practicing right away, although they had to seek royal confirmation within three years or risk losing them. In 1606, this became four years: Bravo Lozano and Hidalgo Nuchera, *De indianos y notarios,* 69. The crown thus maintained a modicum of quality control. However, the need for revenue clearly drove the process of selecting those who would make official Spanish American records: see Tomás y Valiente, *La venta de oficios en Indias (1492–1606),* 131.

110. Parry, *The Sale of Public Office in the Spanish Indies under the Hapsburgs,* 19–20; this provision of "perpetuity" included Spanish American notaries and many other royal officials.

111. Ibid., 20.

112. By the late seventeenth century, the sale of treasury offices and governorships of provinces had become common: ibid., 48–58. The term "patrimonialización" is Tomás y Valiente's: see *La venta de oficios en Indias (1492–1606),* 35–39.

Whether these sales produced a less-qualified set of royal officials is much debated. But historians (as well as contemporary critics) agree that the sale of offices had pernicious, long-term effects; see, e.g., Andrien, *Crisis and Decline*, esp. 103–29.

113. Alemán, *Guzmán de Alfarache*, 1:137.

114. According to J. H. Elliott, *Spain and Its World, 1500–1700*, 29, "There is no doubt that his two years in Salamanca, followed by a long period of training and experience as a notary, first in Seville and then in Hispaniola, gave him a working knowledge of Latin and a close acquaintance with the methods and the technicalities of Castilian law."

2. Interests

1. Guaman Poma, *El primer nueva corónica y buen gobierno*, 2:342–43.

2. Garner, "Long-Term Silver Mining Trends in Spanish America," 898–935. The crown's share of registered silver was known as the *quinto real*, or royal fifth.

3. Lockhart, *Spanish Peru 1532–1560*, 70; for more detail on the lives of these initial Spanish invaders, see Lockhart, *The Men of Cajamarca*.

4. Lockhart, *Spanish Peru 1532–1560*, 13–17. The Spaniards' actions disclose a recognizably medieval economy of rewards in which great lords bestowed favors on those who served them best. But encomiendas numbered only in the hundreds, and thousands of claimants were rushing to the Americas to get a piece of the action. Figuring out how to satisfy them was a time-consuming, politically delicate royal activity. See De la Puente Brunke, *Encomienda y encomenderos en el Perú*.

5. For those who did not obtain an encomienda, the goal was often to return to Spain and live the life of an *indiano*, perhaps purchase an office there. See, e.g., the case of notary Pedro de Salinas and his partner Juan Franco in Lockhart, *Spanish Peru 1532–1560*, 73–75.

6. See Cook, *Born to Die*, and *Demographic Collapse*. On the social dislocation caused by disease, violence, and colonial exactions, see Wightman, *Indigenous Migration and Social Change*.

7. Lockhart, *Spanish Peru 1532–1560*, 61–62. See Konetzke, *Colección de documentos para la historia de la formación social de Hispanoamérica, 1493–1810*, 1:128.

8. On early modern litigiousness as suspicious, un-Christian activity, see Kagan, *Lawsuits and Litigants in Castile, 1500–1700*, 17–20; and Brooks, *Pettyfoggers and Vipers of the Commonwealth*, 132–36.

9. See Luján Muñoz, *Los escribanos en las Indias Occidentales y en particular en el Reino de Guatemala*, 101–5, on mid-century debates about whether to allow Spanish notaries to circulate among indigenous pueblos.

10. Mörner, *La corona española y los foráneos en los pueblos de indios de América*.

11. These were patterned after Castilian models. The earliest such officials

were named for Santo Domingo and the other cities of the Caribbean; for notarial appointments, see Guajardo-Fajardo Carmona, *Escribanos en Indias durante la primera mitad del siglo XVI*, 1:260–308.

12. See Toledo, *Francisco de Toledo*, 2:222–24.

13. Caciques, for instance, did not simply disappear from indigenous community life. Especially in the Andes, they retained considerable power; the new mayors, cabildos, and other town and village officeholders of the late 1500s did not displace them. And there was never neat separation between *españoles* and *indios*. Large numbers of people were neither simply "Spanish" or "Indian" but a mixture, and many were of African descent as well, as Spaniards began relying on people shipped in bondage from the West African coast. See Spalding, *Huarochirí*; Pease, *Curacas, reciprocidad y riqueza*; and O'Toole, "From the Rivers of Guinea to the Valleys of Peru," 19–36.

14. Such courts existed in Cuzco and Lima, but have not been studied. For Mexico, see Borah, *Justice by Insurance*.

15. Konetzke, *Colección de documentos para la historia de la formación social de Hispanoamérica, 1493–1810*, 1:367, 604, 606–7; *Recopilación de leyes de los reynos de las Indias*, 2:153. On contemporary notions of "race" and *mestizaje*, see K. Burns, "Unfixing Race," 188–202.

16. Guaman Poma, *El primer nueva corónica y buen gobierno*, 2:485. As it happens, among the oldest lawsuits remaining in Cuzco's archives is a 1594 case against a magistrate's notary, Francisco Jiménez, charged with doing exactly the kind of thing Guaman Poma denounced. According to witnesses, Jiménez had extorted the indigenous tributaries of nearby Yucay while the magistrate was away: ARC, Cabildo, Justicia Ordinaria, Causas Criminales, expediente de 1594.

17. Calancha, *Coronica moralizada del Orden de San Augustin en el Peru, con sucesos egenplares vistos en esta Monarquia*, 491; I thank Karen Graubart for bringing this passage to my attention.

18. Antonio de Paz y Salgado, *Instruccion de litigantes, o guia para seguir pleitos con maior utilidad de los interesados en ellos, y a menos costa de la paciencia de los Jueces, Abogados, Procuradores, y demas Ministros que sirven en el Fuero*, s / f; this is part of his cautionary Rule 14 for would-be litigants.

19. Fernández de Lizardi, *The Mangy Parrot*, 242.

20. Writing offered the possibility of getting your labor and tribute obligations reduced, or lessening the labor and fees exacted by your priest: see Stern, *Peru's Indian Peoples and the Challenge of Spanish Conquest*, 114–37.

21. As Herzog puts it, *Upholding Justice*, "People involved in administering justice were never isolated individuals, never impartial, never distanced from society. Social networks first constructed the administration and then influenced it" (9). As she notes, this has revisionist implications for "our use of notions such as corruption for an early modern period in which nonpublic interests were at the

core of the administrative system" (10). An analogous case is that of Brazilian magistrates: see Schwartz, *Sovereignty and Society in Colonial Brazil*, esp. chaps. 8 and 13.

22. Stern, *Peru's Indian Peoples and the Challenge of Spanish Conquest*, 95. For a later example involving notaries, see Ramírez, *Provincial Patriarchs*, 244–46.

23. Jorge Polo y la Borda has studied a particular sugar plantation: "La hacienda Pachachaca (segunda mitad del siglo XVIII)," *Histórica* I (1977): 223–47; see also Guevara Gil, *Propiedad agraria y derecho colonial*. Maize, too, was a valuable commodity in Potosí; see Glave and Remy, *Estructura agraria y vida rural en una región andina*.

24. Cieza de León, *Crónica del Perú, primera parte*, 258.

25. This was typical; Lockhart notes, *Spanish Peru 1532–1560*, 70, that "notaries' offices were always clustered together on the town square, near or even in the city council building." See AGI, Lima, 196, n. 29, confirmation of Antonio Pérez de Vargas, which mentions the *portal de los escribanos* (where he won his notarial office at auction) on Cuzco's Plaza del Regocijo.

26. The ARC contains no notarial registers from the 1530s through the 1550s, and only very few and fragmentary records from the 1560s and 1570s. Between them, Corregimiento and Cabildo records contain only three sixteenth-century criminal lawsuits, one of which is misclassified as a criminal case. Civil cases from the late 1500s are a bit more abundant: see Decoster and Bauer, *Justicia y poder*.

27. ARC, Libro de Cabildo #1 (1545–51), fol. 65v.

28. He was a royal notary (*escribano real*), "able and prepared for the said office." This was the standard credential for those assigned the highest offices in a major Spanish American city's notarial corps.

29. Sancho was almost certainly related to one of Cuzco's encomenderos, Pedro de Orue. According to De la Puente Brunke, *Encomienda y encomenderos en el Perú*, 221–22, 363, Pedro was encomendero of Maras; a successful lawsuit was brought against him for exploiting "his" Indians.

30. He was granted the post by Pedro de la Gasca, then Peru's acting governor. Later books of council minutes show that Orue frequently sought and obtained license from the cabildo to name a substitute and absent himself from his duties. The council also began allowing him generous sick leaves as infirmities began to get the better of him. See 1551 permission, ARC, Libro de Cabildo #4 (1561–64), fols. 23–23v, June 9, 1561.

31. The same man might hold and exercise both offices, as often happened in Cuzco. See Guajardo-Fajardo Carmona, *Escribanos en Indias durante la primera mitad del siglo XVI*.

32. AGI, Lima, 178, n. 7. Diego de Burgos, *boticario*, had obtained the post because he was among the creditors of its deceased former holder, Don Lupercio de Quiñones, who had received the post because of the death of Pedro de León.

Pedro de León practiced as a notary in Cuzco; on his credentials, see AGI, Lima, 565, legajo 3, fol. 82, February 21, 1539. The other two men probably never set foot there.

33. According to Quesada, when the Contreras brothers had risen in revolt in Panama in 1550 and tried to rob the royal treasury, he was "in the vanguard and on the front lines"; for context, see *Documentos relativos a Don Pedro de La Gasca y a Gonzalo Pizarro*, 1:55–61. He also happened to be visiting Upper Peru during Sebastián Castilla's 1553 revolt, and opposed the upstart, narrowly escaping death. When an even bigger revolt broke out in Cuzco the following year, Quesada had rushed into the fray with a party of soldiers he had armed at his own expense. His son Gerónimo Sánchez de Quesada later added in his own petitions that his father had been "discoverer and *conquistador* of the province of Carabaya," pacifying its indigenous population, founding a town, and discovering "rivers of gold."

34. Separately, his son would later succeed in obtaining a position as alderman in Cuzco's cabildo.

35. His place as cabildo notary was confirmed to him in a document of 1571 declaring that Orue had been a good servant of the crown for thirty-two years (i.e., since 1539): ARC, Libro de Cabildo #6 (1573–78), fol. 213, entry of March 3, 1578, citing a document from Yucay dated May 28, 1571.

36. ARC, Libro de Cabildo #6 (1573–78), fol. 213. Similarly, in 1574 Toledo granted Joan de Salas the office of *procurador* in Cuzco because he was not only qualified but the son of Martín de Salas, "conquistador destos rreinos y que le mataron los tiranos en la dicha ciudad [del Cuzco] por alçar la voz de su mag[esta]d." AGI, Lima 178, n. 31.

37. ARC, Libro de Cabildo #7 (1581–84), fols. 4v–5, April 17, 1581, petition and approval of Cervantes; fols. 29–32v, September 1581 dispute over exercise of office of cabildo notary in which Cervantes charges Orue with attempting to "vengar sus pasiones" (29v). By fol. 32v, Sancho Ortiz de Orue starts signing again, but not for long.

38. Though one man gained office by knowing the king's pharmacist, as we saw above in the case of Pedro Díaz Valdeón (AGI, Lima, 178, n. 7), and another via the king's "ayuda de cámara" (AGI, Lima, 178, n. 18). Parry indicates that during these years, such dealings were not unusual; *The Sale of Office in the Spanish Indies under the Hapsburgs*, 11.

39. "Yo Pedro quispe escrivano pu[blico] y de cavildo por Su Mag[esta]d en la perroquia de nuestra s[eñor]a de purificacion del Hospital de los Naturales," in ARC-PN, Pedro de la Carrera Ron, protocolo 4 (1586–96), unbound notebook marked with a strip of paper that says Pedro Quispe, 1586–87, fol. 652v, death certificate of "Jhoan ninamanco yndio pechero en la d[ic]ha parroquia," February 20, 1586.

40. Ibid., fols. 650v–51.

41. ARC, Corregimiento, Causas Ordinarias, legajo 2 (1587–1602), expediente 46 (1595), cuaderno 25. This too is a fragment of what was once a more extensive record; it begins on fol. 167 and ends on fol. 190, and contains documents from June and part of July 1595. Peru's "Indian justice" system has yet to be studied. On the General Indian Court of Mexico, see Borah, *Justice by Insurance*.

42. Garcilaso de la Vega considered the term an insult: see Garcilaso de la Vega, *Comentarios reales de los Incas*, 2:627–28.

43. A thriving coca trade developed, and hundreds of mule trains laden with coca baskets were sent toward Potosí: see Glave, *Trajinantes*.

44. On Potosí as seen through its thriving petty commerce, see Mangan, *Trading Roles*.

45. AGI, Lima, 180, n. 35, November 9, 1607. Carrera Ron received his office through a 1597 renunciation in his favor by Juan de Castañeda. See also AL, Signatura CC-149, caja 357 (1608–19), "Libro de toma de razón del Cabildo," fols. 12v–13v: in 1608, Carrera Ron was allowed to name a substitute to cover his routine notarial duties while he tended to his job as cabildo notary.

46. The will is in ARC-PN, Francisco Hurtado, protocolo 116 (1617), fols. 516–25; Carrera Ron's coca investments are on fol. 517.

47. Carrera Ron married Doña Ana de Almirón, the daughter of Francisco de Almirón. According to Donato Amado Gonzáles (personal communication), Almirón was part of the city's merchant community.

48. V. Cummins, "The Church and Business Practices in Late Sixteenth Century Mexico," 438. These bulls, Cummins suggests, "could amount very nearly to public condoning by the Church of the reality of the business world" (439). José Navarro, a native of Castellán de Santiago in La Mancha and a numerary notary in Cuzco, arranged in his will to purchase ten bulas de composición: see ARC-PN, José Calvo, protocolo 50 (1643), fol. 82.

49. AL, Signatura CC-149, caja 357 (1608–19), "Libro de toma de razón del Cabildo de los títulos de corregidores, regidores, escribanos reales y etc.," fol. 42.

50. ARC-PN, Alonso Beltrán Lucero, protocolo 4 (1636–37), fol. 1049, will of December 7, 1637.

51. ARC-PN, Alonso Calvo, protocolo 50 (1650), fol. 87, will of February 17, 1643: "Declara que tiene en administración y arrendamiento el estanco de los naipes de esta ciudad y corregimientos del distrito de la Real Caja por tiempo de 10 años . . . a razón de 1,700 pesos pagados en barra a fin de cada un año."

52. *Recopilación de las leyes destos reynos*, 2:384–85: "Los escrivanos no sean tratantes en oficio de regatoneria, ley 20. titulo 3. libro septimo." Covarrubias defines "regatón," in *Tesoro de la lengua castellana*, 900, as "El que compra de forastero por junto y revende por menudo"; the verb *regatear* means to bargain to drive down the price of something (e.g., "es muy del regatón").

53. ARC-PN, Gerónimo Sánchez de Quesada, protocolo 30 (1592), fol. 337v. The

peso ensayado is a common sixteenth-century unit of account, and a rather confusing one for the historian: it is sometimes defined as the equivalent of 12½ reales, and other times as 450 maravedis. See TePaske and Klein, *The Royal Treasuries of the Spanish Empire in America*, 1:xviii.

54. ARC-PN, Francisco Hurtado, protocolo 116 (1617), fol. 517v.

55. ARC-PN, José Calvo, protocolo 50 (1643), fol. 86v.

56. AGI, Indiferente, 738, n. 123, "Consulta de boca hecha por el licenciado Gasca de Salazar [del Consejo de Indias] a su majestad," March 20, 1571.

57. For Alonso the elder's credentials, see AGI, Lima, 178, n. 12, which contains 1573 testimony on his notarial qualifications. For those of Cristóbal de Lucero, see AGI, Lima, 179B, n. 46: Cristóbal got his office through the renunciation made in him by Antonio Sánchez, who died in 1595. In ARC-PN, Alonso Beltrán Lucero, protocolo 10 (1646–49), fols. 56–56v, September 9, 1642, Alonso the younger declares in his will that he lives in houses on the Plaza del Regocijo that were once his grandfather's.

58. ARC-PN, Alonso Beltrán Lucero, protocolo 10 (1646–49), fols. 55–58. The will orders his executor to give 1,000 pesos to an unnamed person "for the reason that I have told and communicated to him," so it is possible that Beltrán Lucero had a partner, or perhaps a child (or children).

59. AGI, Lima, 196, n. 29.

60. ARC-PN, Gregorio Básquez Serrano, protocolo 52 (1705), will of June 15, 1705.

61. AGI, Lima, 187, n. 144.

62. ARC-PN, Cristóbal de Bustamante, protocolo 16 (1686), fol. 456.

63. Martín López de Paredes did a lot of notarial business for Mesa Andueza; see, e.g., ARC-PN, López de Paredes, protocolo 144 (1659), fols. 814–814v, in which Mesa Andueza hires Pedro Guaman, "indio," to serve for ten years as a worker (*yanacona*) on the hacienda Guandoja in the valley of Anta, and protocolo 145 (1660), fols. 392v–93 and 398v–99, in which Mesa Andueza rents spaces in the city's center for a store (*tienda de pulperia*) and a shoemaker's workshop.

64. See Burns, *Colonial Habits*, 64–67.

65. ARC-PN, Gregorio Básquez Serrano, protocolo 51 (1704), fol. 166v, will of March 28, 1704: "en el [oficio público] estan ympuestos tres mill p[eso]s de censo principal a favor de la caja de censos de yn[dio]s." See also Navarro's will in ARC-PN, José Calvo, protocolo 50 (1643), fols. 83–83v: he declares that when he purchased his office he assumed payments on an 800-peso censo that had previously been imposed on it "en favor de unos indios."

66. ARC-PN , Cristóbal de Bustamante, protocolo 16 (1686), fols. 456v and 458v.

67. AGI, Lima, 187, n. 84, August 8, 1652.

68. According to findings of Friar Domingo de Cabrera Lartaún of Cuzco, "juez visitador de tierras y desagravio de indios," in ARC, Cabildo, Justicia Or-

dinaria, Causas Civiles, legajo 6 (1650–55), expediente 154, cuaderno 32, "Informa-ción hecha a petición de don Juan Marca," Juan López de Paredes took possession of the lands "por empeño que de ellas le hizo don Lorenzo Paucar y otros que se las ha vendido teniendolas adjudicadas a los indios del ayllo Coscoxa cuyas eran." Don Lorenzo Paucar appears in the books of López de Paredes: see, e.g., ARC-PN, Martín López de Paredes, protocolo 140 (1655) [fol. number incomplete], February 4, 1655: obligación y venta de Don Lorenzo Paucar, "cacique governador del pueblo de Andaguayllillas la chica, jurisdicion desta ciudad del Cuzco," a Antonio Hernández Cavezudo, "hacendado en el dicho valle de Andaguaylas." The buyer is said to have previously paid tribute amounts on behalf of Don Lorenzo and his community.

69. ARC, Cabildo, Justicia Ordinaria, Causas Civiles, legajo 6 (1650–55), expedi-ente 154, cuaderno 32, "Información." Each witness gave his version and signed his name: Don Blas Tito, a local ethnic lord (*curaca*) and mayor of Andahuaylillas; Don Juan Ramos, a native of Andahuaylillas of the Salloc ayllu and caretaker of the town's church; and Don Marcos Quispi Tocta, Don Pascual Ninatupa, and Don Juan Quispe, all heads of local ayllus.

70. Ibid. The priest's testimony indicates he knew this because "Manuel de Avendaño and other Spaniards had come to consult him as to whether the sale would be secure." López de Paredes's participation in land sales is confirmed by his own notarial registers: see, e.g., protocolo 143 (1658), fols. 951–52v, the May 6, 1658, sale by Don Marcos Quispetucta, "cacique y principal y governador del pueblo de Andaguayllillas de el ayllo guascar quiguar," to Manuel de Avendaño, "hacendado en el valle de andaguayllillas," of four *fanegadas* of land in Andahuay-lillas.

71. ARC, Cabildo, Justicia Ordinaria, Causas Civiles, legajo 6 (1650–55), expedi-ente 154, cuaderno 32, "Información."

72. On the holdings of the Duke of Alba, see De la Puente Brunke, *Encomienda y encomenderos en el Perú*, 343, 353, 359, 368.

73. ARC, Corregimiento, Causas Ordinarias, legajo 16 (1657–63), expediente 324, cuaderno 20: "Autos seguidos por Martín López de Paredes escribano contra Nicolás Moreno Hidalgo," fol. 4v. López de Paredes obtained a *composición* con-firming his title from land inspector Lartaún in 1659; see fols. 8–9v. For more on Gualpa Nina, see chap. 5.

74. The general picture that emerges in these documents is one of indigenous community leaders' desperation and Spaniards' land hunger. Demographic histo-rians have found that the indigenous population of the region as a whole was decimated by disease and in sharp decline at this time, only recovering sometime around the early eighteenth century: see Wightman, *Indigenous Migration and Social Change*.

75. López de Paredes (and perhaps other notaries) may have resembled the

modern Vietnamese *"secrétaires* and *interprètes* who served as intermediaries between the French officials in the Mekong Delta and their Vietnamese subjects," as described by Scott, *Seeing like a State*, 48: "By concentrating on the legal paperwork, such as title deeds, and the appropriate fees, they occasionally became landlords to whole villages of cultivators who had imagined they had opened common land free for the taking. . . . Whatever their conduct, their fluency in a language of tenure specifically designed to be legible and transparent to administrators, coupled with the illiteracy of the rural population to whom the new tenure was indecipherable, brought about a momentous shift in power relations."

76. The death certificate is contained in AGI, Lima, 194, n. 19, March 2, 1680: "expediente de confirmación del oficio de escribano público de Cuzco a Alfonso de Bustamante" (successor in López de Paredes's notarial office).

77. AAL, Apelaciones del Cuzco, XL:1 (1708–16), fol. 47v. For more about people signing blank pages, see chapter 3. In the Oropesa land case, an ecclesiastical notary (*notario*) named Pedro Carrillo de Guzmán declares himself López de Paredes's *compadre* (fol. 13). Carrillo de Guzmán also appears (AAL, Apelaciones de Cuzco, XXIV:7 [1674]) as the author of a rare private letter, addressed to the cacique of Macarí, notifying him that he will have to pay 300 pesos to get some documents copied, half up front to distribute among *oficiales* (presumably Carrillo de Guzmán's assistants), "y así no se podrá comenzar a sacar sino es dándose adelantado."

78. On Cuzco's confraternities, see Baker, *Imposing Harmony*, 144–47. On the power of the royal Inca standard bearer (*alférez real*) in Cuzco, see Donato Amado Gonzáles, "El Alférez Real de los Incas," 55–80.

79. ARC, Corregimiento, Causas Ordinarias, legajo 46 (1763–65), expediente 1020 (1765), cuaderno 32; and legajo 56 (1775–77), expediente 1273 (1775), cuaderno 5. The latter makes reference to the altar "vulgarly called the Altar of the Escribanos," and notes "the ancient custom in this city" of alternating the expense of the altar from one year to the next, "one year a Notary . . . and the next a Procurador, accompanied by two mule owners and teamsters" (4). On the social statements made by the order of precedence in the annual Corpus Christi procession, see Dean, *Inka Bodies and the Body of Christ*.

80. See ARC-PN, Francisco Hurtado, protocolo 116 (1617), fol. 516v, on Carrera Ron's membership in nine Cuzco cofradías; fol. 517v, regarding 50 pesos owed to Carrera Ron by his fellow notary Alonso Herrero, "which I [Carrera Ron] lent him for the funeral of his wife"; and fol. 519v, regarding an additional 6,500 pesos owed to Carrera Ron by Alonso Herrero.

81. Lorenzo Mesa Andueza had three sons (José, Blas, and Agustín) in the clergy: ARC-PN, Cristóbal de Bustamante, protocolo 16 (1686), fol. 459v. And Doña Francisca de San Pedro López de Paredes, the notary's daughter and a professed nun in Santa Catalina, appears in ARC-PN, Joan de Saldaña, protocolo 296 (1685),

fols. 357–58v, selling a cell inside the convent that her father, by then deceased, had purchased for her. The notary's son, Dr. Martín López de Paredes, *clérigo presbítero*, made out his own will in 1693: ARC-PN, Joan de Saldaña, protocolo 302 (1693), fols. 520–21v.

82. ARC-PN, Alonso Beltrán Lucero, protocolo 10 (1646–49), fols. 55v–56v.

83. ARC-PN, Cristóbal de Bustamante, protocolo 16 (1686), fol. 456v.

84. Pérez de Vargas indicates that the house was first sold for 4,600 pesos not to him but to his wayward son, Ventura Pérez. Then, after Pérez de Vargas had lived in it and improved it, Centeno took advantage of his absence to arrange for the house to be sold to Juan Francisco Ochoa for 10,000 pesos.

85. The Lima notary Pedro Pérez Landero Otañez y Castro (whose records are catalogued in the AGN under "Pedro Pérez Landero") authored a manual for the proper conduct of these exercises: *Practica de visitas, y residencias apropriada a los Reynos del Perú, y deducida de lo que en ellos se estila.* See also Herzog, "La comunidad y su administración," 161–83.

86. ARC-PN, Miguel de Contreras, protocolo 5 (1596–97). Some Cuzco residencia records are in the AGN, but are in such poor condition that they are no longer made available to researchers.

87. Ibid., fol. 1362: Francisco de la Fuente started in Lima as *secretario del crimen* in the Real Audiencia, then the Audiencia's *receptor*, later becoming *escribano del Juzgado de Provincia* and finally cabildo notary in Cuzco.

88. AGN, Real Audiencia, Causas Criminales, legajo 3, 1598, cuaderno 10, fols. 15–15v.

89. Ibid., fol. 6.

90. Ibid., fol. 11v.

91. Ibid., fols. 10v–11.

92. Meanwhile Diego de Espinosa, the antagonist with whom De la Fuente had tangled in July 1596, was found free of any wrongdoing. Ibid., fol. 1766.

93. AGN, Real Audiencia, Causas Criminales, legajo 3, 1598, cuaderno 10, fol. 1351: "Nunca les [h]e llevado . . . mas de tan solamente a tres pessos, y a tres y medio y a quatro y estos me vienen de derecho porque demas de [h]averlo [h]allado en costumbre que se pagaba a [Sebastián] de Vera mi antezesor los dichos derechos son muy moderados en esta ciudad."

94. ARC-PN, Miguel de Contreras, protocolo 5 (1596–97), fol. 1351v. The amount Francisco de la Fuente paid is confirmed by AGI records: Lima, 179A, n. 53. Bidding started in October 1591 with his bid of 12,000 pesos, and the next day rose to his final and winning offer of 16,000 pesos ensayados.

95. ARC-PN, Miguel de Contreras, protocolo 5 (1596–97), fol. 1352: "Y yo no soy de las personas a quien la ley proibe de tratos y contratos." As long as he has been in Cuzco, he reports, "jamas [h]e tenido cien pesos de sobra para poder tratar y contratar con ellos . . . andando siempre adeudado y enpeñado como lo estoy al

pres[en]te pagando censos y baratas que se [h]an [h]echo para la paga del d[ic]ho oficio."

96. On the acquisition of such shared understandings, see Bourdieu's concept of *habitus* in his *Outline of a Theory of Practice*; see also de Certeau, *The Practice of Everyday Life*.

97. Each Audiencia had one, and notaries were supposed to post it in their workplaces. Fee tables (*aranceles*) themselves are elusive; see, however, the Guatemalan one reproduced in Luján Muñoz, *Los escribanos en las Indias Occidentales y en particular en el Reino de Guatemala*, 157–70; also AGI, Charcas, 16, ramo 24, n. 116, which specifies that sixteenth-century cabildo notaries of Potosí might charge from four *tomines* to one peso per page, depending on the type of document. For historical context, see Guajardo-Fajardo Carmona, *Escribanos en Indias durante la primera mitad del siglo XVI*, 1:229–45.

98. See Herzog, *Mediación, archivos y ejercicio*, 51–52, on the fines Quito's seventeenth-century notaries faced.

99. Parry, *The Sale of Public Office in the Spanish Indies under the Hapsburgs*, 70.

100. AGN, Real Audiencia, Causas Criminales, legajo 3, 1658, cuaderno 4, fols. I–I V.

101. It is unclear from Spanish notaries' wills what they brought with them and what they obtained locally, and they invested their resources very differently; some invested much more in Cuzco than others. Yet I have not seen a Spanish notary describe himself as "poor" except for the unfortunate Pérez de Vargas.

102. Luis de Quesada's son, Gerónimo Sánchez de Quesada, also knew Quechua. See ARC-PN, Martín López de Paredes, protocolo 144 (1659), fols. 831v and 936–37v, for examples of document making in which the notary himself served as interpreter for the Quechua-speaking *otorgantes*.

103. In a 1704 codicil to his will, the numerary notary Cristóbal de Bustamante pleads for his debtors to forgive him "because he is poor, burdened with a wife and many children, and with no means whatsoever to repay them." ARC-PN, Gregorio Básquez Serrano, protocolo 51 (1704), fol. 172v. The will suggests that lawsuits over his handling of an estate for which he served as executor strained his resources. Ibid., fols. 164v–65, 169v. Cf. González Cruz, *Escribanos y notarios en Huelva durante el antiguo régimen (1701–1800)*, who finds similarly diverse circumstances among the notaries of eighteenth-century Huelva; according to their wills, about a third of them ended their days in penury.

104. For comparative perspective, see esp. Hardwick, *The Practice of Patriarchy*.

105. It is still difficult to judge Francisco de la Fuente's case. Some of the testimony taken from residencia witnesses supports his case that the Espinosas were menacing figures who held a terrorized city in their thrall. What seems clear is that this particular "power group" had turned against De la Fuente by the mid-1590s. By 1596 Francisco de la Fuente had decided that the best defense was a good offense. He

must have succeeded after a time. He was still in jail as late as January 1598, but some years thereafter he resumed his place as cabildo notary in Cuzco.

106. De la Fuente, after all, had some powerful allies; the documents note that an uncle of his, Pedro Álvarez de Solórzano, was a judge in the Audiencia of Chile. AGN, Real Audiencia, Causas Civiles, legajo 48, 1619, cuaderno 184, fols. 95–99.

107. AGN, Real Audiencia, Causas Civiles, legajo 22, 1585, cuaderno 115, petition presented in Lima on July 7, 1585. One wonders if Ruiz would have been denounced if he had kept up payments on the piece of cabildo property he had annexed to himself.

108. Guaman Poma, *El primer nueva corónica y buen gobierno*, 2:655–56. In a roundabout way, notaries' wills often confirm this by making restitution to particular indigenous communities, presumably for things taken and enjoyed but never paid for: e.g., that of Pedro de la Carrera Ron.

109. Guaman Poma, *El primer nueva corónica y buen gobierno*, 2:677.

3. Custom

1. See Millares Carlo, *Tratado de paleografía española* 3:408, for common abbreviations.

2. Handwriting did shift in the course of the sixteenth and seventeenth centuries from the cursive known as *cortesana* to a more "degenerate" version known as *procesal*, and the even more rapid, rounded *encadenada*: see Cortés Alonso, *La escritura y lo escrito*, 12, 24; and Millares Carlo, *Tratado de paleografía española*, 1:235. But protocolos from similar periods look very much alike, as I was able to see in archival records of Seville, Lisbon, Puebla, Lima, and Cuzco from the sixteenth and seventeenth centuries.

3. See K. Burns, "Notaries, Truth, and Consequences"; and Carolyn Dean, "Beyond Prescription."

4. "Otorongo inga corcoroba" (literally "Inca hunchback jaguar," in a mix of Spanish and Quechua) and "oficial Oturunco falsso ynca hierro Bolssa micha" (a string of insults not easily translated; it contains another Quechua "jaguar" as well as a "false Inca").

5. There may have been some exceptions among the earliest notaries of Spanish America, as the crown was still granting offices as patrimonial favors to favorites. On the whole, though, AGI records from the 1500s and 1600s confirming titles to notarial offices are clear: practicing notaries in Spanish America learned their jobs from an early age, whether in Spain or in the Americas.

6. AGI, Lima, 178, n. 20, fol. 1v. In a later example, AGN, Superior Gobierno, legajo 13, 1769, cuaderno 305, fol. 14, José de Palacios testified in 1769 that at "the age of ten or twelve," he had entered the workshop of the Cuzco notary Pedro José Gamarra to learn how to read and write.

7. AGI, Lima, 178, n. 20, fol. 6v. González then served another stint as an assistant to the notary of the Audiencia in Panama City. Once in Lima, he worked as head assistant to a notary (*oficial mayor*) before seeking his own credentials. By then he had already been at it for fifteen years, not an unusual amount of preparation. See also AGI, Lima, 178, n. 12, on Alonso Beltrán Lucero; and ibid., n. 15, on Joan de Quirós.

8. AGN, Superior Gobierno, legajo 17, 1782, cuaderno 461, fols. 4v–13. One of Gamarra's apprentices, José de Palacios, also writes of working his way up, in AGN, Superior Gobierno, legajo 13, 1769, cuaderno 305, fol. 14: Gamarra, Palacios testified, "viendo mi aplicacion y adelantam[ien]to no solo en escrivir, si no tambien en estender es[critu]ras e inteligenciarme de los demas autos, y papeles de su oficina, se anheló a enseñarme y documentarme con amor y cuydado, de modo que llegue a ser su oficial mayor."

9. Lockhart, *Spanish Peru 1532–1560*, 70. This apprenticeship was not usually formalized by contract, and copyists were rarely referred to as "apprentices." Serving a notary in Baroque Rome was similar: see Nussdorfer, "The Boys at the Banco," and her *Brokers of Public Trust*, chap. 5: "The Office." Likewise becoming a clerk or scrivener in Elizabethan England: see Brooks, *Pettyfoggers and Vipers of the Commonwealth*, 154.

10. See, e.g., AGN, Real Audiencia, Causas Criminales, legajo 9, 1741, cuaderno 70A, fols. 13–15. Witnesses testified that Francisco de Guzmán, who was accused of stealing papers from the notary he served, had worked in his boss's home as well as his office. See also ARC, Corregimiento, Causas Ordinarias, legajo 34 (1742), expediente 720, cuaderno 6, in which Alejo Gonzáles Peñaloza, a royal notary of Cuzco, has his assets seized; the inventory (fols. 8–11) discloses that he kept much (if not all) of his archive at home.

11. See the case of Doña Francisca Calvo Justiniano, ARC, Corregimiento, Causas Ordinarias, legajo 34 (1742), expediente 720, who died just as her *poder para testar* was being finalized; one witness testified that she had sent a servant out to round up "the first white men she encountered" to witness the document (fol. 59). The notary Alejo Gonzáles Peñaloza was accused of falsification; for more on this case, see chapter 4.

12. See, in addition to the above, ARC, Cabildo, Justicia Ordinaria, Causas Civiles, legajo 17 (1716–29), expediente 494 (1728). See also ARC-PN, Joan de Saldaña, protocolo 297 (1686), fols. 630–31, declaración of December 20, 1686 by Don Diego González de Alarcón about the controversial circumstances surrounding the will of the corregidor of Paucarcolla, Don Francisco Antonio Pareja de Rabago.

13. See ARC-PN, Francisco de Unzueta, protocolo 257 (1713–14), fol. 316–316v, in which Bernardo de Benavente, longtime oficial mayor to the Cuzco notary Joan de Saldaña, recounts an outing to a client's house (discussed further in chapter 5) in which, as apprentice, he carried Saldaña's draft book and inkwell. See also ARC,

Corregimiento, Causas Criminales, legajo 77 (1582–1693), expediente of October 15, 1672, fol. 17, in which Sebastián Correa Palomino, who was briefly an apprentice to the Cuzco notary Bartolomé López Barnuevo, declares that "when he went to the office, he sat in the corner where the apprentices sit, and he never handled any papers because the others would not let him."

14. ARC, Cabildo, Justicia Ordinaria, Causas Civiles, legajo 12 (1690–94), expediente 329 (1690), "Autos ejecutivos seguidos por Juan Francisco Luyando, escribano de Su Magestad," fol. 14.

15. One witness indicated that the two shared the same bedroom: ARC, Cabildo, Justicia Ordinaria, Causas Civiles, legajo 38 (1773), expediente 925, "Autos seguidos por el teniente coronel Don Joseph de Tapia y Sarmiento, escribano de S.M."

16. According to the anonymous author of a Spanish manual, *Pirothecnia entretenida, curiosa y agradable de fuegos recreativos, con varias invenciones y secretos, y algunas ideas generales, para que cada uno pueda formarse otras á su modo*, one needed many things to make fireworks (*cohetes*), including "ordinary paper" (82).

17. AGN, Real Audiencia, Causas Criminales, legajo 9, 1741, cuaderno 70A, fols. 8v–9v.

18. AGN, Superior Gobierno, legajo 17, 1782, cuaderno 461, fols. 100v–101.

19. Ibid., fol. 102v.

20. This, too, was an old pattern: see Lockhart, *Spanish Peru 1532–1560*, 73–74. The 1769 testimony of Pedro José Gamarra about his former oficial mayor José de Palacios provides a good job description: "Tubo a su cuydado todos los papeles, Protocolos, y Autos desempeñando la confianza, y en especial en estender las Escripturas, y coordinar los Registros de ellas, y ponerlos en orden, y abecedarlos con toda legalidad, y limpiesa sin que Yo tubiese que notarle." AGN, Superior Gobierno, legajo 13, 1769, cuaderno 305, fol. 14v.

21. Penmen, too, might have theirs: see ARC-PN, Joan de Saldaña, protocolo 297 (1686), fols. 330–330v, June 19, 1686, in which Juan Agustín Cárdenas, "oficial plumario," acknowledged receipt of 80 pesos from Gregorio Díez de Lanta Ron, who bought cattle from him in the province of Chumbivilcas.

22. See Dean, "Beyond Prescription," esp. 299–308, 313–16. For a sense of the work of Pedro Díaz Morante, a famous calligrapher of Madrid whose work circulated widely, and that of his contemporaries Giuliano Sellari and Leopardo Antonozzi, see *Pictorial Calligraphy and Ornamentation*.

23. The verse at the top of figure 15 reads, "Soy el gentil Porroa valiente / / / De levita antigua vestido / / / el mas grosero y atrevido / / / y de este oficio incapie permanente"; on Porroa's frock is inscribed "Porroitas machuchas / / / viejecito maldito orejudo / / / haciendo incapie permanente."

24. "The notary did not do the bulk of the writing himself," as Lockhart notes in *Spanish Peru 1532–1560*, 70; "that was the task of an aide," typically "a young man who had not yet acquired his notary's title."

25. The term is a complicated one, as reflected in Covarrubias's entry, *Tesoro de la lengua castellana o española*, 366–67, which relies largely on axioms to convey meaning. "Costumbre" might refer to a woman's menstrual period; additionally, "La costumbre haze ley, entiéndese quando no [h]ay ley en contrario, ni repugna a la razón y justicia" (366). On the legal definition of custom, see Tau Anzoátegui, *El poder de la costumbre*.

26. *Las Siete Partidas*, 2:122 (Partida 3, Título 19, ley 1).

27. Guajardo-Fajardo Carmona, *Escribanos en Indias durante la primera mitad del siglo XVI*, 1:134–36. Numerous examples are presented throughout the text.

28. The phrase is Clanchy's: *From Memory to Written Record*, 305.

29. Dean, "Beyond Prescription."

30. See Pérez Landero Otañez y Castro, *Practica de visitas*, on how official inspections of notaries should be conducted; among the questions that should be asked: Did notaries have people sign things in blank?

31. Herzog, *Mediación, archivos y ejercicio*, 56, notes that Quito authorities did occasionally condemn a notary to exemplary punishment. In one 1732 case (56n102), a notary's assistant falsified a signature on an overdue document, the draft of which had been lost; as a result, the notary's practice was suspended for two years. However, this was not typical treatment, and the fines assessed and risks run may have been considered by notaries a reasonable opportunity cost.

32. The blank page might also be loose, to be bound into a register later. See, e.g., the testimony of the Cuzco notary Cristóbal de Lucero in a lengthy lawsuit concerning a dowry document, AGI, Escribanía 508A, fol. 27: "Se tiene por costumbre quando se vá á hazer, y otorgar semejantes escrituras de dote a las casas de los otorgantes, otorgarlas en papel suelto, por no llevar los registros los Escrivanos, y despues las ponen en el."

33. Herzog, *Mediación, archivos y ejercicio*, 55, also notes "blank pages with signatures and no contents," squeezed-in handwriting, and half-completed records in the notarial registers of mid-colonial Quito.

34. Pérez Landero Otañez y Castro, *Practica de visitas*, fol. 187.

35. Occasionally one appears: see AGN, Pedro Pérez Landero, protocolo 1510 (1696A), which has a small leather-bound draft book of *minutas* inserted before the table of contents. For useful insight into the history of such draft books, see Escriche, *Diccionario razonado de legislación civil, penal, comercial y forense, con citas del derecho, notas y adiciones por el licenciado Juan Rodríguez de San Miguel*, 440, entry for "minutario."

36. Moreno Trujillo, in "Diplomática notarial en Granada en los inícios de la modernidad (1505–1520)," 81, notes that "la Pragmática [de 1503] admite que se tomen *las tales escrituras por registro o memorial o en otra manera*, es decir, alguna clase o especie de borrador podía ser empleado por el notario en el desempeño de su labor."

37. ARC-PN, Miguel de Contreras, protocolo 5 (1596–97), fol. 1353v.

38. Herzog, *Mediación, archivos y ejercicio*, 55: "En Quito proliferó la práctica según la cual los escribanos recibían la firma de los otorgantes en blanco para luego insertar en el espacio libre el contenido del instrumento, haciendo que las dos cosas (texto y firma) parecieran coetáneas aunque no lo fueran." In one inspection visit, she notes, all of Quito's notaries were fined for doing this, and all said, like De la Fuente, that it would be impossible to run their businesses any other way.

39. AAL, Apelaciones del Cuzco, legajo 4, expediente 14 (1639), appeal "en nombre del Bachiller Cristóbal Vargas de Carvajal de Ocampo, cura de Poma-canche," fol. 47, testimony of witness Pedro Bazán.

40. Ibid., fol. 52.

41. Days might pass before all the steps were completed and a contract pro-duced—enough time for the parties to become anxious about the notary's work, change their minds, even sue between the draft and final copy. See, e.g., AGN, Real Audiencia, Causas Civiles, legajo 237, 1681, cuaderno 887, "Autos seguidos por el Maestre de Campo D. Pedro Gutiérrez de Quintanilla contra el Monasterio de Santa Clara de la ciudad de Huamanga" (about which more in chapter 4).

42. See AGI, Escribanía, 508B (1634), a lengthy lawsuit in which witnesses testified about notarial practice, among other things: "Los escrivanos otorgando las escripturas fuera de sus oficios y aun estando en ellas las toman en papel suelto y luego las agregan a sus rregistros y esto lo [h]a visto hazer este testigo muchas vezes" (253v); "todos los escrivanos rresciven e toman algunas escripturas quando se otorgan fuera de sus oficios y en ellos en papel suelto y luego hazen rregistro dellas y lo [h]a visto como perssona que [h]a negociado en los d[ic]hos oficios" (259v–260).

43. Chartier, "Texts, Printing, Readings," 165.

44. AAL, Apelaciones del Cuzco, legajo 4, expediente 14 (1639), fols. 42–44.

45. AGN, Real Audiencia, Causas Civiles, legajo 70, 1732, cuaderno 541, fol. 11. The notary asserts his innocence of the charges, but Villalobos claims that the minuta presented (fols. 8–10v) is not the original one, but a made-up version created later as cover. The minuta is written in the first person and crossed through, which is what a penman typically did after writing out a fully developed draft in the notarial register.

46. ARC-PN, Miguel de Contreras, protocolo 5 (1596–97), fols. 1360v–61.

47. Ibid., fol. 1360v.

48. See also *Protocolos de los escribanos de Santiago*, which contains a similar abundance of extrajudicial business involving merchants and merchandise: pow-ers of attorney, *obligaciones*, sales, and more.

49. See the 1690 lawsuit in AGN, Real Audiencia, Causas Civiles, legajo 269, 1690, cuaderno 1016, over a broken sales contract that revealed interest taking. See also V. Cummins, "The Church and Business Practices in Late Sixteenth Century

Mexico," esp. 428–36; Tomás de Mercado, *Suma de tratos y contratos.* Tapia Franco cites Lima examples of usurious contracts in "Análisis histórico institucional del censo consignativo en el derecho peruano."

50. Covarrubias, *Tesoro de la lengua castellana o española,* 809. The picaresque Guzmán gives a tutorial on mohatras: Alemán, *Guzmán de Alfarache,* Segunda Parte, Libro 3, capítulo 2, esp. 2:367–76. See also Escriche, *Diccionario razonado de legislación civil, penal, comercial y forense,* 440. I thank Elvira Vilches for her help on the intricacies of early modern credit.

51. V. Cummins, "The Church and Business Practices in Late Sixteenth Century Mexico," 436.

52. See ARC, Cabildo, Justicia Ordinaria, Causas Civiles, legajo 38 (1773), expediente 937, cuaderno 15, for the case of Pedro José Gamarra, who drew up documents for the nuns of Santa Clara to satisfy his censo payments. By 1773 he was dead and his heirs were years behind on payments, despite the nuns' efforts to convince them to pay up.

53. ARC-PN, Lorenzo de Mesa Andueza, protocolo 194 (1661), fols. 1412–13v, August 13, 1661.

54. See, e.g., Nussdorfer, *Brokers of Public Trust,* chap. 5; she finds that "Roman notaries vigorously participated in the credit market," as did their employees. See also Hoffman, Postel-Vinay, and Rosenthal, "Private Credit Markets in Paris, 1690–1840," 293–306, and "Information and Economic History," 69–94; and on the money lending of English scriveners ca. 1600, Brooks, *Pettyfoggers and Vipers of the Commonwealth,* 44.

55. Hardwick, *The Practice of Patriarchy,* 34–35.

56. K. Burns, *Colonial Habits,* 137.

57. Ibid., 138–39.

58. Hardwick, *The Practice of Patriarchy,* 41, finds that "notarial credit brokering became commonplace in the sixteenth and seventeenth centuries." People accepted it "as a matter of practicality"—although she also notes, 38, that "notaries' handling of deposited money between receiving it and lending it could call into question the ideals of notarial objectivity and disinterestedness." There was certainly "potential for malpractice."

59. ARC, Asuntos Eclesiásticos, Junta de Consolidación, legajo 86 (1806–7), expediente 9, June 18, 1806.

60. Pérez Landero Otañez y Castro, *Practica de visitas,* fols. 187–88.

61. ARC-PN, Miguel de Contreras, protocolo 5 (1596–97); Herzog, *Mediación, archivos y ejercicio,* 51–52.

62. Víctor Tau Anzoátegui, *El poder de la costumbre,* shows how important a place custom had in Spanish and Spanish American legality in the sixteenth and seventeenth centuries as a recognized source of law; see also Cutter, *The Legal Culture of Northern New Spain,* esp. chap. 2.

63. Note that he did not have to specify his reasoning. On the determination and sentencing of penal cases, see Herzog, *Upholding Justice*, 47–49.

64. Manual writers provided the proper form for this delegation of responsibility to the notary: the *comisión*. See, e.g., Monterroso, *Pratica civil, y criminal, e instruction de scrivanos*, fol. 14v.

65. For instance, in ARC-PN, Martín López de Paredes, protocolo 134 (1649–50), fols. 144v–45, September 18, 1649, López de Paredes attests that he accompanied Cuzco's constables and a surgeon to inspect the corpse of a murder victim, a black man "they said was named Juan Angola." See also ARC, Corregimiento, Causas Criminales, legajo 78 (1700–45), expediente *de oficio*, August 16, 1745, fol. 1: notary Juan Bautista Gamarra is dispatched with a "médico cirujano" to another murder scene.

66. Álvarez Posadilla, *Practica criminal por principios, o modo y forma de instruir los procesos criminales en sumario de las causas de oficio de justicia contra los abusos introducidos*, 1–2.

67. See, e.g., Juan y Colom, *Instrucción de escribanos en orden a lo judicial*, 33.

68. Gutiérrez, *Practica criminal de España*, 269.

69. ARC-PN, Miguel de Contreras, protocolo 5 (1596–97), fol. 1353.

70. According to Nussdorfer, *Brokers of Public Trust*, chap. 3, "The Laws," Roman notaries' assistants might also be involved in the actual writing of judicial records.

71. In theory, a finished deposition was read back to the witness and then signed by her if she felt it corresponded to her testimony. See, however, the orphaned witness's signature in a series of depositions, with no testimony filled in: ARC, Cabildo, Justicia Ordinaria, Causas Civiles, legajo 14 (1700–1704), expediente 431 (1704), cuaderno 25, fols. 4–4v.

72. AGN, Real Audiencia, Causas Criminales, legajo 3, 1727, cuaderno 21, "Causa criminal seguida contra D. Francisco de los Ríos y Quevedo, D. Francisco Arias de Saavedra, Dr. D. Juan de Mendoza, D. Alejo Fernández Escudero y otros por el delito de homicidio el primero y concusión los restantes," fols. 6–6v.

73. Ibid., fols. 6v–7.

74. Ibid., fol. 251.

75. Ibid., fol. 209v.

76. Ibid., fols. 7v–8, testimony of Don Pedro Rioseco.

77. This is precisely the practice that Monterroso decries in his *Pratica civil, y criminal, e instruction de scrivanos*, fol. 7v.

78. Covarrubias, *Tesoro de la lengua castellana o española*, 541, "escrivir."

79. Ibid., 739, "instruir."

80. Nussdorfer's work on the youthful notarial employees of Baroque Rome (known as *giovani* or *sostituti*) also makes this clear; see *Brokers of Public Trust*, 168: "Most employees, especially those in their teens and twenties, did not stay long

with any given notary; six or seven month stints were not unheard of, and parish census data suggests that two years was common." Elsewhere in the same chapter, Nussdorfer observes: "Perhaps the greatest threat to [a notary's] solvency . . . was the inescapable result of the expanded size of venal offices and the Roman scribal labor market: ignorant, incompetent or immoral employees" (195).

81. AGN, Superior Gobierno, legajo 13, 1769, cuaderno 305, fol. 4.

4. Power in the Archives

1. AGI, Escribanía, 509B (1634), fol. 12, according to Cuzco numerary notary public Luis Díez de Morales.

2. Under Spanish law, a wife's dowry was not considered a part of her husband's assets, even though he was legally empowered to administer her dowry goods.

3. AGI, Escribanía, 509B (1634), fols. 15–16.

4. Ibid., fol. 16v.

5. ARC-PN, Joan de Quirós, protocolo 14 (1583), fols. 741–43v, November 21, 1583.

6. For instance, ARC-PN, Alonso Beltrán Lucero, protocolo 4 (1636–37), fol. 1048v: the 1637 will of the Cuzco notary Alonso Calvo lists two secret *mandas*, or bequests.

7. ARC, Lorenzo Mesa Andueza, protocolo 177 (1650), fol. 96[?] (page no. broken off), July 11, 1650.

8. Albornoz, *Arte de los contractos* , fol. 52.

9. Ibid., fol. 52v.

10. Ibid.

11. Ibid.

12. Yrolo Calar, *La política de escrituras*, 104.

13. Ibid., 105.

14. People recognized this at the time: Mercado, for instance, observes in *Suma de tratos y contratos* that for all the abundant silver production of the Indies, there "great penury is felt, because many days may go by before a bit of silver appears" (2:360).

15. Lockhart, *Spanish Peru 1532–1560*, 81, notices the "strong element of fiction" in commercial transactions, but indicates merchants owned little property; indeed, he says, "merchants tried to avoid . . . extensive investment in real estate" (80). Technically perhaps so, but this appearance could have been produced through confidence games of the sort I am tracing here.

16. ARC, Alonso Beltrán Lucero, protocolo 4 (1636–37), fols. 1050v–51.

17. Clients might also change parties' names so as to use one transaction to pay off the debt owed from a separate, unrelated transaction.

18. ARC, Martín López de Paredes, protocolo 137 (1652), fols. 1208–11v. My thanks to Gabriela Ramos for providing me the reference to this transaction.

19. One's will might be used to set the record straight: see, for example, that of Don Rodrigo de Esquivel, AGI, Escribanía, 508B (1634), fols. 53v–54.

20. V. Cummins, "The Church and Business Practices in Late Sixteenth Century Mexico," 436.

21. Ibid., 424.

22. See, e.g., AGN, Real Audiencia, Causas Civiles, legajo 269, 1690, cuaderno 1016, a Lima case from 1690 in which one man sues another for failing to follow through on a contract and sell textiles within four months for a price that included 20 pesos "por raçon de ynteres" (fol. 1). The defendant testified that he did not recall any interest (fol. 3v); unfortunately, the case is incomplete and the outcome unclear.

23. See Real Díaz, *Estudio diplomática del documento indiano*, 21, on *subrepción* and the closely related *obrepción* (involving the withholding of key information); see also Joaquín Escriche, *Diccionario razonado de legislación civil, penal, comercial y forense*, 479 and 651. On the medieval basis of the prohibition of such fraud, see *Las Siete Partidas*, Partida 3, Título 18, ley 36, "De las cartas que son ganadas por engaño."

24. See Hardwick, *The Practice of Patriarchy*, 36, for details of curious cases, including that of a notary who allegedly fell asleep in the midst of counting a client's money.

25. As Real Díaz points out in *Estudio diplomática del documento indiano*, 21, the authenticity of a notarized document does not guarantee its historical truthfulness; it may be the product of subrepción or obrepción. Notaries might not be at fault if their clients were perpetrating frauds on one another, but the notarial literature insisted that they be vigilant nevertheless.

26. ARC-PN, Gregorio Básquez Serrano, protocolo 51 (1704), fols. 100v–101.

27. I examine the use of exclamations more fully in "Forms of Authority," 149–63, drawing on eighteen cases registered before Cuzco notaries: eleven by women, six by men, and one by a married couple.

28. ARC-PN, Alonso Beltrán Lucero (1642–43), fol. 179v, July 16, 1642.

29. Ibid.

30. As van Deusen makes clear, this was a difficult course to pursue; see *Between the Sacred and the Worldly*, esp. chaps. 3 and 4. See also Mannarelli, *Private Passions and Public Sins*, esp. chap. 4; and Arrom, *The Women of Mexico City, 1790–1857*.

31. ARC-PN, Alonso Beltrán Lucero (1642–43), fols. 7–8v, January 14, 1643.

32. *Las Siete Partidas*, 3:68–69 (Partida 5, Título 11, ley 28). Albornoz, *Arte de los contractos*, 7v, writes that "impossible contracts" include those made in a state of "just fear" (*miedo justo*): "fear of death, or of bodily torture, or loss of a limb, or of infamy, and the like." By contrast, contracts made under fear "they call vain [*vano*]" are valid. Escriche, *Diccionario razonado de legislación civil, penal, comercial y*

forense, 437–38 (citing Partida 7, Título 3, ley 7), uses slightly different terms, differentiating between *miedo grave* vs. *miedo leve*; according to him, *miedo reverential* does not rise to the level of "grave fear." For more on "reverential fear" and its uses, see Premo, *Children of the Father King*. The phrase "weapon of the weak" I borrow from Scott, *Weapons of the Weak*.

33. Carvajal, *Instruccion y memorial para escrivanos y juezes executores, assi en lo criminal como cevil, y escripturas publicas*, fols. 112–112v.

34. Ibid., fol. 112v.

35. *Reclamación, exclamación*, and *declaración* might be used to name the same form. See Amezúa y Mayo, *La vida privada española en el protocolo notarial*, 70–72, for late sixteenth-century examples.

36. ARC-PN, Gregorio Básquez Serrano, protocolo 51 (1704), fol. 56. For extra protection, the document indicates, she had already registered a separate exclamation with the notary Juan Flores de Bastidas.

37. Bakewell, in *Silver and Entrepreneurship in Seventeenth-Century Potosí*, 42, raises this possibility in the case of the desperate Captain Francisco Gómez de la Rocha of Potosí, who was accused of serious crimes: "Even his wife had refused his request, in mid-September 1649, to become a co-guarantor of his debts." In a footnote, Bakewell cites as evidence the wife's *exclamación* against her husband, and observes that "the possibility cannot be discounted, of course, that her refusal . . . was a device to safeguard family possessions" (195–96).

38. On the other hand, Doña Micaela might have known enough about her husband's business to realize that she could register this form of protest against him in the event of violence. One key to interpreting this "exclamation" could be the relationship between her notary, Alonso Beltrán Lucero, and her husband: were they friendly rivals or distant rivals? The will of Juan Flores de Bastidas has not yet turned up, unfortunately; that of Beltrán Lucero is fairly brief and does not mention him: ARC-PN, Alonso Beltran Lucero, protocolo 10 (1646–49), fols. 55–58, will of September 9, 1642.

39. ARC-PN, Pedro de Cáceres, protocolo 30 (1684), fol. 558, September 6, 1684.

40. Ibid., fols. 910–910v.

41. Ibid., fols. 2–2v, January 2, 1696.

42. Ibid., fols. 157–157v, March 10, 1695.

43. ARC-PN, Gregorio Básquez Serrano, protocolo 52 (1705), fol. 53, February 26, 1705.

44. ARC-PN, Joan de Saldaña, protocolo 297 (1686), fol. 435, June 8, 1686.

45. They were in a position to spread the news when a loan had been repaid and fresh capital was available for lending, when an estate was about to be auctioned, and so forth (see chapter 3).

46. Twinam's *Public Lives, Private Secrets* underlines the importance of keeping dishonorable matters, such as out-of-wedlock pregnancy, within the family circle;

if successful, "private pregnancy" kept a woman's reputation intact. Given the importance of keeping dishonorable things secret, perhaps commissioning a notary to register domestic violence was occasionally dangerous.

47. Men's self-representations in exclamations remind us that patriarchy also controlled many kinds of male subjects—hence the "pusillanimous" man; the good, obedient, filial son; and so forth.

48. ARC-PN, Francisco de Unzueta, protocolo 257 (1713–14), fol. 418v, April 12, 1714, petition by Doña Bárbara Antonia de Carrión y Mogrovejo, widow of Don Fernando de Cartagena.

49. See van Deusen, *Between the Sacred and the Worldly*, chaps. 3 and 4.

50. Changes of ink *within* a page are fairly common, however, and might indicate that a penman got tired (or was assigned to complete other business).

51. See, e.g., AGN-PN, Gregorio de Urtazo, protocolo 1906 (1696A), fols. 532–35v, distrato dated May 27, 1696, to undo a prior sales contract. See also AGN-PN, Pedro Pérez Landero, protocolo 1510 (1696A), fols. 30v–31 v, distrato de venta. I have never seen a distrato in Cuzco's archives; Cuzco notaries typically used the margins of documents as the space for cancellation.

52. There was always the possibility of the codicil for less drastic revisions. For Italian cases of the use of wills, see Benadusi, "Investing the Riches of the Poor."

53. ARC-PN, Luis Díez de Morales, protocolo 77 (1633), fol. 652. She had gone against her father's will in marrying her first spouse, Juan de la Concha, in Lima. After his death, she inherited his property and entered into a second marriage, to the Cuzco notary Francisco de la Fuente. At some point before leaving Lima, she gave in to her father's demands that she leave a will, registering it before the Lima notary Pedro González de Contreras.

54. AGN, Real Audiencia, Causas Civiles, legajo 237, 1681, cuaderno 887, fols. 45–45v. The documentation is inconclusive, but it seems likely the nuns got a final contract worded the way they wanted.

55. He claimed his wife had hidden the receipts that showed he had, in fact, made payments. AGI, Escribanía, 510A (1645).

56. AGN, Real Audiencia, Causas Civiles, legajo 257, 1688, cuaderno 965, fols. 4–4v.

57. ARC, Corregimiento, Causas Ordinarias, legajo 26 (1691–92), expediente 528 (1691). For a later attempt to have a document set aside based on the signer's illness and the forcing of his consent, see the case of Don Ramón Vicente Tronconis in ARC, Intendencia, Causas Ordinarias, legajo 5, expediente 14 (1785), fol. 7.

58. ARC, Corregimiento, Causas Ordinarias, legajo 34 (1742), expediente 720, cuaderno 6; witnesses' testimony begins on fol. 3v, the notary's version on fols. 6–7, and the corregidor's order on fol. 196v. The corregidor ordered a new *poder* to be drawn up for the deceased under the instructions of the friar who had been her spiritual advisor and confidant.

59. AAL, Apelaciones del Cuzco, XL:1 (1708–16), fol. 4.

60. Ibid., fols. 4–4v.

61. Verdicts were frequently appealed, moreover, making it even harder to know whose arguments ultimately prevailed.

62. In the summer of 2002, I looked in what seemed the most fruitful place: the well-organized divorce appeals from Cuzco in Lima's Archivo Arzobispal. I gave up, however, after a slow search turned up abundant allegations of violence, but no exclamations. NB: those trying to trace a particular person's affairs can now check the indices of useful catalogs of Cuzco's judicial records; see Decoster and Bauer, *Justicia y poder* (1997).

63. See ARC, Cabildo, Justicia Ordinaria, Causas Civiles, legajo 17 (1716–29), expediente 465 (1719), in which Doña Petrona Gonzáles accuses her half-brother Juan Godines of having duped her into signing a document that cheated her out of a portion of her inheritance; the language on fol. 1v. is the same as that of an exclamation. The verdict is missing, unfortunately, but this case suggests that plaintiffs might indeed mobilize exclamations in the context of lawsuits. Whether or not exclamations worked in a given case may not be clear, but it is likely they worked in *some* cases or people would have used other tactics instead.

64. Diego de la Coba, in turn, adduced his own titles, and the legal claims went back and forth: ARC, Corregimiento, Causas Ordinarias, legajo 22 (1680–84), expediente 459 (1682), cuaderno 9.

65. Ibid. (1691–92), expediente 527 (1691), cuaderno 8, fol. 25.

66. ARC, Cabildo, Justicia Ordinaria, Causas Civiles, legajo 14 (1700–1704), expediente 423 (1702), cuaderno 17.

67. ARC, Corregimiento, Causas Ordinarias, legajo 26 (1691–92), expediente 531 (1692), cuaderno 12, fols. 59–59v. Covarrubias, *Tesoro de la lengua castellana o española*, 898 (under *recaudar*), indicates that a *recaudo* could be either a payment ("el cobro que se da de una cosa") or a message requesting a response.

68. ARC, Corregimiento, Causas Ordinarias, legajo 26 (1691–92), expediente 531 (1692), cuaderno 12, fol. 87, verdict of April 16, 1696.

69. ARC-PN, Juan Flores de Bastidas, protocolo 107 (1675–80), fols. 200–200v.

70. ARC, Corregimiento, Causas Criminales, legajo 77 (1582–1693), expediente of October 15, 1672, fol. 1v.

71. Ibid., fol. 11v.

72. Ibid., fol. 13, testimony of Matías Maceo against Martín de la Borda and Sebastián Correa.

73. See also ibid., expediente of 1660: Don Francisco Tito Condemayta, *gobernador* of the town of Copacabana, accuses his adversary, Juan de Larraíncar, of having negotiated with the penmen of the notarial office where the records of their trial were kept, "so that they would give them to him, as in effect they did give them to him," leaving Don Francisco "defenseless" (s/f).

74. Covarrubias, *Tesoro de la lengua castellana o española*, 785–86, notes that *mano* has many meanings and is used in "infinite" figures of speech; among those he gives first: "Tener mano, tener poder" (786). See Rowe, *Dead Hands*.

75. AGN, Derecho Indígena, legajo 12, 1718, cuaderno 213, fol. 1v.

76. Guajardo-Fajardo Carmona, *Escribanos en Indias durante la primera mitad del siglo XVI*, 1:248, cites the medieval Castilian Fuero Real as well as the Siete Partidas on this point: "Porque el oficio de escribano es . . . público, honrado y común, hagan las escrituras a todos sin dejarlo de ejecutar por amor, desamor, miedo o vergüenza."

77. ARC, Cabildo, Justicia Ordinaria, Causas Civiles, legajo 14 (1700–1714), expediente 433 (1704), cuaderno 27, fol. 1. Bartola Ignacia Sisa repaid the loan using textiles valued at 100 pesos.

78. AGI, Escribanía, 508A and 508B.

79. For its terms, see AGI, Escribanía 508A, fols. 37v–39.

80. Ibid., fol. 64v.

81. Ibid., fols. 64v–65.

5. Archives as Chessboards

1. Mallon, for example, in "The Promise and Dilemma of Subaltern Studies," notes "the historian's disciplinary interest in reading documents as 'windows,' however foggy and imperfect, on people's lives" (1506).

2. See González Echevarría, *Myth and Archive*, 59: "The give and take of legal language issues from its very dialectical and polemical nature. No utterance can occur in legal proceedings without assuming a question or a response. . . . This is no theoretical dialogue, however, but one that is part of legal rhetoric itself; truth, existence in the civil sense, propriety, all emerge from such a confrontation." See also ibid., 8–10, for useful comment on Bakhtin's influential work and its limitations, and Ginzburg, "The Inquisitor as Anthropologist," in his *Clues, Myths, and the Historical Method*, esp. 159–60.

3. The history of chess makes this metaphor especially appropriate: introduced into Iberia by the Moors, it was described in the landmark *Libro de juegos* commissioned by the same thirteenth-century king, Alfonso X, who is associated with the *Siete Partidas*. Chess grew popular in Mediterranean Europe in the late fifteenth century, and the earliest printed book about it was printed in Salamanca in 1497: Luis Ramírez de Lucena's *Repetición de amores y arte de ajedrez*.

4. As Starn points out in "Truths in the Archives," 400, "Diplomatic frankly acknowledges that the archives compound truth with misrepresentation and that archives are products of formal protocols, institutional arrangements, more or less explicit intentions, and historical circumstances of their formation and preservation" (400). If we're open to the notion of sources as constructed texts, we can

use these guides to the construction process. See, for example, the excellent work of Cortés Alonso, esp. *La escritura y lo escrito.*

5. Lockhart, "Between the Lines," in *Of Things of the Indies*, 255.

6. ARC-PN, Pedro López de la Cerda, protocolo 193 (1701), fols. 1024–26v, donation of December 1, 1701. The house was left to Doña Clara and Doña Inés Ñucay by the terms of the 1694 will of their mother, Doña Isabel Ñucay *ñusta*; in 1699, Doña Clara bought out Doña Inés and made the house entirely hers. On beatas and beaterios in Cuzco, see Burns, "Andean Women in Religion," 81–91.

7. See chapter 4; the 1704 will is in ARC-PN, Gregorio Básquez Serrano, protocolo 51 (1704), fols. 100v–101.

8. Hanks, *Intertexts*, 13. As Hanks goes on to note, reading "an intertextual trajectory" in colonial documents forces us "to get beyond notions like the 'situation,' 'speech event,' 'face-to-face,' and even copresence, in order to embed communicative processes in broader social fields. This is easier said than done."

9. Guajardo-Fajardo Carmona, *Escribanos en Indias durante la primera mitad del siglo XVI*, 1:248, cites the influence of the Fuero Real on the *Siete Partidas*, Partida 3, Título 19, leyes 3–4.

10. Hanks, *Intertexts*, 12 (italics mine) and 14; see also Abercrombie, *Pathways of Memory and Power.*

11. Lockhart, "Between the Lines," in *Of Things of the Indies*, 240.

12. ARC-PN, Francisco de Unzueta, protocolo 257 (1713–14), fols. 316–16v, January 13, 1714.

13. ARC-PN, Joan de Saldaña, protocolo 296 (1685), fols. 139–43v, March 8, 1685. The document ends in a series of signatures, including that of Benavente as a witness. Don Cristóbal, the putative seller, wrote a very shaky hand and left a big inkblot on the page. Later it looked to me like a kind of distress signal, and an asterisk in the contract's margin (placed by an unknown hand) seemed to mark the site of a deception. Yet had I not come across Benavente's disclosure first, I would have assumed the 1685 sale had gone through as registered.

14. Escriche, *Diccionario razonado de legislación civil, penal, comercial y forense, con citas del derecho, notas y adiciones por el licenciado Juan Rodríguez de San Miguel*, 142–43; he goes on to give another example, that of a secret, illicit contract by which someone receives an ecclesiastical benefice on condition of leaving its income to someone else.

15. ARC, Corregimiento, Causas Criminales, legajo 77 (1582–1693), expediente with cover letter dated November 23, 1650. Don Diego Gualpa Nina is the cacique who a few years later sold a piece of land to the Cuzco notary Martín López de Paredes: see chap. 2.

16. See Itier, "Lengua general y comunicación escrita"; Durston, "La escritura del quechua por indígenas en el siglo XVII"; and Taylor, *Camac camay y camasca.*

17. Lockhart, *Of Things of the Indies*, 207, believes "there is every reason to think

that a large mundane Quechua documentation existed in the seventeenth century and perhaps earlier and later. What can have come of it is another matter, and the fact that so little has surfaced after so much searching is not a cause for optimism." The ethnographic research of Frank Salomon in the Huarochirí region suggests that local archives' contents may hold very little from early colonial times, whether in Quechua or Spanish.

18. See Toledo, *Francisco de Toledo*, 2:222–24. Any criminal suit that might merit the death penalty or other serious physical harm was supposed to be sent to the corregidor, as well as any civil suit involving more than thirty pesos, allegations against caciques, or disputes between pueblos over land or labor.

19. Ibid., 2:222: "No han de escribir, porque lo han de hacer sumariamente." When criminal cases were serious enough to merit forwarding to the corregidor, arrests and depositions needed to be made while people were still available and memories fresh. Thus in accordance with the Toledan ordinances, pueblo authorities "shall arrest the delinquents," who might be Spaniards or other non-Indians, "and when testimony has been taken they shall send everything to the said Magistrate so that he may punish them." Ibid., 2:224.

20. See Escriche, *Diccionario razonado de legislación civil, penal, comercial y forense*, 359, on the *juicio sumario*: "Aquel en que se conoce brevemente de la causa, despreciando las largas solemnidades del derecho, y atendiendo solamente á la verdad del hecho."

21. The only example I know of this kind of writing comes from Cuzco: in 1595, Pedro Quispe, acting as notary for the city's Indian court, made a written summary of the cases decided by the *juez de naturales*. What remains of it is only fragmentary, but fascinating: see ARC, Corregimiento, Causas Ordinarias, legajo 2 (1587–1602), expediente 46 (1595), cuaderno 25, fols. 167–90.

22. ARC, Cabildo, Justicia Ordinaria, Causas Civiles, legajo 2 (1606–26), expediente 32, cuaderno 5, Don Juan Francisco Arias Maldonado v. Juan de San Pedro, February 1614, fols. 16–21v. I thank Sabine Hyland for sharing with me the paper that she, Brian Bauer, and Donato Amado prepared for the 2005 annual meeting of the American Anthropological Association, which analyzes this source.

23. The exception is wills: see K. Burns, "Making Indigenous Archives."

24. The phrase "contact zone" is Pratt's, from her influential essay "Arts of the Contact Zone," 33–40.

25. Communities did not always get along with the official protector of natives, as Donato Amado has pointed out to me.

26. Spivak, "Can the Subaltern Speak?"; see also Trouillot, *Silencing the Past*.

27. One thing rarely visible in the record is the extra fees notaries might charge: see, e.g., AAL, Apelaciones de Cuzco, XXIV:7 (1674), regarding the ecclesiastical notary Pedro Carrillo de Guzmán, who asked for a substantial advance payment to make a copy of a case that was being appealed to Lima. In a rare

private letter, the notary notifies the cacique of Macarí that he will have to pay 300 pesos to get some documents copied, half up front to distribute among Carrillo de Guzmán's assistants, "y así no se podrá comenzar a sacar sino es dándose adelantado."

28. My point about collaborative agency pertains to lawsuits more generally. Many begin with an official's declaration that he has been apprised of something by an unnamed party: "As I am informed. . . ." These were conducted *de oficio* rather than in response to a plaintiff's petition. Such lawsuits obscure the identity of the person(s) initiating them, who might or might not be the plaintiff.

29. See, e.g., Paz y Salgado, *Instruccion de litigantes* [page number missing], who advises would-be litigants that "above all it is very important to figure out which abogado enjoys the best relationships with the Judges, and to take advantage of his patronage [*patrocinio*]."

30. See ARC, Cabildo, Justicia Ordinaria, Causas Civiles, legajo 18 (1730–38), expediente 501 (1733), cuaderno 4, fol. 2v, testimony of Francisco Maldonado; and ibid., fol. 4, testimony of Pedro José Gamarra.

31. An exception that proves the point is ARC, Corregimiento, Causas Criminales, legajo 78 (1700–1745), expediente de 1701 (s/n), 20 junio 1701, in which plaintiff Isidro Ortiz de Aro successfully sued to recover 744 pesos. The case took two years, and each side was advised by an abogado. Total court costs came to 336 pesos, half of which went to the abogados, with another 50 pesos to the notary.

32. De la Puente Brunke is researching Lima's magistrates, and Renzo Honores is completing a study of colonial Andean procuradores; their work will add much to our understanding of colonial Andean justice.

33. Kagan, *Lawsuits and Litigants in Castile, 1500–1700*, 35, 42. For more on torture, see Tomás y Valiente, *La tortura en España*; Alonso Romero, *El proceso penal en Castilla*, 244–56; and Silverman, *Tortured Subjects*. Herzog and Cutter indicate that judicial torture was rare in the colonial contexts they study: Herzog, *Upholding Justice*, 28–29; Cutter, *Legal Culture of Northern New Spain 1700–1810*, 123. Yet the evidence from Cuzco, while hardly abundant, suggests otherwise. Only two bundles of seventeenth-century criminal cases remain, containing eighty-four cases or *expedientes*: ARC, Cabildo, Justicia Ordinaria, Causas Criminales, legajo 92 (1600–1697), and ARC, Corregimiento, Causas Criminales, legajo 77 (1582–1693). Of the handful of relatively complete cases, two concern defendants who were ordered to undergo torture: an indigenous commoner named Ambrosio de Ecos Olarte and a noble descendant of the Incas, Don Francisco Tito Condemayta, whom witnesses testified was left bedridden for months and permanently lame in one arm. Judges may have been much more liberal in ordering torture of indigenous defendants.

34. Kagan, *Lawsuits and Litigants in Castile, 1500–1700*, 99–103, 138, finds that the appeals court of Valladolid modified or reversed about a third of the cases that

came before it, a significant "reversal rate" that probably encouraged litigants contemplating appeals.

35. ARC, Cabildo, Justicia Ordinaria, Causas Criminales, legajo 92 (1600–1697), expediente 6, October 9, 1699, fol. 1.

36. In the extant record in Cuzco's archives, such petitions and other legal writings are invariably in Spanish, although Quechua might well have been the language in which Asencia Sisa and others first voiced their complaints. For insightful analysis of early modern French pleas for royal mercy, see Davis, *Fiction in the Archives*, 20–21; these narratives, by contrast, did need to be expressed as much as possible in the plaintiff's voice.

37. Carvajal, *Instruction y memorial para escrivanos y juezes executores, assi en lo criminal como cevil, y escripturas publicas*, fol. 1, thus indicates that judges, "especially good ones," give greater credit to sumaria witnesses' depositions.

38. In the ARC's Cabildo and Corregimiento criminal cases from the sixteenth and seventeenth centuries (limited almost entirely to seventeenth-century cases), all but a small handful are incomplete; many contain only a few folios of what was once a much longer record.

39. Herrup, *A House in Gross Disorder*, 6. "Law," she continues, "is a cultural dialect; in seventeenth-century England, it was, along with religion, the most ubiquitous and influential dialect." The same could be said of seventeenth-century Cuzco, Lima, and other centers of the Spanish American lettered city.

40. ARC, Cabildo, Justicia Ordinaria, Causas Criminales, legajo 92 (1600–1697), expediente 7, May 1699.

41. Ibid., fols. 34–34v, 35v–36.

42. Ibid., fols. 19v–20, as per the defense of Cristóbal Pillco offered by the protector of natives Don Gerónimo de Alegría y Carvajal.

43. Ibid., fol. 36.

44. Ibid., fol. 3, sumaria testimony of Antonia Sisa, May 30, 1699: "el d[ic]ho Don Graviel y su muger se fueron a la puna a sacar papas y ocas."

45. See, e.g., the initial question that was to be asked of witnesses presented on behalf of the plaintiff, which was leading in the extreme and over 220 words long: Ibid., fol. 25.

46. Carvajal, *Instruction y memorial para escrivanos y juezes executores, assi en lo criminal como cevil, y escripturas publicas*, fols. 2v–3.

47. Carvajal notes that if too many questions were bundled together in one item, the witness might cause confusion in his testimony by not distinguishing the source of his knowledge: whether he saw things as an eyewitness, learned about them by hearsay, etc. Such distinctions mattered greatly since judges were supposed to weigh testimony depending on its source; eyewitness testimony trumped hearsay, for example.

48. According to Phillips, *Six Galleons for the King of Spain*, 127, the master was a very important shipboard figure in the sixteenth century and early seventeenth, second in command to the sea captain (if one was present), "with responsibility for sailing the vessel, in consultation with the pilot, who actually fixed the course." A master had to be qualified to take the place of the sea captain or the pilot if necessary. By the late seventeenth century, however, "the master's administrative functions inexorably took over from the nautical ones," and his status declined.

49. AGI, Justicia, 836, n. 6, third document set, digitalized image 15. The case is one of several examined by Pulido Rubio, *El piloto mayor de la Casa de la Contratación de Sevilla*, chap. 7, 145–203; see esp. 163–69. Pulido Rubio cites enough significant disparities between prescription and practice to make the testimony of the prosecution's witnesses seem credible. He notes, in the case of the accused interim *piloto mayor*, the man's low salary (165). Clarence Haring also provides a brief summary: see *Trade and Navigation between Spain and the Indies in the Time of the Hapsburgs*, 301–2.

50. The piloto mayor oversaw the final examination of candidates and their formal approval (or rejection): see Pulido Rubio, *El piloto mayor de la Casa de la Contratación de Sevilla*, 134–39. The notary drew up the requisite papers. Pulido Rubio (132–33) cites a 1546 order reiterating a portion of the Casa's governing ordinances: examinations were to take place on *días de fiesta* so that more cosmographers and pilots could be present and vote on the candidates. Additionally, it was specified "que no se de carta de Examen sinque proçeda buena ynformaçion de la legalidad y buenas costumbres y espiriençia dela mar del piloto que asi se Examine." For additional details on the required qualifications, see ibid., 140–43. Despite all royal attempts at quality control, "pilots and masters who had never faced an examination were still permitted to set sail" (144).

51. AGI, Justicia, 836, n. 6, third document set, image 29; the juicy phrase is attributed to the witness Sebastián de Porras, a pilot and resident of Sevilla: "gran robo y bellaqueria."

52. AGI, Justicia, 836, n. 6, second document set, image 107, from the *probanza*, or questionnaire for the defense. Here Díez claims the unvarying amount came to twelves *reales*: four for the *información*, another four for the vote and *autos* related to it, and four more for the exam certificate. Interestingly, in his testimony of December 23, 1551, he specifies a different amount (third document set, image 92): ten maravedis per page.

53. AGI, Justicia, 836, n. 6, third document set, image 97. Díez was at pains to indicate that he did do some of the writing personally, though Ribera in his own testimony did not mention Díez writing.

54. AGI, Justicia, 836, n. 6, second document set, 115, from the questionnaire for the defense; Díez (or the notary) used a different term in his December 23, 1551

testimony: that he had "dictated" to Ribera, "rezandole." Covarrubias gives two definitions for *rezar*, "to pray" and "to recite" (as opposed to singing, e.g., a mass): *Tesoro de la lengua castellana*, 909.

55. AGI, Justicia, 836, n. 6, third document set, image 29, prosecution witness Sebastián de Porras, a pilot and resident of Sevilla.

56. AGI, Justicia, 1154, n. 2, images 13–14. On the Sevilla jail, see Domínguez Ortiz, *Crisis y decadencia de la España de los Austrias*; and Pedro de León, *Grandeza y miseria en Andalucía*.

57. Ibid., image 23, from the prosecutor's accusations against the defendant.

58. Ibid., images 23–24; 5.

59. Not all AGI documents can be accessed through the archive's computer terminals, but brief descriptions of each document (or document bundle) exist, indexed by keywords. These were two of the documents that came up when I searched for "escribano&fraude."

60. See Herzog, *Upholding Justice*, esp. the introduction.

61. I am grateful to Paul E. Hoffman for clarifying this for me: see his "The Archivo de Protocolos de Sevilla," 29–32. The neighborhood notaries of San Juan de la Palma, for instance, clearly did a lot of business for the Casa de la Misericordia, a women's shelter. So many of its residents were given charitable dowries to marry that the notary might use a printed form for the requisite dowry documents to save time: see, e.g., AHS-PN, oficio 1, Bernardo García, 1687 (1 enero–7 julio), fols. 373–93v, for a long run of *cartas de dote* all transacted on the same day, March 16, 1687.

62. Ibid., fol. 439, March 24, 1687: "color membrillo cocho." Cuzco's notarial records typically recorded only the designators *español, negro, mulato, mestizo, and indio*—though Lane, in "Captivity and Redemption," 230, finds a more varied terminology in play for late sixteenth-century Quito, including "the color of cooked quince."

63. The catalog for Oficio 1 (San Juan de la Palma), for example, indicates that fourteen men acted as notaries there between 1504 and 1800. Of these, six might well have been related, including four men whose careers spanned nearly a century: Mateo de la Cuadra (1507–15), Juan de la Cuadra (1515–19), Alonso de la Barrera (1519–45), and Diego de la Barrera Farfán (1545–1602).

64. By the eighteenth century, much less of a boom time for Cuzco than the preceding two colonial centuries, the Gamarra family had launched a kind of notarial dynasty: see K. Burns and Najarro, "Parentesco, escritura y poder," 113–35.

65. As Stoler puts it in "Colonial Archives and the Arts of Governance," 100, "How can students of colonialism . . . turn to readings 'against the grain' without moving along their grain first? . . . Assuming we know these scripts . . . diminishes our analytic possibilities."

66. Álvarez, *De las costumbres y conversión de los indios del Perú*, 268.

67. See Herzog, "La comunidad y su administración."

68. As Tanselle notes in "The World as Archive," 403, "Historians tend to think of primary sources as language alone, rather than as artifacts." He insists that "the artifact has its own story to tell, one that can never be separated from what the words say or what the text as a whole signifies in social terms." See also Starn, "Truths in the Archives," 387–401.

69. See Lockhart's two landmark studies, *Spanish Peru 1532–1560*, and *The Men of Cajamarca*.

70. Lockhart, *The Nahuas After the Conquest*, 6.

71. Ibid., 7–8 (italics mine). See also Restall, "A History of the New Philology and the New Philology in History."

72. Lockhart, *The Nahuas After the Conquest*, 429–30.

73. Van Young, "The New Cultural History Comes to Old Mexico," 234.

74. Lockhart and others do pay some attention to notaries, but relatively little to the ways they worked. See, however, Lockhart's useful methodological piece "Between the Lines," in his *Of Things of the Indies*. His most careful attention to notaries' work comes in his excellent treatment of Spanish notaries in *Spanish Peru 1532–1560*, 68–76.

75. See Lockhart, *The Nahuas After the Conquest*, 40–41; Horn, *Postconquest Coyoacán*, 63–64; Haskett, *Indigenous Rulers*, 110–11; Restall, *The Maya World*, 66–68; and Terraciano, *The Mixtecs of Colonial Oaxaca*, 48, 193–94. See also Gary Tomlinson, *The Singing of the New World*.

76. Hanks notes in *Intertexts*, 14, regarding the colonial Maya, "The fact that the scribes who operated in the Indian Republics were trained in large measure by the [Spanish] missionaries is indicated powerfully by the commonalities of discourse style between missionary and notarial genres."

77. See, for example, Haskett, *Indigenous Rulers*, 53, for the late colonial example of Nahuatl election records. Some types of documents more greatly resembled their Spanish-language counterparts than others: see, e.g., the appendices in Lockhart, *The Nahuas After the Conquest*, 455–74; and Restall, *The Maya World*, 323–331.

78. Stoler, "Colonial Archives and the Arts of Governance," 90. On the "archival turn," see 92–96.

79. "Many notarial documents consist primarily of formula, and with little risk you can skip from the substantive beginning to the signatures and dates at the end," writes Lockhart, in "Between the Lines," in *Of Things of the Indies*, 237; by contrast, "a will must be read all the way through." While I appreciate his point about wills, I would argue that skipping the formulae of other documents entirely *is* a risky strategy, especially for those just beginning to find their way into colonial Latin American archives.

80. I refer here to the kind of general power of attorney made to facilitate legal representation of one person by another (*poder general para pleitos*). On the diverse

kinds of *poder*, see Monterroso, *Pratica civil, y criminal, e instruction de scrivanos*, fols. 121–32.

81. Monterroso, for instance, includes love among several scripted possibilities in the form language he provides for a basic donation ibid., fols. 116v–17: "Be it known to all . . . that because I owe you, so-and-so, resident of such-and-such a place, for the good and loyal services you have provided me. Or because of the love I have for you. Or because you are marrying so-and-so. Or so that you may become a priest. Thusly one specifies the causes for which the donation is being made."

82. Stoler, "Colonial Archives and the Arts of Governance," 103.

83. This is the title of a University of Michigan graduate seminar in which Rebecca J. Scott kindly invited me to participate; for her own recent work involving Louisiana notaries, see "Public Rights, Social Equality, and the Conceptual Roots of the *Plessy* Challenge," esp. 795–97.

Epilogue

1. Mirow, *Latin American Law*, 212. For broader historical context, see Merryman, *The Civil Law Tradition*.

2. From the late nineteenth century, the Bolivian state began aggressively pushing a liberal program to break up communal lands and abolish communal landholding. On this history and the struggles waged by the *caciques apoderados*, see Larson, *Trials of Nation Making*, and Gotkowitz, *A Revolution for Our Rights*. See also Andrés Lira González, *El amparo colonial y el juicio de amparo mexicano* (Mexico City: Fondo de Cultura Económica, 1972).

3. The caciques turned to Leandro Condori Chura, whom they called simply el Escribano, "the Notary." He later told of their deep respect for old documents: "They used to say, 'In the ancient titles it says the Indian is free, he can't just be jailed or ignored.' We found documents to that effect, and they would also say, 'These old titles show that they did not abuse the Indian.'" Condori Chura and Ticona Alejo, *El escribano de los caciques apoderados*, 64.

4. Take the case of the famous Huarochirí manuscript, a rare, anonymous Quechua text from the early 1600s: thanks to diplomatic sleuthing, Alan Durston has recently been able to identify the author as Cristóbal Choquecasa, "a scion of the ruling lineage of the Checa." See Durston, "Notes on the Authorship of the Huarochirí Manuscript," 239. See, too, the controversy generated by the historian Laura Laurencich-Minelli's claims concerning Andean documents from a private collection in Italy; she raised questions about (among other things) Guaman Poma's authorship of the *El primer nueva corónica y buen gobierno*.

5. As Adorno notes in "The Archive and the Internet," 1–2, what was once

deliberately secret or unavailable can now be translated, annotated, and posted online for a worldwide audience—a digital conquest of space that would have dazzled the old cosmographers. The Guaman Poma website she established in collaboration with the Royal Library of Denmark in Copenhagen is an outstanding example; see www.kb.dk / elib / mss / poma /.

GLOSSARY

abogado: Advocate; a man formally schooled in law (also known in Spain and Spanish America simply as a *letrado*, "lettered one"). Such men resembled the barristers of the English legal system. As legal scholars, they were adept at forming arguments based on civil and canon law; they knew Latin, and might own relatively large libraries of legal texts. Their services were expensive enough that many in the colonial Andes sought out a cheaper alternative—such as a *procurador*—when they needed a petition or other legal writing to present before a judge.

escribano: A general term for a public notary (as distinct from *notarios*). These men held public offices, and belonged to what might be called, following C. W. Brooks, "the lower branch" of the Spanish legal system, operating at a less prestigious level than the letrados. Escribanos prepared legally binding documents of an extrajudicial kind for their clients (e.g., contracts of various kinds; wills), and also produced many types of judicial records (e.g., confessions; witnesses' depositions). They learned their job through informal apprenticeship with one or more active notaries. Of the many specific kinds of escribanos at work in colonial Spanish America, those most frequently encountered in Andean archives are *escribanos públicos y del número*, *escribanos reales* (or *de Su Majestad*), and *escribanos públicos y de cabildo*, all varieties of public notaries.

escribano de cabildo: In the Andes, an indigenous notary who held his post for life in a particular indigenous *pueblo* or town, maintaining records of the actions of the local mayor (*alcalde*) and town council (*cabildo*). These men were not royally appointed holders of public offices, and should not be confused with the *escribanos públicos y de cabildo*.

escribano público y de cabildo (or *de consejo*): A notary public holding the office of notary to the municipal council (*cabildo*) of a specific Spanish or Spanish American town or city. These men were responsible for keeping records of the council's actions and decisions (*actas*) and maintaining its archives. They might simultaneously practice locally as *escribanos públicos y del número* or *escribanos reales*.

escribano público y del número: A numerary notary public, who held his office by royal appointment in a specific town or city (as distinct from *escribanos reales*). Compared to the cities of early modern Spain, those of Spanish America had relatively few numerary notaries; sixteenth-century Mexico City, for instance, had only a half dozen.

escribano real (or *de Su Majestad*): A notary public who by royal appointment might act as a notary in any part of his sovereign's realm, as long as he did not infringe on the privileges of the numerary notaries. These men might move around from city to city, unlike the numerary notaries.

juez: Judge; a man empowered by his office—and only during his term of office—to hear and decide suits brought before him. Those who acted as judges in colonial Spanish America (e.g., alcaldes; corregidores) were not necessarily versed in the law; moreover, Spanish justice did not require them to explain the legal reasoning behind their decisions. Thus they leaned heavily on the permanent legal professionals around them (*abogados, escribanos,* and *procuradores*) for help in deciding cases.

legajo: A document bundle; the term may refer to loose or bound records, and is often used in archival classification systems.

letrado: These men studied law at university, and generally occupied a more prestigious place in the Spanish and Spanish American legal hierarchy than the escribanos or procuradores. See above, *abogado.*

minuta (or *nota*): The draft of a client's business before a notary, often dictated by the notary to an assistant who wrote down the basics in a draft book or *minutario.* Such entries were typically crossed out once the fully developed draft was written in the chronologically correct location in the notary's *registro,* for later binding into a *protocolo.*

notario, or *notario eclesiástico*: An ecclesiastical notary. In Spanish America as well as in Spain, the church had its own courts, judges, procedures, archives, and notaries. This study does not deal with these men, whose history for the most part has yet to be written. In colonial Cuzco their training seems to have been the same as that of other notaries: apprenticeship with one or more active notaries (who might be escribanos públicos) to learn the basics.

oficial: A notary's assistant; also commonly known as a penman (*plumario*) or writer (*escribiente*).

oficial mayor: The head assistant in a notary's workshop; he supervised the other assistants' labor and made sure the notary's archive was properly maintained and organized.

plumario: A notary's penman; synonymous terms that show up in Andean archives include *amanuensis*, *escribiente*, and *oficial*.

procurador: A Spanish or Spanish American legal representative comparable to the Elizabethan common law attorney or solicitor. These men drew up papers for presentation in court on behalf of their clients, as long as routine legal issues and forms were involved. Like notaries, they held public offices and learned the ropes of the legal system through practical application; several Cuzco procuradores, for example, were previously notaries' assistants. Their posts cost significantly less than those of numerary notaries, and may have been of slightly lower social standing. Some eventually moved up to become numerary notaries.

protocolo: "The original book of public records [*actos públicos*]," in Covarrubias's definition (*Tesoro de la lengua castellana*, 885), in which "the essentials of the act are recorded, along with the parties and witnesses, with the day, month, year, and place. The notary is obliged to extend [this record] in a document in the standard form, for the satisfaction of the parties and general knowledge of the truth."

registro: One of the fifty-sheet notebooks comprising a notary's bound volume of public acts (protocolo); the term might also be used to refer to the entire protocolo.

registro de indios: In Andean usage, a notebook in which a notary recorded acts (e.g., labor agreements, sales and rental contracts, and wills) pertaining to people classified as "Indians." From the mid-1600s, Cuzco's notaries segregated such registers at the back of their protocolos and identified them on the cover sheets as "Indian registers" (see, e.g., figure 3).

signo: The unique insignia a notary public received at the time of his appointment to office. Along with his signature and his distinctive flourish or paraph (*rúbrica*), a notary's signo attested that a document was duly witnessed and legally true.

WORKS CONSULTED

Primary Sources

Manuscripts

CUZCO, PERU

Archivo Arzobispal del Cuzco

Archivo Regional de Cusco (ARC)

    Asuntos Eclesiásticos

    Cabildo

        Administrativo, Edictos

        Justicia Ordinaria, Causas Civiles

        Justicia Ordinaria, Causas Criminales

    Corregimiento

        Causas Criminales

        Causas Ordinarias [i.e., Civiles]

    Intendencia

    Libros de Actas del Cabildo

    Protocolos Notariales (ARC-PN)

        Luis de Quesada

        Gerónimo Sánchez de Quesada

        Miguel de Contreras

        Joan de Olave

        Pedro de la Carrera Ron

        Cristóbal de Lucero

        Francisco Hurtado

        Luis Díez de Morales

        José de Solórzano

        Alonso Beltrán Lucero

        José Calvo

        Alonso Calvo

        Antonio Moreno

        Lorenzo de Mesa Andueza

        Joan de Saldaña

        Juan Flores de Bastidas

Martín López de Paredes
Pedro de Cáceres
Lorenzo Xaimes [Jaimes]
Cristóbal de Bustamante
Pedro López de la Cerda
Francisco de Maldonado
Gregorio Básquez Serrano
Alejo Fernández Escudero
José Fernández Cataño
Juan Bautista Gamarra
Miguel de Acuña
Francisco de Unzueta
Bernardo José Gamarra
Julián Tupayachi
Luis Ramos Tituatauchi
Escribanos de naturales (1677–1705)

LIMA, PERU
Archivo Arzobispal de Lima (AAL)
Apelaciones del Cuzco
Archivo General de la Nación (AGN)
Derecho Indígena
Protocolos Notariales (AGN-PN)
Diego Sánchez Vadillo
Alonso de la Torre
Pedro Pérez Landero
Francisco Sánchez Becerra
Gregorio de Urtazo
Real Audiencia, Causas Civiles
Real Audiencia, Causas Criminales
Superior Gobierno
Títulos de Propiedad
Archivo de Límites, Ministerio de Relaciones Exteriores (AL)
Sala de Investigaciones, Biblioteca Nacional
SEVILLE, SPAIN
Archivo General de Indias (AGI)
Charcas
Escribanía
Estado
Indiferente
Justicia
Lima

Patronato

Quito

Archivo Histórico de Sevilla (AHS)

    Sección Histórica de Protocolos Notariales (AHS-PN)

        Bernardo García (oficio 1)

        Juan de Vargas Gallego (oficio 3)

        Abecedarios (oficio 4, 1553–70)

        Juan Muñoz Naranjo (oficio 4)

        Juan Pérez Galindo (oficio 4)

PORTUGAL

Arquivo Nacional da Torre do Tombo, Lisbon

UNITED STATES

Latin American Library, Tulane University

Wilson Library, University of North Carolina, Chapel Hill

Printed Works

Acosta, José de. *Historia natural y moral de las Indias*. Seville: Juan de León, 1590.

——. *Natural and Moral History of the Indies*. Edited by Jane E. Mangan; translated by Frances M. López-Morillas; introduction by Walter D. Mignolo. Durham, N.C.: Duke University Press, 2002.

Albornoz, Bartolomé de. *Arte de los contractos*. Valencia: Pedro de Huete, 1573.

Alcaraz y Castro, Isidoro. *Breve instruccion del methodo, y practica de los quatro juicios, civil ordinario, sumario de particion, executivo, y general de concurso de acreedores*. Madrid: Domingo Fernandez de Arrojo, 1762.

Alemán, Mateo. *Guzmán de Alfarache*. 2 vols. 6th ed. Edited by José María Micó. Madrid: Cátedra, 2003 [1599, 1604].

——. *The Rogue, or the Life of Guzman de Alfarache*. Translated by James Mabbe; introduction by James Fitzmaurice-Kelly. 4 vols. New York: Alfred A. Knopf, 1924 [1623].

Al-Tulaytuli, Ahman b. Mugit. *Formulario notarial*. Introduction by Francisco Javier Aguirre Sádaba. Madrid: Consejo Superior de Investigaciones Cientí-ficas, 1994.

Álvarez, Bartolomé. *De las costumbres y conversión de los indios del Perú: Memorial a Felipe II (1588)*. Madrid: Ediciones Polifemo, 1998.

Álvarez Posadilla, Juan. *Practica criminal por principios, o modo y forma de instruir los procesos criminales en sumario de las causas de oficio de justicia contra los abusos introducidos*. Valladolid: Imprenta de la Viuda e Hijos de Santander, 1794.

Arguello, Antonio de. *Tratado de escrituras y contratos publicos, con sus anotaciones*. Madrid: Francisco Martínez, 1630.

Arias, Juan. *Practica ecclesiastica para el uso y exercicio de notarios publicos y apos-tolicos, y secretario de prelados. Con un tractado breve de visitacion de yglesias, muy util y necessario a los Visitadores y Notarios de visitacion.* Madrid: Guillermo Droy, 1585.

Arzáns de Orsúa y Vela, Bartolomé. *Historia de la Villa Imperial de Potosí.* Edited by Lewis Hanke and Gunnar Mendoza. 3 vols. Providence: Brown University Press, 1965.

Ballesteros, Thomas de. *Tomo primero de las ordenanzas del Peru.* Lima: José Contreras, 1685.

Bodin, Jean. *On Sovereignty: Four Chapters from the Six Books of the Commonwealth.* Translated and edited by Julian H. Franklin. New York: Cambridge University Press, 1992.

Cabrera Núñez de Guzmán, Melchor de. *Idea de un perfecto abogado.* Madrid: Eugenio Rodríguez, 1683.

Calancha, Antonio de la. *Coronica moralizada del Orden de San Augustin en el Peru, con sucesos egenplares vistos en esta monarquia.* Barcelona: Pedro Lacavalleria, 1638.

Carvajal, Bartolomé de. *Instruction y memorial para escrivanos y juezes executores, assi en lo criminal como cevil, y escripturas publicas.* Granada: Hugo de Mena, 1585.

Castro, Ignacio de. *Relación del Cuzco.* Lima: Universidad Nacional Mayor de San Marcos, 1978 [Madrid, 1795].

Cervantes, Miguel de. *Exemplary Stories.* Translated by Lesley Lipson. New York: Oxford University Press, 1998.

Cieza de León, Pedro de. *Crónica del Perú, primera parte.* Revised 2nd ed.; introduction by Franklin Pease. Lima: Pontificia Universidad Católica del Perú, 1986.

Columbus, Christopher. *The* Diario *of Christopher Columbus's First Voyage to America 1492–1493, abstracted by Fray Bartolomé de Las Casas.* Transcribed and translated by Oliver Dunn and James E. Kelley Jr. Norman: University of Oklahoma Press, 1989.

Correas, Gonzalo. *Vocabulario de refranes y frases proverbiales (1627).* Edited by Louis Combet; revised by Robert Jammes and Maite Mir-Andreu. Madrid: Editorial Castalia, S.A., 2000 [1627].

Covarrubias, Sebastián de. *Tesoro de la lengua castellana o española.* Edited by Martín de Riquer. Barcelona: Editorial Alta Fulla, 1989 [1611].

De la Ripia, Juan. *Practica de testamentos, y modos de subceder.* Cuenca: Antonio Núñez Enríquez, 1676.

Díaz de Valdepeñas, Hernando. *Summa de notas copiosas muy sustanciales y compendiosas.* Granada: Hernando Díaz and Juan de Medina, 1544.

Digest of Justinian, The. Translation edited by Alan Watson. 2 vols. Revised ed. Philadelphia: University of Pennsylvania Press, 1998.

Documentos relativos a Don Pedro de La Gasca y a Gonzalo Pizarro. 2 vols. Edited by Juan Pérez de Tudela y Bueso. Madrid: Real Academia de Historia, 1944.

Escriche, Joaquín. *Diccionario razonado de legislación civil, penal, comercial y forense, con citas del derecho, notas y adiciones por el licenciado Juan Rodríguez de San Miguel*. Mexico City: Universidad Nacional Autónoma de México, 1993 [1837].

Escudero, Cristóbal. *Estilo y pratica eclesiastica, y civil de procuradores, generalmente para todos los tribunales eclesiasticos, y seglares destos reynos*. Salamanca: Diego Cosio, 1647.

Febrero, José. *Librería de escribanos e instrucción jurídica teórico-práctica de principiantes*. 6 vols. Madrid: Antonio Pérez de Soto, 1769–86.

Fernández de Lizardi, José Joaquín. *El Periquillo Sarniento*. Madrid: Cátedra, 1997.

——. *The Mangy Parrot: The Life and Times of Periquillo Sarniento, Written by Himself for His Children*. Translated by David Frye; introduction by Nancy Vogeley. Indianapolis: Hackett Publishing Company, 2004.

Forner, Juan Pablo. *Discurso sobre la tortura*. Edited by Santiago Mollfulleda. Barcelona: Editorial Crítica, 1990 [1792].

The Function of Documents in Islamic Law: The Chapter on Sales from Tahāwī's "Kitāb al-shurūt al-kabīr." Edited with an introduction by Jeanette A. Wakin. Albany: State University of New York Press, 1972.

Garcilaso de la Vega, el Inca. *Comentarios reales de los Incas*. 2 vols. Edited by Carlos Araníbar. Lima: Fondo de Cultura Económica, 1991.

González de Torneo, Francisco. *Pratica de escrivanos que contiene la judicial, y orden de examinar testigos en causas civiles, y hidalguias, y causas criminales, y escripturas en estilo estenso, y quentas, y particiones de bienes, y execuciones de cartas executorias*. Alcalá de Henares: Juan Gracián, 1587.

González de Villarroel, Diego. *Examen, y practica de escrivanos*. Valladolid, 1652.

Guaman Poma de Ayala, Felipe. *El primer nueva corónica y buen gobierno*. 3 vols. Edited by John V. Murra and Rolena Adorno; Quechua translations by Jorge L. Urioste. Mexico City: Siglo XXI, 1980 [1615].

——. *Y no ay remedio* . . . Lima: CIPA, Centro de Investigación y Promoción Amazónica, 1991.

Gutiérrez, José Marcos. *Practica criminal de España*. 4th ed. Madrid: Fermín Villalpando, 1826.

Gutiérrez de Vegas, D. Fernando. *Los enredos de un lugar, o historia de los prodigios, y hazañas del célebre Abogado de Conchuela el Licenciado Tarugo, del famoso escribano Carrales y otros ilustres personajes que hubo en el mismo Pueblo antes de despoblarse. Dividida en cinco libros, o sátiras contra la prepotencia, la avaricia, la mala fé, la pusilanimidad, y otros bastardos afectos del hombre, destruidores de la Justicia*. [Madrid?] Manuel Martín, 1778.

Hevia Bolaños, Juan de. *Curia filipica donde se trata de los iuizios forenses, eclesiasticos, y seculares, dividida en cinco partes*. Madrid: Melchor Sánchez, 1652 [1603].

Homem Correa Telles [Correia Teles], José. *Manual do Tabellião ou ensaio de jurisprudencia eurematica contendo a collecção de minutas dos contractos, e instru-*

mentos mais usuaes, e das cautelas mais precisas nos contractos, e testamentos. Lisbon: Impressão Regia, 1830.

Huerta, Roque de. *Recopilacion de notas de escripturas publicas, utiles y muy provechosas. Por las quales qualquier escrivano podra ordenar qualesquier escripturas que ante el se otorgaren, de las que se acostumbran en todos estos Reynos.* Salamanca: Juan de Junta, 1551.

Ibn al-'Attar. *Formulario notarial y judicial andalusí del alfaquí y notario cordobés m. 399/1099.* Translated by Pedro Chalmeta y Marina Marugán. Madrid: Fundación Matritense del Notariado, 2000.

Juan y Colom, José. *Instruccion de escribanos en orden a lo judicial.* Valladolid: Editorial Lex Nova, 1993 [1736].

Konetzke, Richard, ed. *Colección de documentos para la historia de la formación social de Hispanoamérica, 1493–1810.* 3 vols. Madrid: Consejo Superior de Investigaciones Científicas, 1953–62.

Lama, Miguel Antonio de la. *Manual del escribano público peruano.* Lima: José M. Nogueira, 1867.

Landa, Diego de. *Relación de las cosas de Yucatán.* 13th ed. Mexico City: Editorial Porrúa, 1986 [1566?].

Lazarillo de Tormes. Edited by Francisco Rico. Madrid: Ediciones Cátedra, 1988 [1554].

León, Pedro de. *Grandeza y miseria en Andalucía: testimonio de una encrucijada histórica (1578–1616).* Edited by Pedro Herrera Puga. Granada: Facultad de Teología, 1981 [1616].

Libro de las bulas y pragmáticas de los Reyes Católicos. 2 vols. Madrid: Instituto de España, 1973.

Martínez, Manuel Silvestre. *Librería de jueces, utilísima y universal para abogados, alcaldes mayores y ordinarios, corregidores é intendentes, jueces de residencias y de visita de escribanos de toda España, receptores de Castilla y Aragon, regidores, Juntas de Proprios, Contribucion y Pósitos, personeros, Diputados del Comun y demas individuos de tribunales ordinarios: añadida é ilustrada con mas de dos mil Leyes Reales, que autorizan su Doctrina.* Madrid: Imprenta de Don Benito Cano, 1791.

Matienzo, Juan de. *Gobierno del Perú.* Edited and with an introduction by Guillermo Lohmann Villena. Paris: L'Institut Français d'Études Andines, 1967.

Melgarejo, Pedro. *Compendio de contratos publicos, autos de particiones, executivos, y de residencias: con el genero del papel sellado, que a cada despacho toca.* Madrid: Los Herederos de Gabriel de León, 1689 [1647].

Mercado, Tomás de. *Suma de tratos y contratos.* Edited by Nicolás Sánchez Albornoz. Madrid: Instituto de Estudios Fiscales, 1977 [1569].

Monterroso y Alvarado, Gabriel de. *Pratica civil, y criminal, e instruction de scrivanos.* Valladolid: Francisco Fernández de Córdova, 1563.

Motolinia [Toribio de Benavente]. *Historia de los indios de la Nueva España.* Edited by Edmundo O'Gorman. 5th ed. Mexico City: Editorial Porrúa, 1990.

Muñoz, Juan. *Pratica de procuradores para seguir pleytos civiles, y criminales. Hecha, y ordenada por Iuan Muñoz, procurador de causas en la ciudad de Guesca. Añadida y enmendada en esta impresion, y con nuevas adiciones, conforme a la nueva Recopilacion.* Madrid: Luis Sánchez, 1591.

Murúa, Martín de. *Códice Murúa: Historia y genealogía, de los Reyes Incas del Perú del padre mercedario Fray Martín de Murúa. Códice Galvin.* Introduction by Juan Ossio. 2 vols. Madrid: Testimonio Compañía Editorial, 2004 [1590].

Navarro, Pedro. *Favores de el Rey de el Cielo, hechos a su esposa la Santa Juana de la Cruz, religiosa de la Orden tercera de Penitencia de N.P.S. Francisco.* Madrid: Mateo Fernández, 1659.

Niebla, Lorenzo de. *Summa del estilo de escrivanos y de herencias, y particiones: y escripturas, y avisos de Iuezes.* Seville: Pedro Martínez de Bañares, 1565.

Ortiz de Salcedo, Francisco. *Curia eclesiastica, para secretarios de prelados, iuezes eclesiasticos, notarios apostolicos, ordinarios, latinos, visitadores, y notarios de visita.* Madrid: por la Viuda de Alonso Martín, 1626.

Palomares, Thomas de. *Estilo nuevo de escrituras publicas, donde el curioso hallara diferentes generos de contratos, y advertencias de las leyes y prematicas de estos Reynos, y las escrituras tocantes a la navegacion de las Indias, a cuya noticia no se deven negar los escrivanos.* Seville: Simón Fajardo Ariasmontano, 1645.

Paz y Salgado, Antonio de. *Instruccion de litigantes, o guia para seguir pleitos con maior utilidad de los interesados en ellos, y a menos costa de la paciencia de los jueces, abogados, procuradores, y demas ministros que sirven en el Fuero.* Guatemala City: Sebastián de Arévalo, 1742.

Pérez, Ignacio. *Arte de escrevir con cierta industria e invencion para hazer buena forma de letra, y aprenderlo con facilidad.* Madrid: Imprenta Real, 1599.

Pérez Landero Otañez y Castro, Pedro. *Practica de visitas, y residencias apropiada a los Reynos del Perú, y deducida de lo que en ellos se estila.* Naples: Nicolás Layno, 1696.

La Picara Justina. 2 vols. Edited by Antonio Rey Hazas. Madrid: Editora Nacional, 1977.

Pictorial Calligraphy and Ornamentation. 86 plates, selected by Edmund V. Gillon Jr. New York: Dover Publications, 1972.

Pirothecnia entretenida, curiosa y agradable de fuegos recreativos, con varias invenciones y secretos, y algunas ideas generales, para que cada uno pueda formarse otras á su modo. Madrid: Imprenta de la Viuda de Ibarra, 1799.

Protocolos de los escribanos de Santiago: Primeros fragmentos, 1559 y 1564–1566. Transcribed by Álvaro Jara y Rolando Mellafe. 2 vols. Santiago, Chile: Ediciones de la Dirección de Bibliotecas, Archivos y Museos, 1996.

Quevedo, Francisco de. *La vida del buscón llamado don Pablos*, 15th ed. Edited by Domingo Ynduráin. Madrid: Cátedra, no publication date [1626].

———. *Obras escogidas*. Introduction by Germán Arciniegas. Mexico City: Consejo Nacional para la Cultura y las Artes (Conaculta) and Editorial Oceano, 1999.

———. *Prosa festiva completa*. Edited by Celsa Carmen García-Valdés. Madrid: Cátedra, 1993.

Recopilación de las leyes destos reynos [Nueva recopilación]. 3 vols. Valladolid: Editorial Lex Nova, 1982 [1640].

Recopilación de leyes de los reynos de las Indias. 3 vols. Madrid: Boletín Oficial del Estado, 1998 [1681].

Regimento que os tabaliaens das notas, e do iudicial ham de ter. Conforme à nova reformação das Ordenações do Reyno. Lisbon: Antonio Alvarez, 1610.

Ribera, Diego de. *Primera parte de escrituras, y orden de particion y cuenta, y de residencia judicial, civil y criminal*. Burgos: Philippe de Iunta, 1586.

Las Siete Partidas. 3 vols. Madrid: Boletín Oficial del Estado, 1985 [1555].

Siguenza [Siguença], Pedro de. *Tratado de clausulas instrumentales, util, y necessario para iuezes, abogados, y escrivanos destos Reynos, procuradores, partidores, y confessores, en lo de justicia, y derecho*. Madrid: Imprenta Real, 1627.

Toledo, Francisco de. *Francisco de Toledo: Disposiciones gubernativas para el Virreinato del Perú*. 2 vols. Transcribed by María Justina Sarabia Viejo; introduction by Guillermo Lohmann Villena. Seville: Escuela de Estudios Hispanoamericanos, Consejo Superior de Investigaciones Científicas, 1986–89.

Two Spanish Picaresque Novels. Translated by Michael Alpert. New York: Penguin Books, 1969.

Villadiego Vascuñana y Montoya, Alonso de. *Instruccion politica, y práctica judicial, conforme al estilo de los consejos, audiencias, y tribunales de corte, y otros ordinarios del reyno, utilissima para los governadores, y corregidores, y otros juezes ordinarios, y de comission, y para los abogados, escrivanos, procuradores, y litigantes*. Madrid: Antonio Marín, 1766 [1612].

Yrolo Calar, Nicolás de. *La política de escrituras*. Edited by María del Pilar Martínez López-Cano, with Ivonne Mijares Ramírez and Javier Sanchiz Ruiz. Mexico City: Universidad Nacional Autónoma de México, 1996 [1605].

Secondary Sources

Abercrombie, Thomas A. *Pathways of Memory and Power: Ethnography and History among an Andean People*. Madison: University of Wisconsin Press, 1998.

Adorno, Rolena. "The Archive and the Internet." *Americas* 61, no. 1 (2004): 1–18.

———. *Guaman Poma: Writing and Resistance in Colonial Peru*. Austin: University of Texas Press, 1986.

———. "The Genesis of Felipe Guaman Poma de Ayala's *Nueva corónica y buen gobierno.*" *Colonial Latin American Review* 2, nos. 1–2 (1993): 53–92.

———. "Images of Indios Ladinos in Early Colonial Peru." In Kenneth J. Andrien and Rolena Adorno, eds., *Transatlantic Encounters: Europeans and Andeans in the Sixteenth Century*, 232–70. Berkeley: University of California Press, 1991.

Alonso Romero, María Paz. *El proceso penal en Castilla, siglos XIII–XVIII.* Salamanca: Ediciones Universidad de Salamanca, 1982.

Amado Gonzáles, Donato. "El Alférez Real de los Incas: Resistencia, cambios y continuidad de la identidad inca." In David Cahill and Blanca Tovias, eds., *Élites indígenas en los Andes: Nobles, caciques y cabildantes bajo el yugo colonial*, 55–80. Quito: Abya-Yala, 2003.

Amezúa y Mayo, Agustín González de. *La vida privada española en el protocolo notarial.* Madrid: Ilustre Colegio Notarial de Madrid, 1950.

Anderson, Perry. *Lineages of the Absolutist State.* New York: Verso, 1979.

Andrien, Kenneth J. *Crisis and Decline: The Viceroyalty of Peru in the Seventeenth Century.* Albuquerque: University of New Mexico Press, 1985.

Andrien, Kenneth J., and Rolena Adorno, eds. *Transatlantic Encounters: Europeans and Andeans in the Sixteenth Century.* Berkeley: University of California Press, 1991.

Armon, Shirfa. "The Paper Key: Money as Text in Cervantes's *El celoso extremeño* and José de Camerino's *El pícaro amante.*" *Cervantes: Bulletin of the Cervantes Society of America* 18, no. 1 (1998): 96–114.

Arrom, Silvia Marina. *The Women of Mexico City, 1790–1857.* Stanford, Calif.: Stanford University Press, 1985.

Artiles, Jenaro. "The Office of Escribano in Sixteenth-Century Havana." *Hispanic American Historical Review* 49, no. 3 (1969): 489–502.

Axel, Brian Keith, ed. *From the Margins: Historical Anthropology and Its Futures.* Durham, N.C.: Duke University Press, 2002.

Baker, Geoffrey. *Imposing Harmony: Music and Society in Colonial Cuzco.* Durham, N.C.: Duke University Press, 2008.

Bakewell, Peter. *Silver and Entrepreneurship in Seventeenth-Century Potosí: The Life and Times of Antonio López de Quiroga.* Dallas: Southern Methodist University Press, 1988.

Bakhtin, Mikhail. *The Dialogic Imagination.* Edited by Michael Holquist; translated by Caryl Emerson and Michael Holquist. Austin: University of Texas Press, 1981.

Barrientos Grandon, Javier. *La cultura jurídica en la Nueva España.* Mexico City: Universidad Nacional Autónoma de México, 1993.

Beal, Peter. *In Praise of Scribes: Manuscripts and Their Makers in Seventeenth-Century England.* New York: Oxford University Press, 1998.

Benadusi, Giovanna. "Investing the Riches of the Poor: Servant Women and Their Last Wills." *American Historical Review* 109, no. 3 (June 2004): 805–26.

Benton, Lauren. *Law and Colonial Cultures: Legal Regimes in World History, 1400–1900*. New York: Cambridge University Press, 2002.

Berger, Adolf. *Encyclopedic Dictionary of Roman Law*, n.s., 43, no. 2. Philadelphia: American Philosophical Society, 1953.

Bicentenario de la muerte de D. José Febrero: Acto de homenaje y catálogo de la exposición bibliográfica. Madrid: Colegio General del Notariado, 1991.

Blouin, Francis X., Jr., and William G. Rosenberg, eds. *Archives, Documentation, and Institutions of Social Memory: Essays from the Sawyer Seminar*. Ann Arbor: University of Michigan Press, 2006.

Bono [Huertas], José. *Breve introducción a la diplomática notarial española. Parte primera*. Seville: Junta de Andalucía, Consejería de Cultura y Medio Ambiente, 1990.

——. *Historia del derecho notarial español*. 2 vols. Madrid: Junta de Decanos de los Colegios Notariales de España, 1979.

——. "La nueva literatura notarial castellana en el Reinado de Felipe II." In *Felipe II y el notariado de su tiempo*, 19–33. Madrid: Consejo General del Notariado, 1998.

——. "La práctica notarial del Reino de Castilla en el siglo XIII. Continuidad e innovación." In *Notariado público y documento privado: De los orígenes al siglo XIV*, 2 vols., 1:481–506. Valencia: Conselleria de Cultura, Educació i Ciència, 1989.

——. "Los formularios notariales españoles de los siglos XVI, XVII y XVIII." *Anales de la Academia Matritense del Notariado* 23, no. 1 (1981): 287–317.

Bono [Huertas], José, and Carmen Ungueti-Bono. *Los protocolos sevillanos de la época del descubrimiento*. Seville: Junta de Decanos de los Colegios Notariales de España and Colegio Notarial de Sevilla, 1986.

Boone, Elizabeth Hill, and Walter D. Mignolo, eds. *Writing Without Words: Alternative Literacies in Mesoamerica and the Andes*. Durham, N.C.: Duke University Press, 1994.

Borah, Woodrow. *Justice by Insurance: The General Indian Court of Colonial Mexico and the Legal Aides of the Half-Real*. Berkeley: University of California Press, 1983.

Bourdieu, Pierre. *Outline of a Theory of Practice*. Translated by Richard Nice. New York: Cambridge University Press, 1977.

Bouza [Álvarez], Fernando. *Communication, Knowledge, and Memory in Early Modern Spain*. Translated by Sonia López and Michael Agnew. Philadelphia: University of Pennsylvania Press, 1999.

——. *Corre manuscrito: Una historia cultural del Siglo de Oro*. Madrid: Marcial Pons, Ediciones de Historia, 2001.

——. *Del escribano a la biblioteca: La civilización escrita europea en la alta edad moderna (siglos XV–XVII)*. Madrid: Editorial Síntesis, 1997.

Bravo Lozano, Jesús, and Patricio Hidalgo Nuchera. *De indianos y notarios*. Madrid: Colegios Notariales de España, 1995.

Brooks, C. W. *Pettyfoggers and Vipers of the Commonwealth: The "Lower Branch" of the Legal Profession in Early Modern England*. New York: Cambridge University Press, 1986.

Brooks, C. W., R. H. Hemholz, and P. G. Stein. *Notaries Public in England since the Reformation*. London: Erskine Press, 1991.

Brownlee, Marina S., and Hans Ulrich Gumbrecht, eds. *Cultural Authority in Golden Age Spain*. Baltimore: Johns Hopkins University Press, 1995.

Burns, Kathryn. "Andean Women in Religion: *Beatas*, 'Decency' and the Defence of Honour in Colonial Cuzco." In Nora E. Jaffary, ed., *Gender, Race and Religion in the Colonization of the Americas*, 81–91. Burlington, Vt.: Ashgate, 2007.

——. *Colonial Habits: Convents and the Spiritual Economy of Cuzco, Peru*. Durham, N.C.: Duke University Press, 1999.

——. "Dentro de la ciudad letrada: La producción de la escritura pública en el Perú colonial." *Histórica* [Lima] 29, no. 1 (July 2005): 43–68.

——. "Forms of Authority: Women's Legal Representations in Mid-Colonial Cuzco." In Marta V. Vicente and Luis R. Corteguera, eds. *Women and Textual Authority in the Early Modern Spanish World*, 149–63. Burlington, Vt.: Ashgate, 2004.

——. "Making Indigenous Archives." Unpublished ms., 2005.

——. "Notaries, Truth, and Consequences." *American Historical Review* 110, no. 2 (April 2005): 350–79.

——. "Unfixing Race." In Margaret R. Greer, Walter D. Mignolo, and Maureen Quilligan, eds., *Rereading the Black Legend: The Discourses of Racial and Religious Difference in the Renaissance Empires*, 188–202. Chicago: University of Chicago Press, 2007.

Burns, Kathryn, and Margareth Najarro. "Parentesco, escritura y poder: Los Gamarra y la escritura pública en el Cuzco." *Revista del Archivo Regional de Cusco* 16 (2004): 113–35.

Burns, Robert I. *Jews in the Notarial Culture: Latinate Wills in Mediterranean Spain, 1250–1350*. Berkeley: University of California Press, 1996.

Burton, Antoinette, ed. *Archive Stories: Facts, Fictions, and the Writing of History*. Durham, N.C.: Duke University Press, 2005.

Cahill, David, and Blanca Tovias, eds. *Élites indígenas en los Andes: Nobles, caciques y cabildantes bajo el yugo colonial*. Quito: Abya-Yala, 2003.

Caillavet, Chantal. *Etnías del norte: Etnohistoria e historia de Ecuador*. Quito: Ediciones Abya-Yala, IFEA, and Casa de Velásquez, 2000.

Cañizares-Esguerra, Jorge. *How to Write the History of the New World: Historiographies, Epistemologies, and Identities in the Eighteenth-Century Atlantic World*. Stanford, Calif.: Stanford University Press, 2001.

Castiglione, Caroline. "Adversarial Literacy: How Peasant Politics Influenced Noble Governing of the Roman Countryside during the Early Modern Period." *American Historical Review* 109, no. 3 (June 2004): 783–804.

Castillo, Antonio, ed. *Escribir y leer en el siglo de Cervantes*. Barcelona: Editorial Gedisa, 1999.

Cavillac, Michel. *Pícaros y mercaderes en el Guzmán de Alfarache: Reformismo burgués y mentalidad aristocrática en la España del Siglo de Oro*. Translated by Juan M. Azpitarte Almagro. Granada: Universidad de Granada, 1994.

Chandler, James, Arnold J. Davidson, and Harry Harootunian, eds. *Questions of Evidence: Proof, Practice, and Persuasion across the Disciplines*. Chicago: University of Chicago Press, 1994.

Charles, John [Duffy]. "Indios Ladinos: Colonial Andean Testimony and Ecclesiastical Institutions (1583–1650)." Ph.D. diss., Yale University, New Haven, 2003.

——. "More *Ladino* than Necessary: Indigenous Litigants and the Language Policy Debate in Mid-Colonial Peru." *Colonial Latin American Review* 16, no. 1 (2007): 23–47.

——. "Unreliable Confessions: *Khipus* in the Colonial Parish." *The Americas* 64, no. 1 (2007): 11–33.

Chartier, Roger. "Texts, Printing, Readings." In Lynn Hunt, ed., *The New Cultural History*, 154–75. Berkeley: University of California Press, 1989.

Chittolini, Giorgio. "The 'Private,' the 'Public,' the State." In Julius Kirshner, ed., *The Origins of the State in Italy 1300–1600*, 34–61. Chicago: University of Chicago Press, 1995.

Chocano Mena, Magdalena. *La fortaleza docta: Elite letrada y dominación social en México colonial (siglos XVI–XVII)*. Barcelona: Edicions Bellaterra, 2000.

Christ, Matthew R. *The Litigious Athenian*. Baltimore: Johns Hopkins University Press, 1998.

Clanchy, M. T. *From Memory to Written Record: England 1066–1307*. 2nd ed. Cambridge, Mass.: Blackwell, 1993 [1979].

Clendinnen, Inga. *Ambivalent Conquests: Maya and Spaniard in Yucatan, 1517–1570*. New York: Cambridge University Press, 1987.

Coe, Michael D. *Breaking the Maya Code*. Revised 2nd ed. New York: Thames and Hudson, 1999.

Condori Chura, Leandro, and Esteban Ticona Alejo. *El escribano de los caciques apoderados: Kasikinakan purirarunakan qillqiripa*. La Paz: Hisbol / THOA, 1992.

Cook, Alexandra Parma, and Noble David Cook. *Good Faith and Truthful Ignorance: A Case of Transatlantic Bigamy*. Durham, N.C.: Duke University Press, 1991.

Cook, Noble David. *Born to Die: Disease and New World Conquest, 1492–1650*. New York: Cambridge University Press, 1998.

——. *Demographic Collapse: Indian Peru, 1520–1620*. New York: Cambridge University Press, 1981.

Cornblit, Oscar. *Power and Violence in the Colonial City: Oruro from the Mining Renaissance to the Rebellion of Tupac Amaru (1740–1782)*. Translated by Elizabeth Ladd Glick. New York: Cambridge University Press, 1995.

Corrigan, Philip, and Derek Sayer. *The Great Arch: English State Formation as Cultural Revolution*. New York: Blackwell, 1985.

Cortés Alonso, Vicenta. *La escritura y lo escrito: Paleografía y diplomática de España y América en los siglos XVI y XVII*. Madrid: Instituto de Cooperación Iberoamericana, 1986.

Cruz, Anne J. *Discourses of Poverty: Social Reform and the Picaresque Novel in Early Modern Spain*. Toronto: University of Toronto Press, 1999.

Cruz Coelho, Maria Helena da. "Os tabeliães em Portugal: Perfil profissional e sócio-económico (sécs. XIV–XV)." In Pilar Ostos Salcedo y María Luisa Pardo Rodríguez, eds., *Estudios sobre el notariado europeo (siglos XIV–XV)*, 11–51. Seville: Universidad de Sevilla, 1997.

Cummins, Thomas B. F. *Toasts with the Inca: Andean Abstraction and Colonial Images on Quero Vessels*. Ann Arbor: University of Michigan Press, 2002.

Cummins, Thomas B. F., and Joanne Rappaport. "The Reconfiguration of Civic and Sacred Space: Architecture, Image, and Writing in the Colonial Andes." *Latin American Research Review* 26, no. 52 (1998): 174–200.

Cummins, Victoria Hennessey. "The Church and Business Practices in Late Sixteenth Century Mexico." *The Americas* 44, no. 4 (1988): 421–40.

Cutter, Charles R. *The Legal Culture of Northern New Spain, 1700–1810*. Albuquerque: University of New Mexico Press, 1995.

——. *The Protector de Indios in Colonial New Mexico, 1659–1821*. Albuquerque: University of New Mexico Press, 1986.

Dagenais, John. *The Ethics of Reading in Manuscript Culture: Glossing the Libro de Buen Amor*. Princeton: Princeton University Press, 1994.

Davis, Natalie Zemon. *Fiction in the Archives: Pardon Tales and Their Tellers in Sixteenth-Century France*. Stanford, Calif.: Stanford University Press, 1987.

——. *The Return of Martin Guerre*. Cambridge, Mass.: Harvard University Press, 1983.

Dayton, Cornelia Hughes. "Rethinking Agency, Recovering Voices." *American Historical Review* 109, no. 3 (June 2004): 827–43.

Dean, Carolyn. *Inka Bodies and the Body of Christ: Corpus Christi in Colonial Cuzco, Peru*. Durham, N.C.: Duke University Press, 1999.

——. "Beyond Prescription: Notarial Doodles and Other Marks." *Word and Image* 25, no. 3 (2009): 293–316.

de Certeau, Michel. *The Practice of Everyday Life.* Translated by Steven Rendall. Berkeley: University of California Press, 1984.

Decoster, Jean-Jacques, and Brian S. Bauer. *Justicia y poder: Cuzco, siglos XVI–XVIII. Catálogo del Fondo Corregimiento, Archivo Departamental del Cuzco.* Cuzco: Centro de Estudios Regionales Andinos "Bartolomé de Las Casas," 1997.

Decoster, Jean-Jacques, and José Luis Mendoza. *Ylustre Consejo, Justicia y Regimiento: Catálogo del Fondo Cabildo del Cuzco (Causas Civiles).* Cuzco: Centro de Estudios Regionales Andinos "Bartolomé de Las Casas," 2001.

De la Cadena, Marisol. *Indigenous Mestizos: The Politics of Race and Culture in Cuzco, 1919–1991.* Durham, N.C.: Duke University Press, 2000.

De la Puente Brunke, José. *Encomienda y encomenderos en el Perú: Estudio social y político de una institución colonial.* Seville: Excma. Diputación Provincial de Sevilla, 1992.

Dening, Greg. *The Death of William Gooch: A History's Anthropology.* Honolulu: University of Hawai'i Press, 1995.

Derrida, Jacques. *Archive Fever: A Freudian Impression.* Translated by Eric Prenowitz. Chicago: University of Chicago Press, 1996.

——. *Of Grammatology.* Translated by Gayatri Chakravorty Spivak. Baltimore: Johns Hopkins University Press, 1974.

Dirks, Nicholas. "Annals of the Archive: Ethnographic Notes on the Sources of History." In Brian Axel, ed., *From the Margins: Historical Anthropology and Its Futures,* 47–65. Durham, N.C.: Duke University Press, 2002.

Domínguez Ortiz, Antonio. *Crisis y decadencia de la España de los Austrias.* Barcelona: Ediciones Ariel, 1969.

——. *The Golden Age of Spain, 1516–1659.* New York: Basic Books, 1971.

——. *Historia de los moriscos: Vida y tragedia de una minoría.* Madrid: Revista de Occidente, 1979.

——. *La sociedad española en el siglo XVII.* Madrid: Consejo Superior de Investigaciones Científicas, 1963.

Doyle, William. *Venality: The Sale of Offices in Eighteenth-Century France.* New York: Oxford University Press, 1996.

Durston, Alan. "La escritura del quechua por indígenas en el siglo XVII: Nuevas evidencias en el Archivo Arzobispal de Lima (estudio preliminar y edición de textos)." *Revista Andina* 37, no. 2 (2003): 207–36.

——. "Native-Language Literacy in Colonial Peru: The Question of Mundane Quechua Writing Revisited." *Hispanic American Historical Review* 88, no. 1 (2008): 41–70.

——. "Notes on the Authorship of the Huarochirí Manuscript." *Colonial Latin American Review* 16, no. 2 (2007): 227–41.

——. *Pastoral Quechua: The History of Christian Translation in Colonial Peru, 1550–1650.* Notre Dame, Ind.: University of Notre Dame Press, 2007.

Eire, Carlos M. N. *From Madrid to Purgatory: The Art and Craft of Dying in Sixteenth-Century Spain*. New York: Cambridge University Press, 1995.

Elliott, J. H. *Imperial Spain, 1469–1716*. New York: New American Library, 1963.

——. *Spain and Its World, 1500–1700: Selected Essays*. New Haven: Yale University Press, 1989.

Enders, Jody. *The Medieval Theater of Cruelty: Rhetoric, Memory, Violence*. Ithaca, N.Y.: Cornell University Press, 1999.

Epstein, Steven A. *Genoa and the Genoese, 958–1528*. Chapel Hill: University of North Carolina Press, 1996.

——. *Wills and Wealth in Medieval Genoa, 1150–1250*. Cambridge, Mass.: Harvard University Press, 1984.

Escribanos y protocolos notariales en el descubrimiento de América: Presentación del Premio de Investigación Histórico-Jurídico, Madrid, 29 de octubre de 1992. Madrid: Consejo General del Notariado, 1993.

Estupiñán Viteri, Tamara. "El uso de papeles fiduciarios en el sistema económico de la Audiencia de Quito. Un estudio de caso: El banquero Cristóbal Martín." *Revista Andina* 34 (2002): 135–49.

Fenger, Ole. *Notarius Publicus: Le notaire au Moyen Âge latin*. Århus: Århus Universitetsforlag, 2001.

Findlen, Paula, Michelle M. Fontaine, and Duane J. Osheim, eds. *Beyond Florence: The Contours of Medieval and Early Modern Italy*. Stanford, Calif.: Stanford University Press, 2003.

Flórez de Quiñones y Tomé, Vicente. "Formularios notariales hispano-musulmanes." *Anales de la Academia Matritense del Notariado* 23, no. 1 (1981): 179–226.

Foucault, Michel. *The Archaeology of Knowledge and the Discourse on Language*. Translated by A[lan]. M. Sheridan Smith. New York: Pantheon Books, 1972.

——. *Discipline and Punish: The Birth of the Prison*. Translated by Alan Sheridan [Smith]. New York: Vintage Books, 1979.

——. *The Order of Things: An Archaeology of the Human Sciences*. New York: Vintage Books, 1973.

——. *Power / Knowledge: Selected Interviews and Other Writings, 1972–1977*. Edited by Colin Gordon; translated by Colin Gordon, Leo Marshall, John Mepham, and Kate Soper. New York: Pantheon Books, 1980.

Friedman, Edward H. "Trials of Discourse: Narrative Space in Quevedo's *Buscón*." In Giancarlo Maiorino, ed., *The Picaresque: Tradition and Displacement*, 183–225. Minneapolis: University of Minnesota Press, 1996.

García-Gallo, Alfonso. *Estudios de historia del derecho indiano*. Madrid: Instituto Nacional de Estudios Jurídicos, 1972.

Garner, Richard L. "Long-Term Silver Mining Trends in Spanish America: A Comparative Analysis of Peru and Mexico." *American Historical Review* 93, no. 4 (1988): 898–935.

Garrett, David T. *Shadows of Empire: The Indian Nobility of Cusco, 1750–1825.* New York: Cambridge University Press, 2005.

Gibson, Charles. *Tlaxcala in the Sixteenth Century.* Stanford, Calif.: Stanford University Press, 1967.

Ginzburg, Carlo. *Clues, Myths, and the Historical Method.* Translated by John and Anne C. Tedeschi. Baltimore: Johns Hopkins University Press, 1989.

——. *The Judge and the Historian: Marginal Notes on a Late-Twentieth-Century Miscarriage of Justice.* Translated by Antony Shugaar. New York: Verso, 1999.

Glave, Luis Miguel. *Trajinantes: Caminos indígenas en la sociedad colonial, siglos XVI–XVII.* Lima: Instituto de Apoyo Agrario, 1989.

Glave, Luis Miguel, and María Isabel Remy. *Estructura agraria y vida rural en una región andina: Ollantaytambo entre los siglos XVI y XIX.* Cuzco: Centro de Estudios Rurales Andinos "Bartolomé de Las Casas," 1983.

González Cruz, David. *Escribanos y notarios en Huelva durante el antiguo régimen (1701–1800).* Huelva, Spain: Universidad de Sevilla, Vicerrectorado para los Centros Universitarios de Huelva, 1991.

González Echevarría, Roberto. *Myth and Archive: A Theory of Latin American Narrative.* 2nd ed. Durham, N.C.: Duke University Press, 1998.

González Jiménez, Manuel, Joseph Pérez, Horst Pietschmann, and Francisco Comín. *Instituciones y corrupción en la historia.* Valladolid: Universidad de Valladolid, 1998.

Gotkowitz, Laura. *A Revolution for Our Rights: Indigenous Struggles for Land and Justice in Bolivia, 1880–1952.* Durham, N.C.: Duke University Press, 2007.

Graubart, Karen B. *With Our Labor and Sweat: Indigenous Women and the Formation of Colonial Society in Peru, 1550–1700.* Stanford, Calif.: Stanford University Press, 2007.

Greenblatt, Stephen J. *Learning to Curse: Essays in Early Modern Culture.* New York: Routledge, 1990.

——. *Marvelous Possessions: The Wonder of the New World.* Chicago: University of Chicago Press, 1991.

Greene, Richard Firth. *A Crisis of Truth: Literature and Law in Ricardian England.* Philadelphia: University of Pennsylvania Press, 1999.

Greene, Roland. *Unrequited Conquests: Love and Empire in the Colonial Americas.* Chicago: University of Chicago Press, 1999.

Groebner, Valentin. *Who Are You? Identification, Deception, and Surveillance in Early Modern Europe.* New York: Zone Books, 2007.

Gruzinski, Serge. *The Conquest of Mexico: The Incorporation of Indian Societies into the Western World, 16th–18th Centuries.* Translated by Eileen Corrigan. Cambridge: Polity Press, 1993.

Guajardo-Fajardo Carmona, María de los Angeles. *Escribanos en Indias durante la primera mitad del siglo XVI.* 2 vols. Madrid: Colegios Notariales de España, 1995.

Guerrero, Andrés. "The Construction of a Ventriloquist's Image: Liberal Discourse and the 'Miserable Indian Race' in 19th Century Ecuador." *Journal of Latin American Studies* 29, no. 3 (1997): 555–90.

Guevara Gil, Jorge A. *Propiedad agraria y derecho colonial*. Lima: Pontificia Universidad Católica del Perú, 1993.

Guha, Ranajit, and Gayatri Spivak, eds. *Selected Subaltern Studies*. New York: Oxford University Press, 1988.

Guibovich Pérez, Pedro. *Censura, libros e inquisición en el Perú colonial, 1570–1754*. Seville: Consejo Superior de Investigaciones Científicas, 2003.

Hamilton, Carolyn, Verne Harris, Jane Taylor, Michele Pickover, Graeme Reid, and Razia Saleh. *Refiguring the Archive*. Cape Town: David Philip Publishers, 2002.

Hanks, William F. *Intertexts: Writings on Language, Utterance, and Context*. Lanham, Md.: Rowman and Littlefield Publishers, 2000.

Hardwick, Julia. *The Practice of Patriarchy: Gender and the Politics of Household Authority in Early Modern France*. University Park: Pennsylvania State University Press, 1998.

Haring, Clarence Henry. *Trade and Navigation between Spain and the Indies in the Time of the Hapsburgs*. Cambridge, Mass.: Harvard University Press, 1918.

Haskett, Robert. *Indigenous Rulers: An Ethnohistory of Town Government in Colonial Cuernavaca*. Albuquerque: University of New Mexico Press, 1991.

Head, Randolph. "Knowing like a State: The Transformation of Political Knowledge in Swiss Archives, 1450–1770." *Journal of Modern History* 75, no. 4 (2003): 745–82.

Headley, John M. *Church, Empire, and World: The Quest for Universal Order, 1520–1640*. Brookfield, Vt.: Ashgate, 1997.

Hebrard, Jean, and Rebecca J. Scott. "The Writings of Moïse (1898–1985): Birth, Life, and Death of a Narrative of the Great War." *Comparative Studies in Society and History* 44, no. 2 (2002): 263–92.

Herrup, Cynthia B. *A House in Gross Disorder: Sex, Law, and the 2nd Earl of Castlehaven*. New York: Oxford University Press, 1999.

Herzog, Tamar. *La administración como un fenómeno social: La justicia penal de la ciudad de Quito (1650–1750)*. Madrid: Centro de Estudios Constitucionales, 1995.

———. "La comunidad y su administración: Sobre el valor político, social y simbólico de las residencias de Quito (1653–1753)." In Beloît Pellistrandi, ed., *Couronne espagnole et magistratures citadines à l'époque moderne: Dossier de mélanges de la Casa de Velásquez*, n.s. 34, no. 2 (2004): 161–83.

———. *Defining Nations: Immigrants and Citizens in Early Modern Spain and Spanish America*. New Haven: Yale University Press, 2003.

———. "Indiani e Cowboys: Il Ruolo dell'Indigeno nel Diritto e nell'Immaginario Ispano-Coloniale." In Aldo Mazzacane, ed., *Oltremare: Diritto e istituzioni dal colonialismo all'età postcoloniale*. Naples: CUEN, 2006, 9–44.

——. *Mediación, archivos y ejercicio: Los escribanos de Quito (siglo XVII)*. Frankfurt: Vittorio Klostermann, 1996.

——. *Upholding Justice: Society, State, and the Penal System in Quito (1650–1750)*. Ann Arbor: University of Michigan Press, 2004.

Hevia, James L. "The Archive State and the Fear of Pollution: From the Opium Wars to Fu-Manchu." *Cultural Studies* 12, no. 2 (1998): 234–64.

Hill, Ruth. *Hierarchy, Commerce, and Fraud in Bourbon Spanish America: A Postal Inspector's Exposé*. Nashville: Vanderbilt University Press, 2005.

Hindle, Steve. *The State and Social Change in Early Modern England, c. 1550–1640*. New York: St. Martin's Press, 2000.

Hirsch, Susan F. *Pronouncing and Persevering: Gender and the Discourses of Disputing in an African Islamic Court*. Chicago: University of Chicago Press, 1998.

Hoenerbach, Wilhelm. "Some Notes on the Legal Language of Christian and Islamic Deeds." *Journal of the American Oriental Society* 81, no. 1 (1961): 34–38.

Hoffman, Paul E. "The Archivo de Protocolos de Sevilla." *Bulletin of the Society for Spanish and Portuguese Historical Studies* 14 (January 1989): 29–32.

Hoffman, Philip T., Gilles Postel-Vinay, and Jean-Laurent Rosenthal. "Information and Economic History: How the Credit Market in Old Regime Paris Forces Us to Rethink the Transition to Capitalism." *American Historical Review* 104, no. 1 (1999): 69–94.

——. *Priceless Markets: The Political Economy of Credit in Paris, 1660–1870*. Chicago: University of Chicago Press, 2000.

——. "Private Credit Markets in Paris, 1690–1840." *Journal of Economic History* 52, no. 2 (1992): 293–306.

Horn, Rebecca. *Postconquest Coyoacán: Nahua-Spanish Relations in Central Mexico, 1519–1650*. Stanford, Calif.: Stanford University Press, 1997.

Hunt, Lynn, ed. *The New Cultural History*. Berkeley: University of California Press, 1989.

Itier, César. *El teatro Quechua en el Cuzco*. Cuzco: Centro de Estudios Rurales Andinos "Bartolomé de Las Casas," 1995.

——. "Lengua general y comunicación escrita: Cinco cartas en Quechua de Cotahuasi, 1616." *Revista Andina* 9, no. 1 (1991): 65–107.

Johnson, Carroll B. "Defining the Picaresque: Authority and the Subject in *Guzmán de Alfarache*." In Giancarlo Maiorino, ed., *The Picaresque: Tradition and Displacement*, 159–82. Minneapolis: University of Minnesota Press, 1996.

Jones, A. H. M. *The Later Roman Empire, 284–602: A Social, Economic, and Administrative Survey*. Vol. 1. Norman: University of Oklahoma Press, 1964.

Jouve Martín, José Ramón. *Esclavos de la ciudad letrada: Esclavitud, escritura y colonialismo en Lima (1650–1700)*. Lima: Instituto de Estudios Peruanos, 2005.

Kagan, Richard L. *Lawsuits and Litigants in Castile, 1500–1700*. Chapel Hill: University of North Carolina Press, 1981.

——. *Students and Society in Early Modern Spain*. Baltimore: Johns Hopkins University Press, 1974.

Kamen, Henry. *Empire: How Spain Became a World Power, 1492–1763*. New York: HarperCollins, 2003.

——. *Philip of Spain*. New Haven: Yale University Press, 1997.

Keen, Suzanne. *Victorian Renovations of the Novel: Narrative Annexes and the Boundaries of Representation*. New York: Cambridge University Press, 1998.

Kelley, Donald R. "Jurisconsultus Perfectus: The Lawyer as Renaissance Man." *Journal of the Warburg and Courtauld Institutes* 51 (1988): 84–102.

——. "'Second Nature': The Idea of Custom in European Law, Society, and Culture." In Anthony Grafton and Ann Blair, eds. *The Transmission of Culture in Early Modern Europe*, 131–72. Philadelphia: University of Pennsylvania Press, 1990.

Kellogg, Susan. *Law and the Transformation of Aztec Culture, 1500–1700*. Norman: University of Oklahoma Press, 1995.

Kellogg, Susan, and Matthew Restall, eds. *Dead Giveaways: Indigenous Testaments of Colonial Mesoamerica and the Andes*. Salt Lake City: University of Utah Press, 1998.

Kirshner, Julius. "Introduction: The State is 'Back In.'" In Julius Kirshner, ed., *The Origins of the State in Italy 1300–1600*, 1–10. Chicago: University of Chicago Press, 1995.

——. "Some Problems in the Interpretation of Legal Texts *re* the Italian City-States." *Archiv für Besellgeschichte* 19 (1975): 16–27.

Kubler, George. *Building the Escorial*. Princeton: Princeton University Press, 1982.

Kuehn, Thomas. *Law, Family, and Women: Toward a Legal Anthropology of Renaissance Italy*. Chicago: University of Chicago Press, 1991.

Lane, Kris E. "Captivity and Redemption: Aspects of Slave Life in Early Colonial Quito and Popayán." *The Americas* 57, no. 2 (2000): 225–46.

Langbein, John H. *The Origins of Adversary Criminal Trial*. Oxford: Oxford University Press, 2003.

——. *Torture and the Law of Proof: Europe and England in the Ancien Régime*. Chicago: University of Chicago Press, 1977.

Larson, Brooke. *Trials of Nation Making: Liberalism, Race, and Ethnicity in the Andes, 1810–1910*. New York: Cambridge University Press, 2004.

Latour, Bruno. "Drawing Things Together." In Michael Lynch and Steve Woolgar, eds., *Representation in Scientific Practice*, 19–68. Cambridge, Mass.: MIT Press, 1990.

Lazarus-Black, Mindie, and Susan F. Hirsch, eds. *Contested States: Law, Hegemony, and Resistance*. New York: Routledge, 1994.

Le Flem, Jean-Paul. "Coyuntura económica y protocolos notariales: El testimonio de dos escribanos segovianos en 1561 y 1680." In *La documentación notarial y la historia*, 2 vols., 2:333–45. Salamanca: Junta de Decanos de los Colegios Notariales de España and Universidad de Santiago, 1984.

Lemaitre, Nicole. *Le scribe et le mage: Notaires et société rurale en Bas-Limousin aux XVIᵉ et XVIIe siècles*. Ussel, France: Musée du Pays D'Ussel, 2000.

Lenz, Hans. *Historia del papel en México y cosas relacionadas (1525–1950)*. Mexico City: Miguel Angel Porrúa, 1990.

Leonard, Irving A. *Books of the Brave: Being an Account of Books and of Men in the Spanish Conquest and Settlement of the Sixteenth-Century New World*. Introduction by Rolena Adorno. Berkeley: University of California Press, 1992 [1949].

Lienhard, Martín. *La voz y su huella: Escritura y conflicto étnico-cultural en América Latina, 1492–1988*. Revised and augmented 3rd ed. Lima: Editorial Horizonte, 1992.

Lira González, Andrés. *El amparo colonial y el juicio de amparo mexicano (antecedentes novohispanos del juicio de amparo)*. Mexico City: Fondo de Cultura Económica, 1972.

Lockhart, James. *The Men of Cajamarca: A Social and Biographical Study of the First Conquerors of Peru*. Austin: University of Texas Press, 1972.

———. *The Nahuas After the Conquest: A Social and Cultural History of the Indians of Central Mexico, Sixteenth through Eighteenth Centuries*. Stanford, Calif.: Stanford University Press, 1992.

———. *Nahuas and Spaniards: Postconquest Central Mexican History and Philology*. Stanford, Calif.: Stanford University Press, 1991.

———. *Of Things of the Indies: Essays Old and New in Early Latin American History*. Stanford, Calif.: Stanford University Press, 1999.

———. *Spanish Peru 1532–1560: A Colonial Society*. Madison: University of Wisconsin Press, 1968.

Luján Muñoz, Jorge. "La literatura notarial en España e Hispanoamérica, 1500–1820." *Anuario de Estudios Americanos* 38 (1981): 101–16.

———. *Los escribanos en las Indias Occidentales y en particular en el Reino de Guatemala*. Revised 2nd ed. Guatemala: Instituto Guatemalteco de Derecho Notarial, 1977.

———. "Los escribanos en pueblos de indios en el Reino de Guatemala durante la colonia." *Memoria del II Congreso de Historia del Derecho Mexicano*, 1980.

Lynch, John. *The Hispanic World in Crisis and Change, 1598–1700*. Cambridge, Mass.: Blackwell, 1992.

———. *Spain, 1516–1598: From Nation State to World Empire*. Cambridge, Mass.: Blackwell, 1992.

Mackey, Carol. "The Continuing Khipu Traditions." In Jeffrey Quilter and Gary Urton, eds., *Narrative Threads*, 320–47. Austin: University of Texas Press, 2002.

Mackey, Carol, Hugo Pereyra, Carlos Radicati di Primeglio, Humberto Rodríguez, and Oscar Valverde, eds. *Quipu y yupana: Colección de escritos*. Lima: Consejo Nacional de Ciencia y Tecnología, 1990.

Maiorino, Giancarlo, ed. *The Picaresque: Tradition and Displacement*. Minneapolis: University of Minnesota Press, 1996.

Malagón Barceló, Javier. *La literatura jurídica española del Siglo de Oro en la Nueva España. Notas para su estudio*. Mexico City: Universidad Nacional Autónoma de México, 1959.

———. "The Role of the *Letrado* in the Colonization of America." *The Americas* 18, no. 1 (1961): 1–7.

Mallon, Florencia E. "The Promise and Dilemma of Subaltern Studies: Perspectives from Latin American History." *American Historical Review* 99, no. 5 (1994): 1491–1515.

Mangan, Jane. *Trading Roles: Gender, Ethnicity, and the Urban Economy in Colonial Potosí*. Durham, N.C.: Duke University Press, 2005.

Mannarelli, María Emma. *Private Passions and Public Sins: Men and Women in Seventeenth-Century Lima*. Translated by Sidney Evans and Meredith D. Dodge. Albuquerque: University of New Mexico Press, 2007.

Mannheim, Bruce. *The Language of the Inka since the European Invasion*. Austin: University of Texas Press, 1991.

Márques Villanueva, Francisco. "Letrados, consejeros y justicias (artículo-reseña)." *Hispanic Review* 53 (1985): 201–27.

Martin, Henri-Jean. *The History and Power of Writing*. Translated by Lydia G. Cochrane. Chicago: University of Chicago Press, 1994.

Martínez Kleiser, Luis. *Refranero general ideológico español*. Madrid: Real Academia Española, 1953.

McKenzie, D. F. *Bibliography and the Sociology of Texts*. Cambridge: Cambridge University Press, 1999.

McNeely, Ian F. *The Emancipation of Writing: German Civil Society in the Making, 1790s-1820s*. Berkeley: University of California Press, 2003.

Merryman, John Henry. *The Civil Law Tradition: An Introduction to the Legal Systems of Western Europe and Latin America*. 2nd ed. Stanford, Calif.: Stanford University Press, 1985.

Merwick, Donna. *Death of a Notary: Conquest and Change in Colonial New York*. Ithaca, N.Y.: Cornell University Press, 1999.

Messick, Brinkley. *The Calligraphic State: Textual Domination and History in a Muslim Society*. Berkeley: University of California Press, 1993.

Metzger, Ernest. *Litigation in Roman Law*. New York: Oxford University Press, 2005.

Mignolo, Walter D. *The Darker Side of the Renaissance: Literacy, Territoriality, and Colonization*. Ann Arbor: University of Michigan Press, 1995.

Mijares Ramírez, Ivonne. *Escribanos y escrituras públicas en el siglo XVI: El caso de la Ciudad de México*. Mexico City: Universidad Nacional Autónoma de México, 1997.

Millares Carlo, Agustín. *Tratado de paleografía española*. 3 vols. 3rd ed. Madrid: Espasa-Calpe, 1983.

Milligan, Jennifer S. " 'What Is an Archive?' in the History of Modern France." In Antoinette Burton, ed., *Archival Stories*, 159–83. Durham, N.C.: Duke University Press, 2005.

Mirow, Matthew C. *Latin American Law: A History of Private Law and Institutions in Spanish America*. Austin: University of Texas Press, 2004.

Morales Padrón, Francisco. "Descubrimiento y toma de posesión." *Anuario de Estudios Americanos* 12 (1955): 321–80.

Moreno Trujillo, María Amparo. "Diplomática notarial en Granada en los inícios de la modernidad (1505–1520)." In Pilar Ostos Salcedo and María Luisa Pardo Rodríguez, eds., *El notariado andaluz en el tránsito de la edad media a la edad moderna. I Jornadas sobre el Notariado en Andalucía, del 23 al 25 de febrero de 1994*, 75–125. Seville: Ilustre Colegio Notarial de Sevilla, 1995.

Mörner, Magnus. *La corona española y los foráneos en los pueblos de indios de América*. Stockholm: Latinamerikanska-institutet i Stockholm, Almqvist and Wiksell, 1970.

Mousnier, Roland. *La vénalité des offices sous Henri IV et Louis XIII*. Revised 2nd ed. Paris: Presses Universitaires de France, 1971.

Mumford, Jeremy Ravi. "Litigation as Ethnography in Sixteenth-Century Peru: Polo de Ondegardo and the Mitimaes." *Hispanic American Historical Review* 88, no. 1 (2008): 5–40.

Mundy, Barbara E. *The Mapping of New Spain: Indigenous Cartography and the Maps of the Relaciones Geográficas*. Chicago: University of Chicago Press, 1996.

Navas, José Manual. *La abogacía en el Siglo de Oro*. Madrid: Ilustre Colegio de Abogados de Madrid, 1996.

Nelson, Cary, and Lawrence Grossberg, eds. *Marxism and the Interpretation of Culture*. Urbana: University of Illinois Press, 1988.

Nicholas, Barry. *An Introduction to Roman Law*. Oxford: Clarendon Press, 1962.

Nirenberg, David. *Communities of Violence: Persecution of Minorities in the Middle Ages*. Princeton: Princeton University Press, 1996.

Notariado público y documento privado: De los orígenes al siglo XIV. Actas del VII Congreso Internacional de Diplomática, Valencia, 1986. 2 vols. Valencia: Conselleria de Cultura, Educació i Ciència, 1989.

Núñez Lagos, Rafael. *El documento medieval y Rolandino (notas de historia)*. Madrid: [n.p.], 1951.

Nussdorfer, Laurie. "The Boys at the Banco: Notaries' Scribes in Baroque Rome."

In Deanna Shemek and Michael Wyatt, eds., *Writing Relations: American Scholars in Italian Archives*, 121–38. Florence: Leo S. Olschki, 2008.

———. *Brokers of Public Trust: Notaries in Early Modern Rome*. Baltimore: Johns Hopkins University Press, 2009.

———. "Lost Faith: A Roman Prosecutor Reflects on Notaries' Crimes." In *Beyond Florence*, Paula Findlen, Michelle M. Fontaine, and Duane J. Osheim, eds., 101–14, 258–59. Stanford, Calif.: Stanford University Press, 2003.

———. "Writing and the Power of Speech: Notaries and Artisans in Baroque Rome." In Barbara B. Diefendorf and Carla Hesse, eds., *Culture and Identity in Early Modern Europe (1500–1800): Essays in Honor of Natalie Zemon Davis*, 103–18. Ann Arbor: University of Michigan Press, 1993.

Obra Sierra, Juan María de la. "Aproximación al estudio de los escribanos públicos del número en Granada (1497–1520)." In Pilar Ostos Salcedo and María Luisa Pardo Rodríguez, eds., *El notariado andaluz en el tránsito de la edad media a la edad moderna. I Jornadas sobre el Notariado en Andalucía, del 23 al 25 de febrero de 1994*, 127–70. Seville: Ilustre Colegio Notarial de Sevilla, 1995.

Offner, Jerome A. *Law and Politics in Aztec Texcoco*. New York: Cambridge University Press, 1983.

Olivera Olivera, Jorge. "Relación de testamentos existentes en el Archivo, siglo XVII." *Boletín del Archivo Departamental del Cuzco* 1 (October 1985): 14–17; 2 (April 1986): 38–41; and 3 (June 1987): 84–89.

Ong, Walter J. *Orality and Literacy: The Technologizing of the Word*. New York: Routledge, 2002 [1982].

Ostos Salcedo, Pilar, and María Luisa Pardo Rodríguez, eds. *El notariado andaluz en el tránsito de la edad media a la edad moderna. I Jornadas sobre el Notariado en Andalucía, del 23 al 25 de febrero de 1994*. Seville: Ilustre Colegio Notarial de Sevilla, 1995.

———. *Estudios sobre el notariado europeo (siglos XIV–XV)*. Seville: Universidad de Sevilla, 1997.

O'Toole, Rachel Sarah. "From the Rivers of Guinea to the Valleys of Peru: Becoming a Bran Diaspora within Spanish Slavery." *Social Text* 25, no. 3 92 (2007): 19–36.

———. " 'In a War against the Spanish': Andean Protection and African Resistance on the Northern Peruvian Coast." *The Americas* 63, no. 1 (2006): 19–52.

Pagden, Anthony. *European Encounters with the New World*. New Haven: Yale University Press, 1993.

———. *The Fall of Natural Man: The American Indian and the Origins of Comparative Ethnology*. New York: Cambridge University Press, 1982.

———. *Lords of All the World: Ideologies of Empire in Spain, Britain, and France, c. 1500–c. 1800*. New Haven: Yale University Press, 1995.

——. *Spanish Imperialism and the Political Imagination: Studies in European and Spanish-American Social and Political Theory, 1513–1830.* New Haven: Yale University Press, 1990.

Pardo, Osvaldo F. "How to Punish Indians: Law and Cultural Change in Early Colonial Mexico." *Comparative Studies in Society and History* 48, no. 1 (2006): 79–109.

Pardo Rodríguez, María Luisa. *Señores y escribanos: El notariado andaluz entre los siglos XIV y XVI.* Seville: Universidad de Sevilla, 2002.

Parry, J. H. *The Sale of Public Office in the Spanish Indies under the Hapsburgs.* Berkeley: University of California Press, 1953.

Pease, Franklin. *Curacas, reciprocidad y riqueza.* Lima: Pontificia Universidad Católica del Perú, 1992.

——. "Utilización de quipus en los primeros tiempos coloniales." In Carol Mackey et al., eds., *Quipu y yupana,* 67–72. Lima: Consejo Nacional de Ciencia y Tecnología, 1990.

Peletz, Michael. *Islamic Modern: Religious Courts and Cultural Politics in Malaysia.* Princeton: Princeton University Press, 2002.

——. *Reinscribing "Asian (Family) Values": Nation Building, Subject Making, and Judicial Process in Malaysia's Islamic Courts.* Notre Dame, Ind.: Erasmus Institute, 2003.

Perera Díaz, Aisnara, and María de los Ángeles Meriño Fuentes. "La cesión de patronato: Una estrategia familiar en la emancipación de esclavos en Cuba, 1870–1880." *Revista de História* 152, no. 1 (2005): 1–27.

Pérez-Bustamante, Rogelio. "Los documentos de Cristóbal Colón y la práctica notarial." In *Escribanos y protocolos notariales en el descubrimiento de América: Presentación del Premio de Investigación Histórico-Jurídico, Madrid, 29 de octubre de 1992.* Madrid: Consejo General del Notariado, 1993.

Pérez Fernández del Castillo, Bernardo. *Historia de la escribanía en la Nueva España y del notariado en México.* 2nd ed. Mexico City: Colegio de Notarios del Distrito Federal and Editorial Porrúa, 1988.

Pérez-Perdomo, Rogelio. *Latin American Lawyers: A Historical Introduction.* Stanford, Calif.: Stanford University Press, 2006.

Peters, Edward. *Torture.* Expanded ed. Philadelphia: University of Pennsylvania Press, 1996.

Petrucci, Armando. *Prima lezione di paleografia.* Rome: Editori Laterza, 2002.

Phelan, John Leddy. *The Kingdom of Quito in the Seventeenth Century: Bureaucratic Politics in the Spanish Empire.* Madison: University of Wisconsin Press, 1967.

Phillips, Carla Rahn. *Six Galleons for the King of Spain: Imperial Defense in the Early Seventeenth Century.* Baltimore: Johns Hopkins University Press, 1986.

Poisson, Jean-Paul. *Notaires et société: Travaux d'histoire et de sociologie notariales.* Paris: Economica, 1985.

Polo y la Borda, Jorge. "La hacienda Pachachaca (segunda mitad del siglo XVIII)." *Histórica* [Lima] 1 (1977): 223–47.

Portelli, Alessandro. *The Death of Luigi Trastulli and Other Stories: Form and Meaning in Oral History*. Albany, N.Y.: State University of New York Press, 1991.

Powers, Karen Vieira. "A Battle of Wills: Inventing Chiefly Legitimacy in the Colonial North Andes." In Susan Kellogg and Matthew Restall, eds., *Dead Giveaways: Indigenous Testaments of Colonial Mesoamerica and the Andes*, 183–213. Salt Lake City: University of Utah Press, 1998.

Pratt, Mary Louise. "Arts of the Contact Zone." *Profession* [Modern Language Association] 9 (1991): 33–40.

Premo, Bianca. *Children of the Father King: Youth, Authority, and Legal Minority in Colonial Lima*. Chapel Hill: University of North Carolina Press, 2005.

Pulido Rubio, José. *El piloto mayor de la Casa de la Contratación de Sevilla: Pilotos mayores, catedráticos de cosmografía y cosmógrafos*. Seville: Escuela de Estudios Hispano-Americanos de Sevilla, 1950.

Quilter, Jeffrey, and Gary Urton, eds. *Narrative Threads: Accounting and Recounting in Andean Khipu*. Austin: University of Texas Press, 2002.

Quispe-Agnoli, Rocío. "Escritura alfabética y literalidades amerindias: Fundamentos para una historiografía colonial andina." *Revista Andina* 34 (2002): 237–49.

Rafael, Vicente L. *Contracting Colonialism: Translation and Christian Conversion in Tagalog Society under Early Spanish Rule*. Ithaca, N.Y.: Cornell University Press, 1988.

Rama, Angel. *La ciudad letrada*. Hanover, N.H.: Ediciones del Norte, 1984.

———. *The Lettered City*. Translated and edited by John Charles Chasteen. Durham, N.C.: Duke University Press, 1996.

Ramírez, Susan E. *Provincial Patriarchs: Land Tenure and the Economics of Power in Colonial Peru*. Albuquerque: University of New Mexico Press, 1986.

Ramos, Gabriela P. "Death, Conversion, and Identity in the Peruvian Andes: Lima and Cuzco, 1532–1670." Ph.D. diss., University of Pennsylvania, Philadelphia, 2001.

Rappaport, Joanne. *Intercultural Utopias: Public Intellectuals, Cultural Experimentation, and Ethnic Pluralism in Colombia*. Durham, N.C.: Duke University Press, 2005.

———. *The Politics of Memory: Native Historical Interpretation in the Colombian Andes*. Durham, N.C.: Duke University Press, 1998.

Rappaport, Joanne, and Tom Cummins. "Between Images and Writing: The Ritual of the King's *Quillca*." *Colonial Latin American Review* 7, no. 1 (1998): 7–32.

Real Díaz, José Joaquín. *Estudio diplomática del documento indiano*. Seville: Escuela de Estudios Hispanoamericanos, 1970.

Restall, Matthew. "A History of the New Philology and the New Philology in History." *Latin American Research Review* 38, no. 1 (2003): 113–34.

——. *Maya Conquistador*. Boston: Beacon Press, 1998.

——. *The Maya World: Yucatec Culture and Society, 1550–1850*. Stanford, Calif.: Stanford University Press, 1997.

Restall, Matthew, Lisa Sousa, and Kevin Terraciano, eds. *Mesoamerican Voices: Native-Language Writings from Colonial Mexico, Oaxaca, Yucatan, and Guatemala*. New York: Cambridge University Press, 2005.

Reyerson, Kathryn L., and Debra A. Salata, eds. and trans. *Medieval Notaries and Their Acts: The 1327–1328 Register of Jean Holanie*. Kalamazoo, Mich.: Medieval Institute Publications, 2004.

Richards, Thomas. *The Imperial Archive: Knowledge and the Fantasy of Empire*. New York: Verso, 1993.

Rivarola, José Luis. *Español andino: Textos de bilingües en los siglos XVI y XVII*. Madrid: Iberoamericana, 2000.

Rodríguez Adrados, Antonio. "El derecho notarial castellano trasplantado a Indias." In *Escribanos y protocolos notariales en el descubrimiento de América: Presentación del Premio de Investigación Histórico-Jurídico, Madrid, 29 de octubre de 1992*, 47–70. Madrid: Consejo General del Notariado, 1993.

——. "La Pragmática de Alcalá, entre Las Partidas y la Ley del Notariado." In *Homenaje a Juan Berchmans Vallet de Goytisolo*, 8 vols., 7:517–813. Madrid: Junta de Decanos de los Colegios Notariales de España, 1988.

Roedl, Bohumír. "Causa Tupa Amaro: El proceso a los tupamaros en Cuzco, abril–julio de 1781." *Revista Andina* 34 (2002): 99–121.

Romero Tallafigo, Manuel, Laureano Rodríguez Liañez, and Antonio Sánchez González. *Arte de leer escrituras antiguas: Paleografía de lectura*. Huelva: Universidad de Huelva, 1995.

Rowe, Katherine. *Dead Hands: Fictions of Agency, Renaissance to Modern*. Stanford, Calif.: Stanford University Press, 1999.

Said, Edward. *Orientalism*. New York: Vintage Books, 1978.

Salomon, Frank. *The Cord Keepers: Khipus and Cultural Life in a Peruvian Village*. Durham, N.C.: Duke University Press, 2004.

——. "Patrimonial Khipu in a Modern Peruvian Village." In Jeffrey Quilter and Gary Urton, eds., *Narrative Threads*, 293–319. Austin: University of Texas Press, 2002.

Scardaville, Michael C. "Justice by Paperwork: A Day in the Life of a Court Scribe in Bourbon Mexico City." *Journal of Social History* 36, no. 4 (2003): 979–1007.

Schwartz, Stuart B. *Sovereignty and Society in Colonial Brazil: The High Court of Bahia and Its Judges, 1609–1751*. Berkeley: University of California Press, 1973.

Schwartz Lerner, Lia. "El letrado en la sátira de Quevedo." *Hispanic Review* 54 (1986): 27–46.

Scott, James C. *Seeing like a State: How Certain Schemes to Improve the Human Condition Have Failed*. New Haven: Yale University Press, 1998.

——. *Weapons of the Weak: Everyday Forms of Peasant Resistance*. New Haven: Yale University Press, 1985.

Scott, Rebecca J. *Degrees of Freedom: Louisiana and Cuba after Slavery*. Cambridge, Mass.: Harvard University Press, 2005.

——. "The Provincial Archive as a Place of Memory: The Role of Former Slaves in the Cuban War of Independence (1895–98)." *History Workshop Journal* 58 (2004): 149–66.

——. "Public Rights, Social Equality, and the Conceptual Roots of the *Plessy* Challenge." *Michigan Law Review* 106, no. 5 (2008): 777–804.

Scott, Rebecca J. and Michael Zeuske. "Property in Writing, Property on the Ground: Pigs, Horses, Land, and Citizenship in the Aftermath of Slavery, Cuba, 1880–1909." *Comparative Studies in Society and History* 44, no. 4 (2002): 669–99.

Seed, Patricia. *Ceremonies of Possession in Europe's Conquest of the New World, 1492–1640*. New York: Cambridge University Press, 1995.

Sell, Barry D., and Louise M. Burkhart, eds. *Nahuatl Theater*. Vol. 1. *Death and Life in Colonial Nahua Mexico*. Norman: University of Oklahoma Press, 2004.

Shapin, Steven. *A Social History of Truth: Civility and Science in Seventeenth-Century England*. Chicago: University of Chicago Press, 1994.

Shipley, George A. "Garbage In, Garbage Out: 'The Best of Vidriera.'" *Cervantes* 21, no. 1 (2001): 5–41.

——. "Vidriera's Blather." *Cervantes* 22, no. 2 (2002): 49–124.

Sicroff, Albert. "Spanish Anti-Judaism: A Case of Religious Racism." In Carlos Carrete Parrondo et al., eds., *Encuentros and Desencuentros: Spanish Jewish Cultural Interaction throughout History*, 589–613. Tel Aviv: University Publishing Projects, 2000.

Sieber, Harry. "Literary Continuity, Social Order, and the Invention of the Picaresque." In Brownlee, Marina S., and Hans Ulrich Gumbrecht, eds., *Cultural Authority in Golden Age Spain*, 143–64. Baltimore: Johns Hopkins University Press, 1995.

Silverman, Lisa. *Tortured Subjects: Pain, Truth, and the Body in Early Modern France*. Chicago: University of Chicago Press, 2001.

Smail, Daniel Lord. *Imaginary Cartographies: Possession and Identity in Late Medieval Marseille*. Ithaca, N.Y.: Cornell University Press, 1999, 2000.

Spalding, Karen. *Huarochirí: An Andean Society under Inca and Spanish Rule*. Stanford, Calif.: Stanford University Press, 1984.

Spiegel, Gabrielle M. *The Past as Text: The Theory and Practice of Medieval Historiography*. Baltimore: Johns Hopkins University Press, 1997.

Spivak, Gayatri Chakravorty. "Can the Subaltern Speak?" In Cary Nelson and

Lawrence Grossberg, eds., *Marxism and the Interpretation of Culture*, 271–313. Urbana: University of Illinois Press, 1988.

———. *A Critique of Postcolonial Reason: Toward a History of the Vanishing Present.* Cambridge, Mass.: Harvard University Press, 1999.

———. "The Rani of Sirmur: An Essay in Reading the Archives." *History and Theory* 24, no. 3 (1985): 247–72.

Starn, Randolph. "Truths in the Archives." *Common Knowledge* 8, no. 2 (2002): 387–401.

Steedman, Carolyn. *Dust: The Archive and Cultural History.* New Brunswick, N.J.: Rutgers University Press, 2002.

Stein, Peter. *Roman Law in European History.* New York: Cambridge University Press, 1999.

Steiner, Emily, and Candace Barrington. *The Letter of the Law: Legal Practice and Literary Production in Medieval England.* Ithaca, N.Y.: Cornell University Press, 2002.

Stern, Steve J. *Peru's Indian Peoples and the Challenge of Spanish Conquest.* Madison: University of Wisconsin Press, 1982.

Stock, Brian. *Listening for the Text: On the Uses of the Past.* Baltimore: Johns Hopkins University Press, 1990.

Stoler, Ann Laura. *Along the Archival Grain: Epistemic Anxieties and Colonial Common Sense.* Princeton: Princeton University Press, 2009.

———. "Colonial Archives and the Arts of Governance: On the Content in the Form." *Archival Science* 2 (2002): 87–109.

Suárez, Margarita. *Desafíos transatlánticos: Mercaderes, banqueros y el estado en el Perú virreinal, 1600–1700.* Lima: Pontificia Universidad Católica del Perú, 2001.

Swart, K. W. *Sale of Offices in the Seventeenth Century.* The Hague: Martinus Nihjoff, 1949.

Tanodi, Aurelio. *Comienzos de la función notarial en Córdoba.* Córdoba, Argentina: Universidad Nacional de Córdoba, 1956.

Tanselle, G. Thomas. "The World as Archive." *Common Knowledge* 8, no. 2 (2002): 402–6.

Tapia Franco, Luis Alfredo. "Análisis histórico institucional del censo consignativo en el derecho peruano." B.A. thesis, Pontificia Universidad Católica del Perú, Lima, 1991.

Tau Anzoátegui, Víctor. *El poder de la costumbre: Estudios sobre el derecho consuetudinario en América Hispana hasta la emancipación.* Buenos Aires: Instituto de Investigaciones de Historia del Derecho, 2001.

Taylor, Gerald. *Camac, camay y camasca y otros ensayos sobre Huarochirí y Yauyos.* Cuzco: Centro de Estudios Regionales Andinos "Bartolomé de Las Casas," 2000.

———. *El sol, la luna y las estrellas no son Dios: La evangelización en quechua (siglo XVI).* Lima: IFEA and Pontificia Universidad Católica del Perú, 2003.

Tedlock, Dennis. "Torture in the Archives: Mayans Meet Europeans." *American Anthropologist* 95, no. 1 (1993): 139–52.

TePaske, John J., and Herbert S. Klein. *The Royal Treasuries of the Spanish Empire in America*. 4 vols. Durham, N.C.: Duke University Press, 1982.

Terraciano, Kevin. *The Mixtecs of Colonial Oaxaca: Ñudzahui History, Sixteenth through Eighteenth Centuries*. Stanford, Calif.: Stanford University Press, 2001.

Thomson, Sinclair. *We Alone Will Rule: Native Andean Politics in the Age of Insurgency*. Madison: University of Wisconsin Press, 2002.

Todorov, Tzvetan. *The Conquest of America: The Question of the Other*. New York: Harper and Row, 1984.

Tomás y Valiente, Francisco. *La tortura en España*. Barcelona: Editorial Ariel, 1973.

——. *La venta de oficios en Indias (1492–1606)*. Madrid: Instituto de Estudios Administrativos, 1972.

——. "La venta de oficios en Indias, y en particular la de escribanías." In *Escribanos y protocolos notariales en el descubrimiento de América: Presentación del Premio de Investigación Histórico-Jurídico, Madrid, 29 de octubre de 1992*, 95–103. Madrid: Consejo General del Notariado, 1993.

——. *Manual de historia del derecho español*. Madrid: Tecnos, 1981.

Tomlinson, Gary. *The Singing of the New World: Indigenous Voices in the Era of European Contact*. New York: Cambridge University Press, 2007.

Trouillot, Michel-Rolph. *Silencing the Past: Power and the Production of History*. Boston: Beacon Press, 1995.

Twinam, Ann. *Public Lives, Private Secrets: Gender, Honor, Sexuality, and Illegitimacy in Colonial Spanish America*. Stanford, Calif.: Stanford University Press, 1999.

Uribe-Uran, Victor M. *Honorable Lives: Lawyers, Family, and Politics in Colombia, 1780–1850*. Pittsburgh: University of Pittsburgh Press, 2000.

Valls i Subira, Oriol. *La historia del papel en España*. 3 vols. Madrid: Empresa Nacional de Celulosa, 1978–82.

van Deusen, Nancy E. *Between the Sacred and the Worldly: The Institutional and Cultural Practice of Recogimiento in Colonial Lima*. Stanford, Calif.: Stanford University Press, 2001.

Van Young, Eric. "The Cuautla Lazarus: Double Subjectivities in Reading Texts on Popular Collective Action." *Colonial Latin American Review* 2, nos. 1–2 (1993): 3–26.

——. "The New Cultural History Comes to Old Mexico." *Hispanic American Historical Review* 79, no. 2 (1999): 211–47.

Varón Gabai, Rafael. *La ilusión del poder: Apogeo y decadencia de los Pizarro en la conquista del Perú*. Lima: Instituto de Estudios Peruanos, 1996.

Vassberg, David E. *Land and Society in Golden Age Castile*. New York: Cambridge University Press, 1984.

Waquet, Jean-Claude. *Corruption: Ethics and Power in Florence, 1600–1770*. Translated by Linda McCall. University Park: Pennsylvania State University Press, 1991.

Weber, Samuel. *Institution and Interpretation*. Expanded ed. Stanford, Calif.: Stanford University Press, 2001.

White, Hayden. *The Content of the Form: Narrative Discourse and Historical Representation*. Baltimore: Johns Hopkins University Press, 1987.

Wightman, Ann M. *Indigenous Migration and Social Change: The Forasteros of Cuzco, 1570–1720*. Durham, N.C.: Duke University Press, 1990.

Wood, Robert D. *"Teach Them Good Customs": Colonial Indian Education and Acculturation in the Andes*. Culver City, Calif.: Labyrinthos, 1986.

Zamora, Margarita. *Reading Columbus*. Berkeley: University of California Press, 1993.

Zimmermann, Reinhard. *The Law of Obligations: Roman Foundations of the Civilian Tradition*. Cape Town: Juta, 1992.

INDEX

Abancay, 47, 52, 119
abogados. *See* advocates
Acosta, José de, 8
adoption, 109–10
advocates, 3, 25–26, 31, 132–33, 155n19,
 167n61, 197n29, 205; reputation of,
 15, 162n13; role of, in Cuzco lawsuits, 92, 197n31
agency, 3–4, 24, 39, 94, 127, 134–35,
 197n28; contractual means for disguising or revealing of, 99–113; indigenous, 131–32
Aguiar y Acuña, Doña Elena de, 116
Aguilar, Cristóbal de, 140–41
Aicardo, Marcelo de, 60–61
Alarcón, Francisco de, 130–32
Alba, Duke of, 56–57
Albornoz, Bartolomé de, 20, 98–
 100
Alemán, Mateo, 22, 24, 41
alguaciles. *See* constables
Álvarez Posadilla, Juan, 88–89, 93
Andahuaylillas, 55, 177–78nn68–70
Anta, 55, 69, 177n63
apprenticeship, notarial. *See* notaries:
 training of
aranceles (price lists), 39, 41, 170n100,
 181n97
archives, 38, 46, 81, 93, 118, 124–25, 138–
 43; fiction in, 11, 95–104, 108, 129,
 143; history and ethnography of, 11–
 19, 27–29, 143–47, 158nn52–53; indigenous, 4–11, 50–51, 130–31, 153n1,

195–96nn17–19, 201nn76–77; manipulation of, 95–123; as notaries' property, 26, 41, 88; as repositories of
 truth, 2–3, 11, 16, 18, 96, 194n4;
 thefts from, 72, 120–21, 193n73
Archivo Arzobispal de Cuzco, 160n73
Archivo Arzobispal de Lima, 160n73,
 193n62
Archivo General de Indias (Seville), 15,
 138–41
Archivo Histórico de Sevilla, 141,
 200n61
Archivo Regional de Cusco, 15, 17, 52,
 148, 160n77, 174n26, 198n38
Arias de Lira, Ambrocio, 70–71, 75
Arias de Lira, Don Juan, 111
Arias de Saavedra, Don Francisco, 92
assets, seizure of: 91; means of avoid-
 ing, 95–96, 100–101, 108, 113, 122, 129
assistants, notarial. *See* oficial mayor;
 plumarios
Atahualpa, 7
Atao, Bartolomé, 130–31
Audiencia (high court) of Lima, 58, 64
Augustinian friars, 45, 55
Ayacucho. *See* Huamanga
ayllus, 55–56, 130, 177–78nn68–70
Aymara (language), 8
Aztecs, 5–6

Balbín, Don Pedro (corregidor), 109
Básquez Serrano, Gregorio, 16, 126
beatas, 104–5, 122, 125–27

Bejarano y Castilla, Miguel, 119–20
Belén (Cuzco parish), 50
Beltrán Lucero, Alonso, 54, 58, 105–6
Benavente, Bernardo de, 68, 128–30, 143
Blanco, Francisco, 115
blank space: in documents, 27, 38, 57, 75–80, 87, 90–93, 117; in notaries' protocolos, 16–17, 185nn32–33, 186n38
Bologna, 25–26, 164n30
book trade, 24, 29, 40
bribes, 45–46, 63, 87, 93, 97, 139–41
Buenavista, Marqués de, 92, 119
Buscón llamado don Pablos, La vida del (Quevedo), xi, 21–24
Bustamante, Alfonso de, 60
Bustamante, Cristóbal de, 55, 65, 77, 181n103

cabildo, 44, 47–50, 55, 59, 97, 133, 142; notaries of, 48–50, 58–64, 66–67, 121–22
Cáceres, Doña Petronila de, 95–96
Cáceres, Pedro de, 75–76, 78, 109–11
caciques, 5, 16, 40, 45–46, 173n13, 179n77; involvement of, in lawsuits, 55–56, 130–32, 136–37, 150, 177–78nn68–70
Calancha, Antonio de, 45
Calvo, Alonso, 53, 60, 101
Calvo Justiniano, Doña Francisca, 116, 183n11
Camberos, Cristóbal, 97
Cañete, 66
Cano Velarde de Santillana, Doña Luisa, 115
Carlos, Don Florián, 118
Carlos Inca, Don Lorenzo, 128
Carlos Ynquiltopa, Don Lázaro, 118
Carlos Ynquiltopa, Don Lucas, 118

Carrera Ron, Pedro de la, 51–52, 54, 57–58, 60, 65, 76, 176nn45–47
Carrión y Mogrovejo, Doña Bárbara Antonia de, 113
Carvajal, Bartolomé de, 13–14, 32–33, 107, 137, 198n47
Casa de la Contratación (Seville), 138–41
Casinchigua (ingenio), 116
censos, 55, 71, 76, 78, 83, 86, 106, 187n52
Centeno, Juan Francisco (captain), 58
Cervantes, Miguel de, 14, 24
Cervantes, Pedro de, 49–50
Chamancalla, 128–29
Chanca Topa, Don Gerónimo, 50–51
Charles V (emperor), 44
children, 68–73, 75, 93–94, 97, 109–10, 122–23
Cieza de León, Pedro de, 47
Clanchy, M. T., 2, 153n1, 155n12, 155n21
coca, 18, 47, 51–52, 58, 82–83
cofradías (confraternities), 57–58
Columbus, Christopher, 1–5, 42, 158n58
confianzas (bogus contracts), 18, 97–104, 113, 123, 128–30, 143
constables, 55–56, 59, 63, 88, 110–11, 188n65
contracartas, 98–99
contracts: xi, 24–26, 50, 65–66, 141, 190n22, 190–91n32; making of, 16, 37–39, 45, 74–87, 97–104, 125–30; un-making of, 104–23, 192n51. *See also* confianzas; exclamations
Contreras, Lorenzo de, 119
Corpus Christi, 57, 137, 179n79
corregidores (magistrates), 44–46, 63, 67, 72, 90–92, 183n12; of Cuzco, 53, 56, 58–59, 120
corruption, 12, 45, 59, 63, 66–67, 139–42, 173–74n21

Cortés, Hernán, 5, 41–42, 172n114

Coscoja (ayllu), 55, 177–78n68

Costilla, Don Gerónimo (marqués de Buenavista), 119–20

Costilla, Don Juan, 119–20

Council of the Indies, 139

Covarrubias, Sebastián de, 42, 83, 93

credit, 55, 76, 78, 83–87, 100, 102, 115, 187n54. *See also* censos

criminal suits, 135–38, 147; initial testimony in (*sumaria información*), 33–36, 88–93, 140, 167n67, 168–69nn78–79, 198n38

criollos, 46, 54, 58, 65, 128–30

Cusipaucar, Francisca, 72

custom, local, 62–67, 73–94, 96, 125, 139, 142, 185n25, 186n38, 186nn41–42

Cutiporras, Don Andrés, 121–22

Cuzco, 8, 15–19; bishop of, 55, 111–12; cabildo of, 47–50, 55

Davis, Natalie Zemon, 11, 108, 198n36

Daza, Antonio, 116

Dean, Carolyn, 73–74

deathbed confessions. *See* notaries: deathbed dealings of

declarations, notarized, 100, 109–10, 120, 128–30

De la Borda, Martín, 121

De la Borda y Andía, Juan, 97, 101

De la Coba, Diego, 118

de la Fuente, Francisco, 58–67, 78–79, 82–83, 90, 141, 180n87, 181–82nn105–6

De la Puente, Don Felipe, 110

De la Ripia, Juan, 38

depositions. *See* witnesses: testimony of

Díaz Dávila, Alonso, 101–2

Díaz de Valdepeñas, Hernando, 28

Díaz Valdeón, Pedro, 49

dictation, 70, 72, 89–90, 93, 199–200n54

Díez de Morales, Luis, 60, 80

Díez, Juan, 139–40

disease, 5, 7, 20, 44, 178n74

divorce, 106, 109, 112–13, 116, 160n73, 193n62

doctors (medical), 15, 123, 188n65

Dominican friars, 8, 55, 81

donations, 98–105, 117–19, 125–27

doodles, notarial, 16, 68–75, 142

dowry, 3, 25–26, 59, 86, 95–96, 122; contractual defense of, 105–8, 118–19

draft book, notarial, 77–79, 81, 87, 115, 128, 185nn35–36

Dueñas Palacios, José de, 94

Durán, Lorenzo, 111

embargo. *See* assets, seizure of

encomiendas, 43–44, 47, 95

Eraso, Don Pedro de, 111

Escovedo, Rodrigo de, 1, 4

escribanías. *See* workshops, notarial

escribanos. *See* notaries

escribanos de cabildo. *See* Indians: as notaries

Escriche, Joaquín, 129

Espinosa, Diego de, 59

Espinosa, Don Cristóbal de, 59

Espinosa, Francisco de, 60–61

Espinosa, Juan de, 59

Espinosa, Luis de, 59, 61

Esquivel, Doña Antonia Gregoria de, 122–23

Esquivel, Doña Leonor de, 122–23

Esquivel, Don Rodrigo de (father), 95–96, 113, 120–23

Esquivel, Don Rodrigo de (son), 95–96, 122–23

Esquivel y Alvarado, Doña Constanza de, 108

exclamations, 18, 104–13, 117, 142, 191nn35–38, 193n63

extrajudicial records, 37–39, 46, 74–87, 95–123, 125–27, 141, 146. *See also under specific types of records*

fear, reverential, 107–11, 190–91n32. *See also* violence, marital

Fernández de Lizardi, José Joaquín, 46

Fernández Escudero, Alejo, 90–92

fireworks, 72, 184n16

Flores de Bastidas, Juan, 60, 105–6, 120

forgery, 95–96, 185n31

formulae, notarial. *See* notaries

Franciscan friars, 5–6, 22–23

fraud, 45, 56, 83, 91–92, 98–100, 104–5, 121–22, 126; measures to prevent, 78, 80, 89, 154n7, 190n23, 190n25

Gallén de Robles (licenciate), 82–83

Gamarra, Bernardo José, 69, 74, 81

Gamarra, Joaquín de, 69

Gamarra, Juan Bautista, 72, 144, 188n65

Gamarra, Pedro José, 69–70, 94, 184n20, 187n52

García del Corral, Doña Mariana, 109–10, 112

García del Corral, Juan, 101

Gonzáles Peñaloza, Alejo, 116–17

González de Torneo, Francisco, 33–34

González Echevarría, Roberto, xi, 3, 155n15, 194n2

Gualpa, Don Bernabé, 56

Gualpa Nina, Don Diego, 56, 130–32

Guaman, Don Juan, 119

Guaman Poma de Ayala, Felipe, 8–10, 43, 45–46, 66–67, 147, 157n45, 202–3n5

Guanahani (island), 1–4

Guandoja (hacienda), 55, 177n63

Gutiérrez de Quintanilla y Sotomayor, Don Pedro, 115

Gutiérrez, José Marcos, 89

Guzmán de Alfarache (Alemán), xi, 21–24, 41, 90, 161n8

handwriting, 77, 79, 90, 93–95, 134, 140–41, 143, 182n2. *See also* signatures

Hanks, William, 126–27, 195n8, 201n76

Hardwick, Julie, 84, 86, 187n58

Hernández Machón, Diego, 55–56

Herrero, Alonso, 60–61

Herrup, Cynthia, 136

Herzog, Tamar, 12, 24, 88, 158nn62–63, 163n21, 173–74n21, 185n31, 186n38

Hevia Bolaños, Juan de, 83

Hinojosa, Agustín de, 121

Hospital de Naturales (Cuzco parish), 50, 119

Huamanga, 64, 115, 121–22

Huanta, 63

Huayna Capac, 7

Hurtado, Francisco, 60

Hurtado de Salcedo, Don Gerónimo (corregidor), 116

illegitimacy, 97, 109–10

Incas, 7–8, 15–16, 42–43, 47, 55, 68, 104, 125–30, 195n6; as litigants, 118, 136–37, 197n33

Indians, 40, 43–46, 55–57, 66–67, 118–19, 121, 125–38, 144–47; courts for, 9–10, 50–51, 196n21; as notaries, 6–11, 44, 50–51, 119, 130–31, 145–46, 156–57n35, 157n44, 161n83, 201n76

indios ladinos (bilingual Indians), 8, 40, 157n42, 157n45

indulgences (*bulas de composición*), 52

inheritance, 38, 54, 96, 101, 104–5, 110–11, 122–26, 193n63

insanity, 116

inspections, 87, 139–40, 180n85, 185nn30–31

insults, 59, 61, 68, 73, 75, 92, 182n4, 184n23

interrogation techniques, 32–37, 137–38, 167n66, 168n73, 198n47

Irolo Calar, Nicolás de. *See* Yrolo Calar, Nicolás de

Jaimes, Lorenzo, 68, 79

Jaimes Ramírez de Zavala, Don Gaspar, 108

Jaquijaguana, 48, 52

Jara de la Cerda, Don Agustín (father and son), 128–30

Jesuits, 8, 57, 117–18, 130

Juan y Colom, José, 34

judges, 31–36, 46, 91–92, 100, 116–19, 132–35, 166n59, 167nn61–67, 206; of Indians (*jueces de naturales*), 9–10, 44, 50, 196n21. *See also* cabildo; corregidores

judicial records, 4, 22–23, 80, 114–24, 130–38, 193n62, 197n28, 197n31; involving Indians, 9–10, 50–51, 55–56; making of, 31–36, 88–94, 167nn62–67, 188n70; theft of, 120–21, 140, 193n73

Junco, Don Melchor del, 116

justicia sumaria, 9–10, 31, 50–51, 131, 196n21

juzgados de indios, 9–10, 44, 50–51

Kagan, Richard, 133, 147, 160n70, 162nn16–18, 197–98n34

Lamero, Hernando (admiral), 82–83

land titles, 6, 16–17, 55–56, 97–105, 150, 155n12, 178–79n75, 202n3; lost or stolen, 118–21; as surety for loans, 119, 122

Laso, Don Diego, 63

Laso de la Vega, Doña Luisa, 106–7

lawsuits. *See* judicial records; litigation; petitions

lawyers. *See* advocates; letrados

Lazarillo de Tormes, xi, 20–21, 24

legitimacy, 97, 109–10

letrados, 3, 26, 44, 122, 155n19, 206. *See also* advocates; judges

Lima, 7, 58, 64, 68, 114, 116

literacy, 6, 23, 61, 72, 80–83, 126–32, 143, 153n1, 156–57nn33–35

litigation, 3–4, 72, 88–96, 114–22, 137–41, 160n70, 167n61, 197–98n34; guidelines for conducting, 30–36, 44–45, 166n58, 167nn62–67; involving Indians, 9–10, 130–37

Lockhart, James, 4, 42–43, 125, 127, 144–45

López Barnuevo, Bartolomé, 120–21

López de la Cerda, Pedro, 60, 104–5, 125–27

López de Paredes, Doña Josefa, 57, 117–18

López de Paredes, Juan, 55, 177–78n68

López de Paredes, Martín, 55–67, 84, 101, 117, 177n63, 178n70, 179–80n81, 188n65

López de Rivera, Andrés, 121–22

López de Solórzano, Juan, 59

Losada y Castilla, Doña María Josefa de, 110–12

Loyola, Juan de, 112

Lucero, Cristóbal de, 54, 60

Lugo, Don Alonso Luis de, 140–41

Luyardo, Juan Francisco, 72

Madrid, 21, 68

Maldonado, Francisco, 117

Maldonado y Álvares, Doña Sebastiana, 111

manuals, notarial. *See* notaries: manuals for

Marca, Don Juan, 55, 177–78n68

marriage, 27, 57–58, 114, 116–17

masters of ships, 138–39, 199n48

Mayas, 6, 144–45, 201n76

Mayontopa, Don Francisco, 16

Mayorazgo (entail), 120

Mendo, Miguel, 53

Mendoza, Don Antonio de, 92

Mendoza, Don Juan de, 101

Mercado, Tomás de, 38, 146

Merced, La, monastery of, 58, 92

Mercedarians, 8, 58

merchants, 38, 63, 65, 82–83, 101, 186n48, 189n15

mercury, 49, 63

Mesa, Alonso de, 55

Mesa Andueza, Lorenzo de, 55, 57–58, 60, 108, 177n63, 179n81

Mesoamerica, 5–6, 144–46, 153n1, 156–57nn33–35

mestizos, 45, 51, 72

Mijancas Medrano, Juan de, 101

minuta (draft), 37–38, 82, 123, 186n45, 206

minutario. *See* draft book, notarial

mohatras, 83, 187n50. *See also* fraud

Monterroso y Alvarado, Gabriel de, 17, 29–40, 73, 83–84, 114–15, 143, 146, 166n52, 166n57

Montoya, Bartolomé de, 60

Montoya, Doña Clara de, 104–5, 117, 125–27, 195n6

Moscoso y Venero, Don Fernando de (marqués de Buenavista), 92

mulattos, 45

mules, 18, 53

Murúa, Martín de, 8

Nahuatl (language), 6, 144–45, 156–57nn33–35, 201n77

Navarro, José, 54, 60

New Spain, 42, 44

nobles, 13, 56, 65, 104–6, 118–22, 125–30, 136–37, 145, 197n33

nota. *See* minuta

notarial records: xi, 10, 16, 48, 52, 63, 141–42; contestation of validity of, 114–18; making of, 26–39, 68–94, 183n11; manipulation of, 95–113, 122–23, 125–28, 143; possession taking and, 1–4, 44; revocation and cancellation of, 101–3, 114; sale of, 41, 121; theft of, 119–21, 183n10

notaries, 13–15, 21–24, 58–64; bad reputation of, 27, 30–31, 34, 38, 41–46, 161–62n8; cabildo, 48–50, 52, 66–67, 121–22, 159n66, 205; as credit brokers, 84–86, 187n54, 187n58; deathbed dealings of, 27, 116–17, 119, 123, 128–30, 183n11; ecclesiastical, 13, 15, 160n73, 179n77, 206; fees charged by, 13, 39–41, 139, 170n100, 181n97, 196–97n27, 197n31, 199n52; as *fides publicae*, 4, 13, 26, 156n24; fines paid by, 87, 89–90, 186n38; indigenous, 6–11, 44, 50–51, 119, 130–31, 156–57n35, 161n83, 201n76, 205; manuals for, 17, 24, 29–40, 87–89, 93, 97–100, 138, 143, 146, 166n52; numerary, 13, 26, 47–49, 52–55, 57, 63, 72, 120, 141, 149, 161n83, 164–65n35, 206; in picaresque fiction, xi, 46; possession taking and, 1–4, 44; requirements for office of, 27, 29, 44–47, 159n68, 165n40; royal, 48–49, 53–54, 63, 72, 116, 206; social status of, 27, 101–2, 159n68; in Spanish legal history, 25–41; training of, 68–94, 149, 160n73; use of templates by, 2–3, 24, 29–30, 38–40, 68, 99–100, 107–8, 125–27, 202n81

notarios. *See* notaries: ecclesiastical

Ñucay, Doña Inés, 125, 195n6
Ñucay, Doña Isabel, 125, 195n6
Nussdorfer, Laurie, xiv, 4, 156n24,
    187n54, 188n70, 188–89n80

Ocllo, Doña Inés, 136–37
oficial mayor (notary's head assistant),
    69–73, 82, 91, 95–96, 113, 121, 184n20,
    206–7
oficios. *See* public offices: sale of;
    workshops, notarial
Olave, Joan de, 52–53
Olivares, Don Pedro de, 130–32
Ollantaytambo, 16
Orna Alvarado, Don Pablo de, 111–12
Oro, Domingo de, 60, 80
Oropesa, 56, 130–32
Orue, Sancho (Ortiz) de, 48–50, 54, 65,
    174nn28–30
Oyardo (Aramburu), Don Pedro de,
    104–5

Palomino, Doña Micaela, 105–6
Palomino, Juan José, 72
Paniagua, Alonso de, 95–96
Paniagua de Loaysa, Don Gabriel, 59, 61
papelitos, 80–82, 97
Paucartambo, 47, 52, 72, 97
Paullo Topa Inca, Don Cristóbal, 128–
    30, 195n13
pawning, 119, 122
Paz y Salgado, Antonio de, 45
Pérez, Blas (captain), 110
Pérez de Vargas (Machuca), Antonio,
    54–55, 58, 60
Pérez Landero (Otañez y Castro),
    Pedro, 87
Periquillo Sarniento, El (Fernández de
    Lizardi), 46
petitions, 24–25, 31, 46, 92, 119, 130–35,
    166n58, 198n36

Petrucci, Armando, 3, 18, 126
Philip II (king of Spain), 12–13, 40, 44
picaresque, xi, 3, 14–15, 20–24, 31, 46,
    142
Pillco, Cristóbal, 136–37
pilots of ships, 138–39, 199nn48–50
Pizarro, Francisco, 7, 42
playing cards, 18, 53
Plaza de Armas (Cuzco), 119, 150
Plaza del Regocijo (Cuzco), 47, 120,
    174n25, 177n57
plumarios (notarial assistants), 67–97,
    120–21, 139–40, 182–183nn6–10, 183–
    84n13, 184n21, 188–89n80, 193n73,
    207
Poma Inca, Don José, 137
Ponce de León, Don Luis, 59
Porroa (y Sánchez), Antonio, 71, 73, 75
possession, act of taking, 1–4, 25,
    155nn12–13
potato fields, 118, 137
Potosí, 42, 47, 49, 51–52, 59, 64
power groups, 17, 46–47, 56, 59–67
power of attorney (*poder*), 27, 52, 68,
    85, 99, 146
Prado, Gaspar de, 60–61
Pragmatic Sanction (1503), 27–29, 37,
    39, 80, 165nn46–47
price inflation, 20, 39
priests, 6, 20–22, 44, 98; in Andes, 40,
    55–57, 67, 80, 104–5, 111–12, 125–27
procuradores, 3, 26, 31, 59, 71–72, 88,
    121, 133, 164n34, 175n36, 207
Protector de Naturales (royal de-
    fender of natives), 130–32, 136–37,
    196n25
protocolos (notarial registers), 28–29,
    50, 52, 68, 71–72, 74, 81–82, 90,
    170n92, 182n2, 207
psalms, as code phrases, 114
public offices, sale of, 4, 12–13, 27, 40–

public offices (*cont.*)
41, 44–45, 50, 54, 59–64, 156n24,
159n62, 171nn107–12

Quechua (language), 8, 17, 46, 55, 65,
68, 133–34, 181n102, 182n4, 195–
96n17, 202n4
Quesada, Luis de, 49–50, 175nn33–34
Quevedo, Don Francisco de (cor-
regidor), 90–92
Quevedo, Francisco de, 21, 46, 90
quipus, xi, 8–9, 11, 131, 153n1, 157n38,
157n47
Quirós, Joan de, 95–96
Quispe, Pedro, 50–51, 196n21
Quispe Topa, Don Martín, 118
Quispicanche, 55, 84

Rama, Angel, 3, 155n20
Raya, Diego de (captain), 109
Real Audiencia. *See* Audiencia (high
court) of Lima
refranes (popular sayings), 14–15, 22,
36, 39, 65, 68, 162nn12–13
registros de indios, 15–16, 207
renunciations (*renuncias*), 40, 81–82, 85
república de españoles, 44
república de indios, 44, 201n76
residencias, 58–64, 67, 82–83, 90
restitution, 52, 55, 119–20, 176n48,
182n108
Rodríguez de la Bandera, Pedro, 111
Rodríguez de Villegas, Tomás, 111
Rolandino dei Passaggieri, 25, 164n31
Roman law, 2, 25, 105, 154n10, 163nn24–
26
Roque Inga, Don Bartolomé, 119
royal notaries. *See* notaries: royal
Ruiz de Garfias, Doña Catalina, 57
Ruiz, Miguel, 66–67

Sacsayhuamán, 118
Salatiel Bonaniense, 25, 164n31
Saldaña, Joan de, 112, 119, 128
sale of offices. *See* public offices, sale
of
sales, contracts of, 25, 50, 52, 68, 74, 85,
190n22, 192n51; bogus, 97–100, 128–
30
Samalvide, Juan de, 112
San Agustín, monastery of, 55
San Blas (Cuzco parish), 136–37
Sánchez, Antonio, 54
Sánchez Vadillo, Diego, 116
San Cristóbal (Cuzco parish), 104–5,
125–27, 137
San Gerónimo (Cuzco parish), 118–19
Santa Catalina, convent of, 57, 84, 86
Santa Clara, convent of, 16, 55, 76, 78,
86, 150
Santo Domingo, monastery of, 55
secrecy, professional, 27, 31, 87, 112,
165n40
servants, 63, 70, 136–37, 183n11
Seville, 15, 24, 26, 68, 138–42
Sicllabamba (ingenio), 133
Siete Partidas, Las, 13, 25, 27, 29–30, 74,
107, 159n68, 165n40
signatures, 73–82, 91–95, 116–17, 126,
133–35, 185n31, 185n33, 188n71, 193n63,
195n13
signo, 3, 74–76, 82, 94, 207
Silva Córdoba y Guzmán, Don Bernardino, 120–21
Silva y Obando, Don José, 110–11
silver, 20, 42, 47, 49, 63, 172n2, 189n14
Sisa, Asencia, 134–35
Sisa, Bartola Ignacio, 122
Sisa, Magdalena, 136–37
slaves, 99, 141–42
Soto, Doña Isabel de, 58, 61, 114,
192n53

Spain: Golden Age of, 20–24, 161nn1–2; imperial administration of, 138–42; justice system of, 24, 30–37; legal history of, 25–41
Stern, Steve J., 17, 46
Stoler, Ann Laura, 18, 143, 146–47, 200n65
sugar, 18, 47, 52–53, 62, 116, 133, 174n23
sumaria información. *See* criminal suits: initial testimony in
summary justice. *See* justicia sumaria

Tamboconga (hacienda), 119–20
Tapia y Sarmiento, José de, 72
templates. *See* notaries: use of templates by
Tlacuilos (Nahua notaries), 5–6
Tocto Coca, Isabel, 50
Toledo, Francisco de, 9, 12, 49, 131, 196nn18–19
toma de posesión. *See* possession, act of taking
torture, judicial, 34–37, 133, 169n81, 197n33
trial records. *See* judicial records
tribute, 56, 177–78n68
Trujillo (Peru), 45
truth, 2–4, 16, 18, 37, 65, 75, 95–96, 126–28, 146–47, 190n25; disputation of, in litigation, 88, 91–92, 104–5, 115, 137; means for disguising of, in documents, 97–123; means for extraction of, from witnesses, 32–37
Túpac Amaru, 49
Tupa Yupanqui, Don Gabriel, 136–38
Tupia, Juan, 50–51

Unzueta, Francisco de, 128

Valencia, Lázaro de, 101–2
Valer, Doña Josefa de, 128–30
Valer Melgarejo, Don Mateo de, 106
Valladares, Don Gerónimo, 118–19

Vargas Carvajal, Cristóbal de, 80
Vásquez, Diego Cayetano, 81–82
Vela de Córdoba, Doña Francisca, 97
venality. *See* public offices, sale of
Venero de Valera, Don Manuel, 91
Vera, Sebastián de, 54
Vicho (hacienda), 57, 117–18
Vicho, Don Francisco, 119
Vilcabamba, 47, 49
Villa, Gabriel de, 60
Villadiego Vascuñana (y Montoya), Alonso de, 32
violence, marital, 105–13
visitas. *See* inspections

wheat, 53
widows, 61, 97, 113, 116–17, 119
wills, xi, 3, 6, 17, 24, 38, 47, 50, 52–55, 58, 61, 71, 101, 105, 115, 125–27, 146, 156n34, 201n79; contested, 95–96, 116, 122–23, 183n12; mysterious bequests in, 22–23, 97; revocation or revision of, 114
wine, 62–63
witnesses, 32–37; "rustic," 33–34; testimony of, 3, 24, 55–57, 61–62, 88–96, 116–23, 132–40, 167nn62–67, 188n71, 198n47
women: "exclamations" against notarial records by, 104–13; legal rights of, 116
workshops, notarial, xii, 18, 26, 37, 45, 59, 61, 70–73, 89–90, 112, 141–42, 146–49, 158–59n61, 174n25; as relatively safe archives, 120; thefts from, 72, 120

Xaimes, Lorenzo. *See* Jaimes, Lorenzo

Yanamanchi (ayllu), 130
Yrolo Calar, Nicolás de, 99–100, 146
Yucay, 111

Kathryn Burns is an associate professor in the Department of History at
the University of North Carolina. She is the author of *Colonial Habits:
Convents and the Spiritual Economy of Cuzco, Peru* (Duke, 1999).

Library of Congress Cataloging-in-Publication Data
Burns, Kathryn, 1959–
Into the archive : writing and power in colonial Peru /
Kathryn Burns.
p. cm.
Includes bibliographical references and index.
ISBN 978-0-8223-4857-3 (cloth : alk. paper)
ISBN 978-0-8223-4868-9 (pbk. : alk. paper)
1. Peru—History—1548–1820—Sources. 2. Archives—Peru—
History. 3. Notaries—Peru—History. 4. Power (Social
sciences)—Peru—History. I. Title.
F3444.B87 2010
985'.031—dc22   2010014583